THE
CHIEF
EXECUTIVES

Books by ISADORE BARMASH

Nonfiction
    The Chief Executives
    For the Good of the Company
    The World Is Full of It
    Welcome to Our Conglomerate—You're Fired!
    The Self-Made Man

Fiction
    Net Net (a novel)

Anthology
    Great Business Disasters

THE
CHIEF
EXECUTIVES

ISADORE BARMASH

J. B. LIPPINCOTT COMPANY
PHILADELPHIA AND NEW YORK

To ELAINE, STANLEY, MARILYN, and PAMELA

Copyright © 1978 by Isadore Barmash
All rights reserved
First edition
9 8 7 6 5 4 3 2 1
Printed in the United States of America

U.S. Library of Congress Cataloging in Publication Data

Barmash, Isadore.
    The chief executives.

    Includes index.
    1. Executives—United States. I. Title.
HF5500.3.U54B34   658.4'2'0973   78-12231
ISBN 0-397-01285-3

Contents

An Introduction	7
1. The Besieging of an American Elite	9
2. In the New Style	34
3. The Web Tightens	48
4. When the Government Comes Knocking	59
5. Many Strident Voices	76
6. Multinationals, Dollars, Payments, Oil, and All	91
7. How Good Are American CEOs?	108
8. The 80/20 Syndrome (Or Methuselah's Law, It's as Old as Human Activity)	133
9. Only So Far and No Further	145
10. How Honest Are They?	159
11. Getting There, Poor or Rich	171
12. The Pivotal Crisis	186
13. The Private Company—Dynasties Without Stockholders	203
14. How They Live	220
15. The Passing of the Imperial Chief Executive	237
Index	249

An Introduction

This book is a journalistic adventure behind the scenes into the behavior, minds, hearts, consciences, attitudes, and styles, both professional and personal, of a singular group of people.

As a peer group, America's top businessmen have rarely been open to the people. Their reluctance to allow the public to penetrate their executive suites and boardrooms has been a direct reason, although not the only one, for a creeping decline in their credibility with that public. It has also fed the rapid growth of government regulation and hard scrutiny that have forced their way into those suspect chambers.

Although I have been a newspaperman for three decades and an author for the most recent one, I decided that I could not rely on my past meetings with many corporate chief executives, and I started afresh. For eighteen months, I examined them, reportorially speaking, along these lines. As the highly vaunted skills of the American economy appeared to have been dented in the mid- and late-1970s, it seemed natural to question whether the decline in national productivity, technology, and profitability, as well as the inability to cure the disease of inflation, might not be directly related to an erosion in the performance and dynamism of those who run American business.

Was the irrepressible strain of the American business hotshot running thin? If not, why was the United States slipping in its economic and competitive role in the world? Had the energy problem sapped the initiative from the nation's chief executives?

And yet, in other ways, America's chief executives are still considered the best the world has, still studied by their counterparts in other nations for their methods of operation and their conceptual thinking and the actions that implement it.

Knocking on corporate doors, I was surprised to be admitted into many. Once admitted, I rarely found anyone who avoided giving answers, although they not all were of equal quality or articulation. Those who wouldn't talk to me (a mere handful) gave only vague reasons—too busy . . . don't really want to discuss the subject . . . heard you were a smart-ass reporter . . . just don't want to get involved . . . and so on. Some never gave any reasons, vague or otherwise.

But almost from the outset, the candid, frequently spontaneous response produced information, insights, and ideas for additional approaches that turned the exercise into the exciting adventure it became. I hope some of that sense of discovery and human interaction will be communicated to those who read this book, despite the seriousness, if not somberness, that will be found here too.

The approach, then, is to place the American corporate chief executive officer—the CEO or "The Chief," as he may be called—into the context of his world and the world at large. My hope is that the result will operate on two levels: as a spotlight on the men and women who run American business for better or worse and as an examination of how the American business world has changed in the last twenty-five years.

I take full responsibility for both the reporting and the interpretation in it and hereby express my deep gratitude to all who helped, advised, and cooperated with me during that process.

1

The Besieging of an American Elite

The Long Climb to Precarious Heights

Few are as wildly applauded and roundly scorned. Few are considered as vital to the health and wealth of the American economy and to the well-being of over 200 million Americans and indirectly of billions of people abroad. And few are as embroiled in a constant controversy over perquisites, promises, and performance.

Whether he be slim or fat, tall or short, diplomatic or axiomatic, altruistic or mercenary, confident or insecure, ept or inept—and he is all of these—the chief executive in corporate America is, for better or worse, one of the country's elite. He is also its troubled elite and lately in many ways its besieged elite.

Falling somewhere in the perception of fans and critics between the Red Baron of Lufthansa and the mighty *patron* of southern Europe and Latin America, but with a flavor all its own, the image of the American corporate chief hasn't quite fallen from that of national treasure to national burden. But in recent years this highly visible member of the American family, second perhaps only to the politician, has been both praised and castigated to the extreme.

Few other Americans receive as many academic, humanitarian, and community awards, and few others are blamed and verbally whipped for as many of our regional and national ills. Social, environmental, moral, and productivity failures are heaped upon him. Conversely, triumphs in the same areas are credited to him. Grateful for the recognition, he blithely accepts what he considers his due as he not-so-blithely takes the blame.

Rarely one to admit to pessimism, he wears professional optimism on his sleeve, often on both sleeves. But sometimes, privately, he wilts and sulks. The forces arrayed against him seem overwhelming—governmental, ideological, labor, societal. So he complains with frustration, What the hell *do* they want, anyway: socialism, Castroism, High Wilsonism—what? And then, rationalizing, he ponders the principle of the price to be paid for working under the free-enterprise system and calms down, or tries to. What is it but the lofty spirit battling the bruised flesh, or something of that nature? he tells himself with some shaky self-indulgence.

He sits on the dais of the Economic Club, the annual dinner of the Business Council or the Business Roundtable, and enjoys the perks, the encomiums of his office, the moment's recognition of his awesome responsibilities, the prideful camaraderie of his peers, the dazzling flashes of the cameras, the needling but implicitly respectful questions from the reporters who push forward, and perhaps most of all the envy and grudging acclaim that flows like a warm wind from the audience. And what can he do but look down upon it all with a soft-bold arrogance, the critiques and the nit-picking forgotten? After all, how long, how many sacrifices, how much intellectual honesty, how much bending of the will did it take to be able to sit so high in the grand ballroom of the Waldorf, the Mark, the Ritz, or the Greenbrier and enjoy the stares from the hushed multitude? He sighs and answers, Plenty, plenty.

How did he get there anyway?

Most showed a particular flair early, combined with a strong display of the work ethic. And they were able to demonstrate initial ability while broadening their knowledge and skills. But, more strategically, when opportunities came their talents and background had become visible enough to create the right tactical exposure needed to propel them into the "ultimate job." And for those who regard accounting, finance, law, and engineering as highly specialized but restrictive professions, such is hardly the case any more. Many of today's CEOs started that way but ultimately copped the "big job."

David Mahoney, a poor Manhattan youth, got through college on an athletic scholarship and took a job on Madison Avenue. He developed a skillful marketing know-how that attracted the interest of Norton Simon, the conglomerator and art patron. When the California entrepreneur decided to retire, he tapped the restless, creative Mahoney at one of the highest salaries in the nation to succeed him as chairman of the big company fashioned in the image and name of Norton Simon.

A gangling, earnest David W. Wallace shifted from engineering to law after World War II. He had been attracted to the logic and order of the legal process when he had served as an infantry officer guarding war prisoners at the Nuremberg war-crimes trial. Discharged from the armed services, he studied law and became an important lawyer to railroads and holding companies. This led to his election in 1973 as chief executive of Bangor Punta Corporation, a highly diversified producer.

Reginald H. Jones, the head of General Electric Company, an $18-billion-a-year colossus, was born in England and studied accounting and finance at the Wharton School of the University of Pennsylvania. Solemn, thoughtful, deliberate, he learned a good deal about General Electric's insides as its traveling auditor for several years. He moved into general management, becoming financial vice-president, a vice-chairman, and a member of the corporate chief executive's "office" before he was elected chairman in 1972.

Some like accounting, some don't. Bernard L. Schwartz, chairman of Loral Corporation, a moderate-sized maker of electronics systems, started as an accountant and made his way up through the corporate ranks with his ability to equate operations and balance sheets. But Russell Banks, who decided that accounting wasn't as interesting as law, continued to work at the first while studying at night for the second. Eventually, he became the top man at Grow Chemical Corporation in New York.

One of the nation's youngest business chiefs at age thirty-eight, William M. Agee studied at the University of Idaho and at Harvard Graduate School, where he earned a master's degree in business administration. When W. Michael Blumenthal, chairman of Bendix Corporation, a $3-billion-a-year defense and industrial-equipment maker, wanted a bright, independent young financial man, he lured Agee away from his top financial role at Boise Cascade Corporation. Gradually, he gave Agee more and more management responsibility. And when Jimmy Carter in turn lured Blumenthal away as his Secretary of the Treasury, Agee, to no one's great surprise despite his age, found himself occupying Blumenthal's chair at Bendix.

Others are basically entrepreneurs. In 1967, Peter S. Redfield left his post as director of administrative services at the Transamerica Corporation in Los Angeles to start his own computer-leasing company, Itel Corporation. Wanting to be his own boss, Redfield is one now, running a company with sales of over $300 million and employing more than two thousand people.

An unusual success on a number of counts, Irving S. Shapiro in 1973 became chairman and chief executive of E. I. du Pont de Nemours & Company, Wilmington, Delaware, the nation's largest chemical company. He was the first lawyer, the first Jew, and only the second nonfamily executive to head the two-hundred-year-old company. Born in 1916 in Minneapolis, the oldest of three sons of Lithuanian immigrants, Shapiro developed pragmatic but scholarly instincts as a lawyer at the Office of Price Administration and in the Justice Department before joining Du Pont's legal department in 1951.

Du Pont, it was widely alleged over the years, had exhibited anti-Semitic tendencies. "In the 1920s and 1930s," Shapiro told this writer, "Du Pont was reluctant to hire and promote Jews. But the company came after me. A B'nai B'rith friend advised me not to take the job, but I did. I figured there is no mystery about a guy named Shapiro. I came there simply as a young lawyer." But obviously he proved his worth beyond that, and Du Pont proved something that business doesn't often prove—that individuals mean a good deal more than labels.

Perhaps the classic indigenous case in recent years involves John D. deButts, chairman and chief executive of the American Telephone and Telegraph Company, one of the world's largest corporations, with annual sales of over $33 billion, a quarterly net profit of $1 billion, 930,000 employees (a work force larger than that of the U.S. Army), and 3 million stockholders. A tall, courtly Southerner with an easy, charismatic manner, whose North Carolina accent has only softened slightly from exposure to Washington, Chicago, and New York, deButts had twenty-two jobs in his thirty-six years with AT&T, integrating smoothly with the intricate layers of the telephone company's spartan society.

Earmarked early for a high role and literally chosen after a lifetime of training, deButts first attracted company attention halfway through his career when he was instructed to prove that the Justice Department would be unwise if it proceeded with its declared intent to break up the Bell System. After three months of intensive work at the task, he produced a thirty-page statement that both management and the legal staff decided presented a cogent argument against ever separating Bell's research, manufacturing, and field operations.

Justice failed to push forward with its case. But deButts had proven himself. His depth research in the field, in Bell Laboratories, and in AT&T's cavernous, cathedral-like New York headquarters, the surprising degree of application to a corporate assignment usually handed to someone on a higher executive rung, propelled him forward in big, firm steps into the CEO's chair.

How important to the nation are such classic American success stories? Of all the well-known businessmen and perhaps a hundred more described, interviewed, or observed in these pages, three emerged in the late 1970s as the most significant and most highly regarded in the country: Reginald Jones of General Electric, John deButts of AT&T, and Irving Shapiro of E. I. du Pont. Each became a prototype business-statesman, bigger than life-size figures welcomed in the White House in the Jimmy Carter administration, carefully listened to in Congress, and frequently considered for high government office. When the President finally decided to remove the peppery, conservative Arthur Burns as chairman of the Federal Reserve Board, he offered the post early in 1978 to Jones and Shapiro. Both declined, citing their commitments to their companies. Yet it was a signal honor, confirmation perhaps that their long career climb was a source of national pride.

Interviewed at length in the process of researching this book, Jones, deButts, and Shapiro receive more mention here than any other figures. Their national and international stature, however, was only one reason for this. Another was their candidness and openness. A third has been their catalytic effect on other chief executives. A fourth reason, perhaps, is the recognition of that indigenous trait of persistence and devotion, now often scorned, which kept them at the same company all their working lives, to advance from bottom to top. Shapiro, the exception, worked for the government first but gave Du Pont more than a quarter century.

Horatio Algerism, in other words, never really departed from the American success saga. But the achievement's manner and the tone have changed radically in the latter half of the twentieth century. In the first fifty years, the entrepreneur, the company founder, and his sons and even grandsons generally occupied the top office in the American company. Since the early 1950s it has been the professional, career-trained and carefully culled from the ranks, as well as the first waves of career managers whose training began from the moment they first walked onto the campus, who have succeeded to the "ultimate job."

Now, in the century's final quarter, the genre is shifting again. The MBAs, the valued pros whose triumphs in one company bring them successively to others, the company saviors with a sharply honed ability to jog a business out of its careening path to disaster, and the so-called overage top executive still possessing the viscera and marrow to provide a strategic caretaker role—all these have come forth in a period of high-cost, high-tax, highly regulated operations. The exigencies of the time, in fact, seem to have coughed up more than a few candidates who might in other times have had to wait long for promotion or who languished in a static situation or found themselves overpriced and overqualified in a declining market and about to be left "on the beach."

Women, too, have come up. But the accession was difficult. Whether it was Mary Wells Lawrence in advertising, Muriel Siebert on Wall Street or in banking, Estee Lauder in cosmetics, Hilda Kirstein in retailing, or Pat Carbine in publishing, they and their sisters had to demonstrate that they were at least as good managers and as entrepreneurially gifted as men. Women executives have always been suspect. Either they would prove too emotional, incapable of coping with high-stress situations, or they would resort to feminine wiles or coyness or show an insufficiently dominant personality, or whatever. Worst of all, they might even become pregnant at the most unstrategic time.

All those fears, with the exception of pregnancy perhaps, were largely disproven. Women executives have generally established the fact that they are quite as effective or noneffective as men, maybe even more effective. And in the process a change occurred. Their defensiveness in business has gone.

"Women in business used to be so intent on impressing you that they were as good as men. Now they seem to be over that hurdle," observes C. Wallace Bates, president of the Business Roundtable, an organization of 170 CEOs active in molding government-business relationships. "Women executives now concentrate on problems. They feel they are much more accepted, they don't have to establish their ability any more and they are received more as equals. That's certainly progress," Bates added.

One way or another, their sex notwithstanding, the CEO genus *Americana* differs from his or her predecessor of the pre-1950s—a more professional, more diversely oriented individual and a more pressure-laden one.

But whether different or not, are these CEOs as good as those who came before, as effective and as capable of generating corporate growth with its consequent stimulus on the national economy?

It's a moot point—with, however, some clear indications that many CEOs are so vexed by pressures, particularly government and regulatory intervention, high taxation, and still-soaring inflation, that they have scaled down their capital expenditures, their research-and-development and technology budgets. Is this evidence of an inability to cope? Businessmen don't think so. They either defend their conservatism as logical or heap blame on a Washington administration and its predecessors for not understanding the needs of business. But some disagree.

In 1977, or more than two years after the nation's economy picked up from a recession trough, American business wasn't investing in growth as it did in previous economic recoveries. Economists generally expressed fears that the new investment level—although up that year by 9 percent after adjusting for inflation—wasn't sufficient to sustain the economy at a high level and keep unemployment at a low level.

But in an editorial late that year, *Business Week*, one of the nation's most respected business magazines, defended businessmen, declaring:

> The reluctance of U.S. business to step up its investment in new plant and equipment cannot be dismissed as a temporary loss of nerve or a minor variation in the busi-

ness cycle. Business is giving a completely rational response to a political and economic climate that holds the return on new investment to inadequate levels and creates the maximum uncertainty in the minds of investors.

At the heart of the problem is the U.S. tax system, which now takes 48 cents out of each dollar of corporate profits. In effect, this doubles the rate of return that a company must expect to earn before it invests in a new project. With stocks selling at about 10 times earnings on the average, a new investment must offer a pretax return of 20% to pay its way.

Add to this the uncertainties created by a decade of continuing inflation and a hostile attitude in Congress, where outspoken members label any gain in profits "obscene." In such a climate, the relatively modest increases in capital spending this year are more than the nation had any right to expect.

Some economists regarded the businessman's response to these problems as a new, even admirable, rationality. But others, such as Walter Hoadley and Alan J. Greenspan, viewed it with alarm. In opposition to the theory that the nation's slower economic growth is better than deliberate government stimulus, they predicted that conservative capital budgets by business will hurt the country's efforts to liberalize trade, which in itself will hurt domestic employment and production.

Other businessmen clearly blame today's CEOs and the corporate climate they largely helped to build.

"The man who runs the big public company has a built-in rear-view mirror," says Frank C. Nicholas, chairman of Beech-Nut Foods Corporation. "He's an inordinate politician who is careful that no one will take a bite out of his rear end, and he makes his decisions based on what it will do for his career. He loses his desire to take risks. He quickly develops an ability to avoid making decisions but gives off an appearance that he's grappling with them."

In the view of Reuben Gutoff, president of Standard Brands, Inc., it's nothing but a "glib cop-out" when businessmen heap abuse on government economic policies and cite the difference between the American business-government adversary relationship and the Japanese system of government subsidies and broad support for business. "The CEOs who complain about government regulation really are fogging their own futures and that of their companies," he said.

A prominent consultant who has dealt with many U.S. chief executives as well as foreign businessmen is convinced that the American CEO is on the verge of losing his international superiority. "The American is still the top guy around the world," declared Marvin Schiller, vice-president of A. T. Kearney, Inc., a Chicago-based consulting firm. "But he won't be for long, I'm afraid. A decade ago, U.S. expertise was considered the model around the world. Executives and consultants from the states were selected by European companies on the basis of the American's marketing know-how, their greater responsiveness, and their hard-nosed analytical ability. But now, for example, in West Germany, the American isn't nearly as much in demand. The Germans, with their strong economic record since World War Two, are convinced that they have a lot of the strong business traits the Americans had and possibly more."

Yet, if the American CEO is obviously under more pressure than his predecessors and more subject to serious questioning about his ability, his behavior and manner of handling his office are curiously lacking any outward signs of awareness of the problem or unusual nervousness. Only occasionally does he let his hair down with outsiders, perhaps on a graying late afternoon when his fatigue and frustration come together and he droops, dropping his guard. But otherwise and in the main, he bears himself with confidence and aplomb. He may be a troubled, even besieged elite, but he carries it well.

Mornings, he strides into his office high in the glass tower with the confident step of authority, the tight mask of responsibility. He acknowledges with a firm but unrevealing nod the respectful, even awed, greetings of receptionist, clerks, secretaries, office managers, and vice-presidents. His own secretary, or administrative assistant if he chooses to uplift her with the more prestigious title, knows him best but can say the least. She—sometimes it is a he—greets the CEO with the veiled fondness or open familiarity that he knows well and may secretly resent. She or he has carefully layered the day into one-hour, half-hour, and even quarter-hour segments, leaving as little or as great a gap for simple isometric breathing or exercise or introspection as the CEO has indicated he wants. Shepherded and shielded by the tight calendar and the smiling watchperson outside his door, he orchestrates his day, coping with internal and external pressures. Often he appears to be grappling with an operational disorder that makes him wonder why people can't think straight or at least realize that common sense is a lot more conducive to promotion than politics.

His ability to cope with the counterpoint of all his players can range from that of Toscanini to Victor Borge. Their varying temperaments, thinking processes, alacrity or slowness, the quality of their response or input to the specific or general problem, their sense of independence or lack of it—all pelt against him like heavy rain on a hollow drum. An optimist because he has to be, he sometimes despairs of people but never of himself. It is a luxury he can't afford. It would be, in a sense, like letting the ship go down.

Nonetheless, throughout the morning and into the afternoon, as the calendar unfolds its human content and matters at hand roll up, he is clearly himself, the chief, calm, assured, judicious. But at lunch, the most rewarding hour to two hours of the day, when he usually holds court, he is at his best.

At 21, or in the Links Club, the Board Room, or the Pinnacle Club, or at the Duquesne Club or the Petroleum Club or in the clubs of his alma mater, be it Harvard, Yale, Princeton, or NYU, he is ushered with respect at the head of his guests by the maitre d' to a choice table. Drinks are ordered with a flourish—hard liquor if a rough day, wine if soft, although that formula is hardly rigid—and food is ordered at a more relaxed pace.

All at the table take their cue from him, but he is sensitive to their mood. If it is strictly a lunch to discuss business, a continuation of his layered schedule, nonetheless it begins with a few social or nonbusiness comments. The President's latest verbal flub. How the Knicks or the Lakers did. A glib but not nasty comment about the new $32.50 top for the latest Broadway musical. The pervasion of the topless or bottomless bars into the edge of the business district. The degree of the new security in the big office buildings—now they're not letting anyone in, even if you work there. And with that bit, jokes begin passing across the table—a young computer says to an old computer, "Listen, if you tell me what's in your memory bank, I'll tell you what's in mine." And the old computer answers, "I'd like to help you out, son. But you know, when you get old, your memory begins to go."

And then the business talk begins. It's an axiom that some days more progress is made over lunch—and more careers go down the drain—than at any other time or place. It is, after all, really another layer in that schedule, and the CEO listens hard while he appears relaxed. Depending upon who his guests are, he will discuss problems, awaiting solutions from those directly involved, never forgetting that one moment or another is just as propitious for the thought, the meaningful idea. The words flow to him and around him—plant productivity . . . materials accounting . . . market share . . . price/earnings multiples . . . responsibility delegation . . . expense budget . . . domestic pressures . . . communications, always that problem of communications. And while the CEO tries to relax as he eats, he doesn't, nor do the others. For the boss, everything is a matter of evaluation and analysis, and everyone there realizes it. So, as the talk proceeds amid the clink of glasses, the waiter's questions, the buzz in the immediate background, the never-ending idea-jockeying between the chief and the staff really doesn't diminish but frets along like a worried undertone.

As lonely as the chief executive must be, he is proud of his role because, like his title and its encomiums, it's a mark of the office.

Many CEOs attempt to offset the loneliness by finding an alter ego, a confidant or two, with whom to let his guard down. The result, in all too many cases, is that he builds a small team of sycophants, loyal, usually innocuous staff members, with whom he frequently eats and pretests his ideas and proposals. Unfortunately, while realistically he seeks a measurable response, all he gets is often too-willing approval. Unless he recognizes it for what it is, it works against him. Carried to its extreme—as happens many times—the certain conclusion is disappointment for him and sometimes even disaster for the company and its employees.

An even more sensitive challenge to his intellectual honesty are the members of the board of directors. For decades, they were mostly company executives, chosen equally for their responsibility and loyalty to the chairman, while a smaller number were outside company heads, suppliers, bankers, or professors of economics, also selected for their prestige and known respect for the CEO. But policy discussions were often honest and objective, although rarely in the 1950s and most of the 1960s were there any notable instances of a board rebelling over a chairman's unwise plans and actions. Peace, fanned by loyalty, reigned in the boardroom.

Starting in the late 1960s, a series of corporate calamities and a resultant clamor for director culpability created a different environment among directors. Given the massive disasters and the accompanying questions of fraud involving Penn Central Transportation, Equity Funding Corporation, W. T. Grant, and United Brands, to name just a few, a harsh spotlight fell upon the role of the director, especially the outside director. His obligation really was to provide a dimension of objectivity. But was he doing that? Companies quickly instituted or increased management and directors' liability insurance. Yet the moral was clear. Boards had to be more independent in the interests of stockholders, not to mention the public, rather than merely function as the CEOs' rubber stamp. Since then, corporate boards have undergone beneficial changes. Directors are more aware of their real responsibilities, and outside directors are being chosen with a new set of criteria. But whether all this will really benefit the company, the stockholder, and the public remains to be seen.

The Statue Topples, the Public Recoils

If that spotlight a few years ago fell upon the director, it descended in full force upon the CEO. The disasters and the suspected frauds raised the biggest questions. Was the CEO effective, sufficiently dedicated, not just flushed with power and perks? Had the American dream—unimaginable success and wealth accruing to a man of relatively humble circumstances who thrived on hard work and had an unusual ability to surmount challenges—created a glutton whose sense of noblesse oblige dominated his actions and whose conscience was a matter of serious question?

With the shock of the big corporate failures and many

minor ones, the moral sense of the socioeconomic effect of businessmen's performance burst upon the public. It was hard to believe that such economic catastrophes, with their damage to many thousands of people, came from the greed and power lust of just a few men.

For example, the jousting for power at Penn Central between Stuart T. Saunders and Alfred E. Perlman, the respective heads of the Pennsylvania Railroad and of the New York Central, both merged into the vast transportation system, was a prime reason for the insolvency of the nation's largest railway line.

But the seeds of chaos were first planted in 1963, fully five years before the merger took place, when Saunders embarked on an acquisition splurge. His plan was that the Pennsy would be wise to diversify out of low-profit railroading into high-profit real estate. As a result, choice industrial parks, amusement centers, and prime-location buildings from New York to Los Angeles were bought.

These earned a good return on investment for several years, but in the queasy 1969 economy everything seemed to come apart. Cash dwindled in both the railroad and the real-estate operations. And then inefficiency in the railroad, combined with growing infighting between Saunders and Perlman, complicated matters. In 1970, a White House–approved loan for $200 million to bail out Penn Central was withdrawn when Congress balked on an issue that had become painfully clear: Why should the public pay for the mismanagement of a huge corporation?

But the public paid anyway.

It paid in government subsidies granted to a strong labor union to keep Penn Central's 90,000 workers employed, whether or not they were essential to the railway system that remained, Conrail and Amtrak. It paid in the economic displacement of towns no longer included as links in the reorganized rail system. And what the public paid in terms of discomfort, delays, and poor service until Conrail and Amtrak were flagged into their right tracks cannot be estimated.

Equity Funding was another and, from a moral standpoint, even more serious matter. A scandal sometimes referred to as the Watergate of American business, the Equity Funding disaster was born in the crafty, fertile brain of Stanley Goldblum, the company's chairman and chief executive and an ex-weightlifter, butcher, and scrap dealer. But what turned it into an infamous chapter in the darker side of business history was that at least a thousand of Equity Funding's executives and employees knew about the company's web of fraud, were involved in it, and fostered it over a period of years.

It all began with Department 99 in the life insurance subsidiary of Equity Funding Corporation of America, a financial services company started by Goldblum. When the affairs of Department 99 were finally brought to light in a court trial that began in April 1973, Goldblum and some of his top associates were accused of scheming to create bogus insurance policies by the thousands. Equity sold about 56,000 policies, for cash, to other major life insurers that considered them fully legitimate. No fewer than a hundred banks and insurance companies, including some of the country's best-known financial firms, found themselves with about 2 million shares of Equity stock that had absolutely no value. Potential losses to thousands of stockholders totaled about $300 million. In addition to the insurance companies, some of Wall Street's most prestigious brokerage houses, which kept recommending Equity stock even after the first startling news stories broke, had also been duped.

The bogus nature of the policies was known and carried on at various levels of Equity Life Insurance. Those closest to the plan's machinations covered up the con game by all sorts of subterfuge, including intimidation of employees, threats of violence, forgery, illegal scrutiny of auditors' findings, and faking of computer tapes. In time, the scheme became a company joke, a put-on successfully fostered on the public. Testified a former Equity executive, "People laughed and laughed about it." The *Wall Street Journal,* which carried the first story on the fraud on April 2, 1973, headlined it "A SCANDAL UNFOLDS" and ended its disclosure with a quote from one source, "My God, the audacity of it." Goldblum, known as a well-tailored loner, a "private person," and "not easy to know," was able to ponder it all during a three-year jail term.

A taciturn, cautious executive, Richard W. Mayer's personal characteristics seemed perfect for his role as a retail credit man. But when he became president of the W. T. Grant Company, he changed drastically. He pushed the old, conventional variety-store chain into big-ticket household goods and expanded the credit program to a long-term installment plan to make it convenient to sell refrigerators and washers. And then, as if to send the train hurtling blindly around the bend, he opened hundreds of big new stores in a two-to-three-year period, as many as twenty-eight in one day.

Why the aggressive push in three separate risky directions by one of the industry's most conservative companies? As Mayer explained to the same coterie of close associates at business breakfasts and lunches, W. T. Grant had been behind the parade so long that it didn't even rally much under the previous management when a major rival, S. S. Kresge Company, embarked on a massive expansion in its K Mart discount stores. But, as Grant executives said later, Mayer and his New York staff didn't pretest their ideas in the field; they announced them by simple fiat.

Executives in the 1,200 Grant stores across the country could only do their best. But many reacted bitterly or without much interest. Poor timing complicated the problem. It was questionable whether a Grant customer who bought stationery, candy, and greeting cards would also buy a refrigerator in the same store. But just about the time that Grant began offering its Bradford line of appliances, household durables began to sag under the pressure of the recession that ended the 1960s. Sales flattened and sagged, and Grant couldn't pay its bills. Trade suppliers refused to ship merchandise. Major bank lenders, which had incurred criticism because of their forbearance, suddenly called in their loans. Six months after Grant filed for bankruptcy status, with debts of over $1 billion, it was declared a bankrupt company and liquidated. Seventy-five thousand employees lost their jobs.

If all this wasn't enough, the public shock was to become even greater. Apparent fraud was disclosed in the cases of Penn Central and W. T. Grant. While the nation's largest railroad plunged toward disaster, fifteen corporate insiders sold more than 40,000 shares for a total of $2 million. In defiance of Securities and Exchange Commission regulations, the executives disposed of their stock on the basis of their inside knowledge at prices between $40 and $70, while the public knew nothing of the company's big troubles. Within days after Penn Central's insolvency was disclosed, investors found that their shares were worth less than $6 each.

Drained by several hundred unprofitable stores, W. T. Grant discovered that several members of its real-estate department had accepted kickbacks—free station wagons, home remodelings, and expensive vacations—from shopping-center developers for recommending that the company sign leases in malls built by their benefactors. The executives were all fired and sued. But, despite a private settlement that largely quashed the proceedings, an uncomfortable question arose: Was executive greediness the reason for the choice of so many bad store sites, pushing W. T. Grant to the brink and over? Like an ugly, erupting boil on the neck of American business, the question festered. Was that executive appetite for favors and gratuities, even if they represented bribes, related to the growing problems of American business?

Whether or not the typical CEO felt a chill running down his spine over the indiscretions of others, his attitude was characteristic. Privately, he deplored the insulated judgments, the internal bickerings, and the demand for more and better executive privileges. But publicly he kept mum. To do so, it seemed to him, was to reduce the problem to its proper perspective. Disasters like Penn Central, Equity Funding, and W. T. Grant, unfortunate as they were, weren't typical. They might have helped to weight the average, but not really too much. They were exceptions, deplorable exceptions.

But the love of perks is not such an exception. Idolized, even exalted, in his own organization either because of sincere respect or actual fear or both, the American business CEO had always had the problem of how well to control the tokens and trappings of his power. Favors, gifts, gratuitous services were constantly being offered from the outside, while the aura that surrounded him within his own company was ego-building to the extreme. Only the most spartan of company heads could resist it all.

Despite a growing clamor in the nation's media and threats by the Internal Revenue Service and the Securities and Exchange Commission, perks remain an important mark of recognition and show few signs of departing from the executive way of life. Company jets, yachts, limousines, lodges, and Caribbean resorts, with only the faintest lines to mark whether they are used for business or pleasure, are only a few of the means in which CEOs and their top associates derive a so-called non-cash compensation. Other perks include lush vacations or expanded weekends (often legitimized by including a business session or two), free transportation for wives and other family members, company-paid memberships in country, luncheon, and dinner clubs, personal loans (at low or lower-than-average interest rates), residential mortgages at less-than-prevailing rates; and free income-tax-return preparation by the company's outside accountants. Some companies also buy villas in Spain for their exhausted executives, lease salmon streams in Iceland for top brass and their business guests, pay security costs at executives' homes, and invite executives to buy all sorts of merchandise—from autos to recliner chairs—through the company purchasing agent at sizable discounts.

The degree and quality of these perks closely reflect the corporate pecking order. Consequently, the CEO is entitled to the best and the most, the president almost as much, the executive vice-president somewhat less, and so on. Executives, while claiming they watch that perks don't go out of line, defend them, mostly on the basis that it is either small compensation for the many extra hours spent on behalf of the company or that much of it is to save time for and wear and tear on the key men. Generally, non-cash compensation is estimated to be growing annually at about 7½ percent.

But while perks are considered by businessmen to be essential fringe benefits, both the IRS and the SEC have been watching them more closely, trying to ensure that perks aren't actually taxable income or that shareholders aren't simply paying for executives' pleasure. The agencies' scrutiny received tacit backing from the Carter administration, which proposed that tax reform include a 50-percent maximum deduction on business lunches. But the President's curb on the so-called three-martini lunch irked business executives because it appeared to indicate that business was all fun, play—and drink.

Is there any clear link between a CEO's efficiency or productivity and his liking of perks? Occasionally—but not often—an excess of perks is cited for pushing a business to disaster. The

Barwick Corporation, an Atlanta-based carpet producer, met with heavy financial problems in 1975. Two years later, its new president, J. Robert Schultz, charged that executive overindulgence had brought it to the brink. Eugene Barwick, the founder, had a large yacht, a ninety-seat jet, and lush apartments in New York and Chicago. Those who know Barwick, whose linebacker dimensions and personal zest made him one of his industry's feistier characters, weren't surprised by his love of perks and the good life. It all appeared natural for this dynamic company builder who was considered one of the carpet industry's best salesmen.

"Too many luxuries for a company's top executives," Schultz, who succeeded Barwick at the company, told the *Wall Street Journal,* "are often a sign of deeper problems in a company —specifically, a poor attitude on the part of management toward the work that needs to be done." Shortly after taking over his post, Schultz eliminated almost all the company's perks—and about half its executives as well.

Much as business heads say they take pains to avoid excesses of perks and deplore them when they happen, there is among those in the upper stratosphere of a business occasional confusion between executive privileges and the canons of personal behavior. The result, if it reaches an extreme, can be personal disaster.

Anthony Conrad, the chairman of RCA Corporation, failed over a five-year period to submit federal income-tax returns, even though he had made withholding payments. When this was disclosed in September 1976, RCA's board demanded his resignation. Was Conrad just too busy, or did he feel that as RCA's chief he could avoid the onerous paperwork that 100 million Americans must undertake every spring? Unquestionably, it was a foolish oversight, and probably no one would admit it more quickly than Conrad himself.

While he never explained his action, Conrad did deny any intent to defraud and claimed that he had met his liabilities through his withholding and other payments accompanying his belated returns. Charged by New York State with attempting to evade state income taxes for the years 1973, 1974, and 1975, Conrad refused extradition from his Gibson Island, Maryland, home to appear in New York City for trial.

Kenneth S. Axelson, a respected financial senior vice-president for the J. C. Penney Company and a onetime New York City deputy mayor for finance, got himself into hot water over a minor matter of perks.

During a grand-jury investigation of bribes by a building contractor to Penney's and Avis executives, evidence emerged that Axelson had his Central Park apartment remodeled by the same contractor who had done much work at Penney's New York headquarters. Axelson had paid only $6,000 for the renovations, but the actual cost should have been about $10,000. Unfortunately, Axelson was under consideration for a post in the new Carter administration as deputy secretary for the Treasury Department. Hearing that the *New York Times* was preparing a story on his exercise of perks, he withdrew his name from nomination. Penney's, however, cleared him of any wrongdoing, and he remained in his company post.

But John Schumacher, a career fashion merchant, wasn't as fortunate. After the *Times* published a full-page feature on his Park Avenue triplex apartment—in which the chairman of Bonwit Teller entertained designers, celebrities, and major suppliers—Genesco, Inc., the parent company, received letters of complaint from customers and stockholders questioning whether Schumacher wasn't overdoing it and allowing the sumptuous pad to distract him. And when Genesco, a southern-based company with a Baptist background and financial problems, received hints that Bonwit employees had also spent time and effort helping Schumacher build and decorate his apartment, it lowered the boom on him. He was summoned home from the Paris couture showings, fired the next day, and told to vacate his office that weekend, despite the fact that his $240,000-a-year contract had another three years to run.

The vast majority of CEOs and other top executives do not fall into such personal disasters. But the threat—the fine line that must be observed between exercise of office and personal propriety—is an ever-present one. Cast into a role of high visibility, the American CEO constantly works in a fishbowl. But now the public has been aroused and is questioning whether all businessmen aren't connivers and gluttons. The fishbowl has gotten bigger.

The Yawning Gap—Promises and Performance

If perks are a personal need whose appetite the corporate chief executive must watch, what he promises and what he delivers are an infinitely greater hazard.

Unlike the politician, whose golden oratory in campaigns isn't entirely held against him in office, the top executive is on the griddle on all his promises and commitments, especially if he heads a public company. During the so-called high-flying 1960s, the head of a large public firm suddenly became bereft of his normal sense of calculation and flatly predicted at a meeting with Wall Street analysts that that year his company would have 50-percent increases in both sales and profits. When the results proved to be considerably less, he could only keep his silence. But his critics didn't. He lost his credibility—at least 50 percent of it.

During his honeymoon period, generally anywhere from one to three years, the typical CEO can make no mistake. Life is pleasant, even bucolic. He basks in the deep satisfaction of having reached the very top of the heap. The inner glow, fed by the obeisance of everyone around him, nourishes his ego. When he damns the previous management, or merely mentions it in gracious but subtly deprecating terms in referring to the company's still-existing problems, he is treated as though it was another, worse company that everyone knows he would have administered better. And every word he utters receives the immediate applause he savors, every demand the instant action he craves. A white knight on a gallant horse thundering into the courtyard to the swell of a mighty organ may seem fanciful, but viewing the high glamour of his acceptance is only a matter of one's taste for hyperbole. "He," as everyone on down the line refers to him, is *it,* the man (sometimes the woman) in the "ultimate job" who taps the buttons which turn the wheels that move the trillion-dollar economy.

Invited to join clubs, inner circles, boards of other companies; asked to accept trusteeships and directorships in the symphony society, museums, and foundations; finding himself the idol of headwaiters, receptionists, and elevator operators—even the cop on the beat and the newstand dealer seem to know him right away—his head can be turned and it often is. Speaking to analysts, to his own executives, to his board, extravagant promises rise to his lips, and if he is fortunate enough to stifle them he will be able to avoid eventual complaints and recriminations. But it is difficult to control one's emotions in a highly charged situation.

As those initial years pass, things change, imperceptibly at first, then with a definiteness that shocks him. His ideas, so freely accepted before, now obtain mixed reactions. His demands find slower action. He is troubled by the mental inertia of people he thought were movers, by the slowness of his directors to accede to his proposals, by the seeming sudden shift by some of his constituencies from approval to hesitation, or questioning or skepticism. He realizes, too, that he is even lonelier than he thought and that a CEO has no peers and no way of sharing his responsibility with anyone else. There is really no one with whom he can discuss his problems on equal, no-recourse terms.

"What I never appreciated before but what I do now is the difference between being chief executive and being president of the company," observed Ellmore C. Patterson, former chairman of J. P. Morgan & Company, and of its subsidiary, Morgan Guaranty Trust Company of New York, the nation's fifth largest bank and its preeminent corporate bank. "The president is concerned with everything that goes on and does many things that the CEO does. But the chief executive has enormous powers over the company's affairs and over the employees. I believe in ideas floating up as well as down to help decisions. But the CEO's challenge and responsibility are absolutely constant.

"Sometimes, the big ones came to me when I was riding a horse, reaching for a paper, or lying down," he said. "And they could be very major decisions, the results of which cannot show up for four or five years and which can make my successor a boob or a hero. That is the power of the job."

But then comes the change of events in roughly the third or fourth year, and the chief executive finds he is no longer the white knight. The scars already show, and his disappointments will not easily be forgotten. His future may already bear some shadows. But how he reacts to the new stacking of the cards and how effective and productive he will be now more than anything else will determine his true worth during the remainder of his usually short tenure.

What is his true worth? Is it any less than that of his predecessor of one, two, or three decades ago?

The questions were put to Harold Stieglitz, vice-president for management and personnel research of the Conference Board, the nonprofit, business-research organization. A pipe-smoking, respected business analyst who has studied and dissected the American CEO for years, Stieglitz preferred to answer the questions in reverse order.

"Twenty and thirty years ago, the chief executive of a large or small business could be more personally involved and more personally effective in his company's affairs," he said. "He took a heavy hand in specific functions. Today, the situation calls for different kinds of skills, and the CEO's effectiveness depends greatly on his ability to operate through other managers. He's no longer managing a business but an organization, no longer a manager of things or functions but a manager of managers. In the old days, he would, for example, decide on and estimate what his research and development needs were. Nowadays, the CEO finds that R & D is only one element in which resources and needs must be coordinated. So he has to manage strategic resources and decide, 'Where do we bet our bucks? . . . How do we organize the entire ball of wax? . . . Who are the key people we have to rely on to do not only the R & D job but sales, planning, production, et cetera?'"

In Stieglitz's view, today's CEO isn't any less effective or productive than his predecessors. His job, his role, and his priorities have changed because the character of business organizations has become more complex. "The typical corporation of today in this country is operating in a competitive, governmental-restraint, and social atmosphere that's totally different from the atmosphere that faced the company of previous decades," Stieglitz added. "That means that the man who runs the business these days has to be a different kind of executive and individual."

Since that is the case, he was asked, what's the man's true worth? And how can his effectiveness be measured?

The bottom line, the immediate profit results, isn't the real measure, Stieglitz replied. "To effectively test his role in today's context of government restraints and the socioeconomic environment," he said, "you have to question how viable he has made the company, its growth, its ability to perpetuate itself and whether he has created the proper managerial atmosphere to take the business on to higher realms. That's the real measure."

But does he really earn the $400,000, $600,000, even the $800,000 that some on top of the heap get? Stieglitz shrugged. "Are you asking me, Is he producing equal to what he earns or what someone else will pay him?" he inquired, smiling. "The guy who is right for the job and is meeting that true measure is worth it, all right. But what most of them are getting paid represents the competitive value that he commands in the market. In other words, if his company won't pay him that kind of remuneration their competitors most likely will."

If today's corporate chief has his own financial bargaining power like that of today's top professional athletes, television personalities, and rock singers, he can truly sit in splendor in his soundproof, interruption-proof suite. But it can only be a momentary respite from the state of siege, which exists just outside his door or at the shrill ring of his telephone or when he confronts one of his growing chorus of "constituencies."

Few large American corporations today do not have guards against those constituencies. Public-relations men, investor-relations experts, consumer-affairs officers or advisers, industrial-relations men, lobbying connections, a coterie of house or outside lawyers—each a specialist in one of those constituencies —a staff or consulting psychologist, personnel specialists, and so on.

And added to those in the most recent years is an increased security force, maintained either by the company or by the building in which its headquarters is located. Terrorism, violence in the form of bombs, bomb scares, telephone threats, and sometimes kidnappings—plus fears fed by the rampant terrorism and kidnappings in several European countries—have created the need for security control in many American companies. Whether in New York, Chicago, or Los Angeles, visitors to a large and growing number of buildings must pass muster with either identification cards or confirmed appointments before they are allowed to enter building elevators.

Yet most American CEOs, including most this writer has interviewed, do not readily admit to being "besieged." The word, they imply, is perhaps too strong. But isn't it tantamount to the welter of new pressures, complexities, constituencies (to use their own word), increasing governmental intervention, and regulatory strictures? Perhaps, some say.

Despite all his disclaimers, all his efforts, and all his attainment, the man who sits at the top of American business is hardly his own man these days. Harried, harassed, and constantly pressured, he finds his ability to maneuver constrained. Many feel that he has lost substantial freedom of movement and of decision-making and much of his own impact on his business and even on the country's economy.

"Today's corporate chief is probably in the worst position he's been in in thirty-five years," declared Pierre Rinfret, a leading economist and director of five companies. "Not since World War Two has the American business head had so little freedom, maneuverability, and independence.

"He's caught in a vise consisting of the increasing imposition of government regulation, investment bankers who care more about financial gain than economic progress, stockholders who want a straight-line growth and constantly higher dividends, and social advocates who insist that profits mean less than social responsibility," Rinfret says.

Contrary to general public opinion, the economist adds, the American businessman's input into national government policy has been considerably less than he wanted. His impact on the White House has been puny because the social environment on which several recent administrations rode to power is "contrary to those things that business wants and advocates," adds Rinfret.

No doubt the term "besieged" jars with the pride and the sense of satisfaction that corporate chiefs still feel about their lofty role in American society. Despite everything, the CEO is still one of the country's premiere elite. Academics carp. Consumers and stockholders file angry class-action suits. Consumer advocates rail. Government overregulates. Unions step up wage demands and organizing efforts. Young people scoff at the profit motive and lay it to corporate greed. Minority and feminist forces bitterly demonstrate.

But then whose influence remains a sensitive reflection of the nation's economic well-being or illness and of its projection on the world scene? Who, after all, has so much power, responsibility, and opportunity to affect the lives of Americans and millions of others all wrapped up in one man?

Who indeed?

2

In the New Style

The Three Ages of Men and Business

In the history of men who rule the corporations, there appear to be quantum leaps—light-year changes in behavior and style: from Andrew Carnegie (rampant, piratical empire-building to rampant philanthropy) to Thomas Murphy of General Motors (the professional product of test-tube executive training), for example. Or John D. Rockefeller (arch business conspirator) to David Rockefeller (the prototype of the urbane banker-statesman). David Sarnoff ("I knew I would never quit . . . no matter what they thought of my radio music box") to Dr. Edwin Land of Polaroid (retiring, reclusive, happiest in the lab). Gerard Swope of General Electric ("Mr. Swope to you, sir!") to Reginald H. Jones, also of GE ("Just call me Reg"). The range of difference in personality and manner seems of epic proportions, defying the mere passage of time.

But the difference is really not so much a quantum leap as new eras in the lives of men and corporations . . . three distinct, functional ages. Dealing with things. Dealing with people. Dealing with situations.

Although the ages blur, depending upon the survival of the men at the top and the maturing of each company, the first age lasted for the first half of the twentieth century at most American companies.

The second age characterized the 1950s, the 1960s, and even the early 1970s.

But the advanced age—the dealing with situations where breadth of vision and optional dexterity were needed more than ever before—fell in the middle of the decade that began with a worldwide energy crisis and the need for cybernetics in the midst of a worldwide hunger problem.

And since the men who bestride the corporations must bend to the internal and external pressures that inevitably shape their roles, the American corporate chief began to change in substance and especially in style.

More than anything else, the chief executive had become a victim of his own environment. His office became a crucible of pressures that could not be ignored any more than the evolution of his own physical and mental prowess.

Public-policy issues were one pressure. The demands of his business and its government relationships or, as business pundits like to call it, "the interface." The need to psychologically blend an organization, its diverse human and physical assets. The urgency of managing a board of directors no longer just a rubber stamp. The calls for attention from many strident voices.

In response to all these, the American corporate chief slowly adopted new characteristics, and his personal and professional style altered:

He became an "intellectual" instead of an autocratic individual. With the growth of complexity, the growth of government and his company's entry into other countries, he could no longer be even a symbolic dictator. He had to open his mind, make it agile, and keep his options free. Dealing in situations, he had to engage in situation analyses in which, while no expert himself, he had to ride herd on experts. Should the business build a new venture from the ground up or acquire one? Which was cheaper, which was more success-prone? Should the company plan on its fuel needs with coal or nuclear energy? Should it base its capital budgeting on historical results or on zero-based considerations? The CEO's seat could no longer be held by the raucous, hard-nosed dum-dum, if, despite what critics had charged in the past, it ever was.

Intellectual? If knowledge of art, culture, history, anthropology, science, or philosophy marked the classic intellectual stereotype, the businessman-intellectual was characterized by his knowledge of business dynamics, marketplace strategies, human relationships. But the change in his style was really due to a change in attitude more than to any precise knowledge. His inner and outer worlds were too intricate for any one man to retain a closed mind. It was too dangerous.

All his pressure points left him little time for the ongoing supervision of the business, so he switched from hands-on to hands-off management and attempted, often succeeding, to inflate the capacity of his mind and the range of his overview.

But unless he protected himself, the reaching for a loftier viewpoint, holding himself above the baying of the company's internal and external hounds, left him too exposed to personal risks. And so the second trait in his new style emerged.

He built himself his own constituency within the company—a disciplined group of supporters. The formation went beyond the mere setting up of a "chairman's office" or "executive office," in which the input would reflect the activities of the company's major entities. It is also something more than a clique, although it has some of those earmarks, too. This homogeneous group actually has two types of members, consisting of senior management, which understands the demands on the CEO's time and attention and could help him meet them, and of others who are personally so loyal to the chief that he could always depend upon them for support. Often the subgroups consist of the same people. But because the typical CEO can't count on his closest associates to be both equally expert and loyal, he has to ensure that he has both close at hand.

Are they mostly yes-men? Ask the question and the CEO recoils. Perish the thought. What good would that do? That is the common retort.

But there is irony in his surrounding himself with a top tier through which everything funnels to him through a sort of human sieve. If he is to have the broad overview and the open options, can he really obtain them if the interpretation of events and challenges are colored by the personal predilections and prejudices of others? But perhaps the real question is could it be otherwise? The complexities and demands of running an American company today are too onerous for total involvement by the company chief. Given the need for the loyal cabal and the field marshals who supply the communiqués and the need to decide how to allocate his time and energy, the top man believes he has made the best of all possible choices.

One of the risks, unquestionably, is the matter of objectivity. Is there room for dissent in such a group? An opportunity for some spice to season the dish? Despite the chief executive's protestations that the top groups aren't just sycophants, one wonders if constant loyalty really isn't the tie that binds such corporate constituencies.

"Despite all the changes, a corporation is still something more of a dictatorship than an open democracy, but the company chairman who doesn't allow dissent is a manager who is foolish indeed," observes Kenneth A. Randall, president of the Conference Board. A former chairman both of the State Bank of Provo, Utah, and of the Federal Deposit Insurance Corporation, Randall adds, "The company head needs occasional, valid dissent. He expects it. But after full discussion, he also expects the dissent to cease and the ranks to close on a majority viewpoint." Of course the final choice remains the chairman's, says Randall. Exposing his viewpoint to wide discussion, the CEO of the late 1970s has also adopted a "healthy" skepticism toward accepted precepts. He knows that too many of them haven't stood up to the test of time or the rapidity of change, Randall adds.

But perhaps the unwillingness to go for the accepted has created the third change in the CEO's management style.

He has assumed the role of a professional economist in the traditional dimension because he no longer trusts the "new" economists. The young economists of the day have substantially alienated the major American CEO because they appear to be captors of the computer and of econometrics. What are econometrics? The application of statistical methods to the study of economic data and business problems. CEOs concede that econometrics and the computer have a role in tracking economic trends, but they believe that this is more properly accomplished by people who understand business dynamics and market dimensions.

"The young economists are some of the brightest people you have ever seen," said one chief executive, who requested anonymity. "But they are worshipers in the cult of the model. They remind you of Robert McNamara's reliance while Secretary of Defense on bomb drops and body counts to forecast the winning of the Vietnam War or the dependence of the real-estate investment trusts (REITs) on massive real-estate feasibility studies while forgetting the impact of the energy problem and of inflation."

Where does the chief executive get his sudden knowledge of economics, anyway?

He gets it from the residue of his education and his participation in management seminars, but most of all from living with its practical demands on his daily management performance. He has learned which economic rules fit, bend, work, and which do not. And if he mistrusts the young cultist economist, he is also increasingly cynical about the older economist-statesman who has failed him in at least the last three recessions. Generally, he likes Paul McCracken (whom he deems a realist with balance). He is intrigued by but not respectful of John K. Galbraith (a populist liberal with histrionic pretensions). He wonders fitfully about Milton Friedman (a redoubtable conservative). And he listens respectfully if abstractly to Walter Heller (a middle-of-the-roader with somewhat indistinct parameters).

But oddly enough, in an era where all economists are suspect, today's American CEO retains a fond respect for the credos of the pioneers, principally Adam Smith (national progress is best secured by freedom of just, private initiative); Thomas Robert Malthus (population increases at a faster rate than the means of sustaining it, hence self-restraint needs to be cultivated), and John Maynard Keynes (income and employment levels depend entirely on private and public expenditure).

He may not agree with them in toto. But in terms of principle the older, classical economists appear to have a better survival rate in credibility at the CEO level than the crop of the 1950s and 1960s and especially of the 1970s.

Perhaps in essence the chief executive's taking on the role of economist is his way of escaping from the clutches of the professional economic adviser, who possibly shouldn't be faulted for his lack of universal success, although he was long considered a pillar in the corporate edifice. Or perhaps it is another symptom that the head of American business simply decided to be his own man.

But this instinct to be all-protected, all-pervasive without overdue involvement in any one, specific activity has not been entirely successful.

And, most recently, this has involved a further change in his style.

He has had to become a personal mass communicator. He was in most cases ill prepared for that role, but he had to learn, because it became clear that sending his chief of staff or his public-affairs vice-president didn't give the company the credibility that the stiffening opposition demanded. When he did dispatch "a hired gun," it only seemed to confirm the stereotyped complaint that businessmen liked to retreat from the battle. He didn't want to be bloodied and so he sent his lieutenant whose blood, it appeared, was cheaper.

So the CEO began to take professional lessons from voice coaches, elocutionists, advertising, and public-relations specialists. As the news about his company moved from the financial to the front page, he began to appear personally before Congress, allowed himself to be interviewed on "Meet the Press," granted interviews with magazines and newspapers, spoke on the public-broadcasting radio and television networks, and even began to appear on television commercials. He was both a delight and a trial to his communications advisers, perhaps more the latter than the former, because he was stiff, self-conscious, not really effective.

But there was no way out. And he knew it.

The real need for his personal participation had begun to hit home. If American industry was to sell its story—that business growth (i.e., profit performance) was vital to the nation's growth (meaning the average American's economic well-being) —it would have to develop its own star-mode, articulate people who could attract sympathetic media treatment because they were appealing and newsworthy in their own right. Businessmen would have to develop their own Ralph Nader, Frank Sinatra, Norman Mailer, Jacqueline Onassis, Walter Cronkite, Barbara Walters, Edward M. Kennedy, and so on.

It was a tough order, too. The hard-pressed television producer who already knows that a commercial loses its punch if it lasts over thirty seconds would allow only seventy-five seconds for one fact to register and the personality to make its impact. Viewer patience lags after that brief span because what the senses perceive must be nurtured by what the emotions and intellect provide. And can businessmen, regardless of how important they might be, compete for charisma with Mary Tyler Moore, the Jeffersons, the Archie Bunkers, and Telly Savalas? Will they in time also be able to achieve the appeal and the excitement that makes for star quality? Probably not—but it could happen.

In the meantime, one can easily see them. Frank Borman, the astronaut-turned-chief-executive of Eastern Airlines, may seem stiff and his eyes a bit glazed as he wanders on television around his airline's ticket counters, expressing his sincerity about service. John D. deButts, the CEO of American Telephone and Telegraph, may seem languid and uncertain as he tells the television audience about boons of telephone automation. Reginald Jones, the chairman of General Electric Company, may seem impressive but heavily pedantic as he appears before a congressional subcommittee or on a TV network news conference. Or the TV viewer might opt for Frank Perdue, the chicken man, or Tom Carvel, the ice-cream man, both of whom make their own commercials. But they and many of their peers are trying—trying to do something that was never before a part of their natural makeup.

It's no longer enough for the American CEOs just to do a good job running a company. They must become superstars too.

Good-bye to Privacy, Maybe

Yet as they reluctantly move more and more into the limelight, they stand to lose the thing they love most—their privacy. It's not so much a matter of hiding, although it is that, too, but a deep desire to want to preserve at least a modicum of family life. Already intermittent and fragmented, however, the CEO's private life will erode even more as he increasingly becomes a public personality.

Caught between having to be both a public presence and the steward of vast private resources, he has become at the same time a removed figure and an eager follower of the latest social mores. The paradox, of course, is obvious to everyone but him, perhaps because he doesn't want it to be. But the clash of desires and drives in the way he lives today makes for more than occasional discomfort and awkwardness.

And so he has built and sustained a film, an invisible barrier, between himself and others. Sometimes he is not even conscious of it. More often, he arranges it himself, keeping a safe vacuum for reflection, protection, and distance. Even his closest associates find it difficult to build a close relationship with him. Knowing it and even savoring it, the chief executive reassures himself that he needs the opportunity to brood for the good of the company and the opportunity to retreat for the good of his own nervous system.

Often preoccupied with their problems, the big guns in American business give off an odd aspect to associates—they aren't really with you when they are with you. Other than their challenges and problems, it appears, everything else is frivolous. One quickly develops the feeling that he is only important to the company head if he is part of the inner, mental world in which the chief executive lives.

But unfortunately, in a good many cases that barrier is carried over into the businessman's home. Bemused, diverted, hung over with his weighty matters, he becomes no companion of dreams. The woman who looks forward to his homecoming finds that only half a mind and heart has returned to the hearth. And more and more, the marriage breaks up, even after many years.

Nonetheless, the company chief knows the hazard of keeping the shield constantly before him. He doesn't always want it to be there, especially with his family. But he knows that while the barrier is a protection it is also an obstacle against being part of change, especially social change. And so he tries in his own way to reflect social mores rather than stand off from them.

George Lang, a famous New York restaurateur, cited some of the eating and drinking habits of many of the top businessmen he catered to in that city and from out of town. "When wine drinking became the in thing," he said, "many of them took wine courses with well-known wine personalities and experts. They bought wines at auctions in London and the United States. They studied wine lists before dining so that they could be facile and at home when they ordered."

The same eagerness to be with the times is demonstrated by businessmen with regard to restaurants and gourmet cooking, Lang said. They seek out the names of the newest, most talked-about eating places. Some take expensive courses in gourmet cooking, Lang added, so that they can intrigue their friends with their chic home pursuits. And wives, who otherwise might object, look on with warm amusement, enjoying their husbands' more human side.

On the other hand, as George Lang noted, another common trait of the businessman's changing habits is that he doesn't want to seem interested in being part of the scene. Not only is the veil dropped—the frown or the vague stare of bemused executives is frequently observed in the restaurant, nightclub, or occasional rock concert—but his presence there is patently offhand (which it isn't really, of course).

If the changing personal style of the typical American CEO appears contradictory, however, it is no more so than in the way he has preferred to live in recent years. The administrator of vast funds, he has lately preferred a modest home or several apartments of modest proportions and decor. European and Asian businessmen tend to have their homes more expressive of their station, with many owning palatial residences staffed with crews of servants and retainers. But many American CEOs, including some earning over $500,000 a year, have homes more befitting executives earning $50,000 a year. Comfort, unpretentiousness, and practicality are the flavors of those residences.

Gone are almost all the lavish, colonial homes in the Hamptons of Long Island—shuttered, torn down, or replaced by country clubs, golf courses, and garden apartments. There are exceptions in the suburbs of New York and in Bethesda, Shaker Heights, and Beverly Hills, where shaded enclaves contain four-, five- and six-acre plots with plush executives' homes. But generally the lavishness that heads of major companies enjoyed and paid for in their homes has given way to more economical, multi-apartment living better suited to the greater mobility that executives have had in recent years.

It may be simply the result of the pursuit of egalitarianism, the desire to shun ornateness and pretension in a time of striving for equality by peoples and classes. On the other hand, life can be pleasant indeed in the finer condominiums of New York, Palm Beach, Saint Petersburg, and in the Sun Belt states, where a good many top executives own residences with from four to as many as ten rooms.

And life there, in between the trips that often take both

husband and wife away from home, is simple but not plain. A maid and/or cook comes in several times a week. The executive's wife often does the cooking herself and takes care of her own shopping. Some couples, too, have given up their chauffeur and do their own driving.

The return to a simpler way of living in corporate America, however, isn't universal. The businessman who is his own star salesman, promoter, and business developer still lives lavishly. Hugh M. Hefner, the founder-chairman of Playboy Enterprises, lives in a pair of mansions, both paid for by the company, one a seventy-four-room affair in Chicago and the other a twenty-nine-room home surrounded by pools, a grotto, and exotic gardens. Bernard Cornfeld, the founder of Investors Overseas Services, had villas in Europe and the Caribbean and, even after he was displaced by the scandals that rocked his giant complex of mutual funds, banks, and insurance companies, lived in a former movie star's Beverly Hills mansion.

In such cases, as in others of more limited proportions, the home is an ostentatious extension of the company, especially of its sales effort. Entertaining of customers, VIPs, and other guests is an ongoing business effort, and there is scarcely a large American company that isn't willing to pay for apartments used by its key executives for a combination of personal living and entertainment.

Yet by and large, the American executive's home life is modest, even spare, in contrast to his counterpart in other countries. Kenneth Randall, of the Conference Board, who often travels abroad for the business-research organization, said, "I can't help noticing the change that has taken place in the way our businessmen live compared to Latin American countries and even the less-developed countries. There, it's common to see businessmen living in big estates with cadres of servants. And it's the same way with their wives—in the U.S., she does a lot of her own housecleaning but in most foreign countries the businessman's wife has servants for all her needs."

And so the typical CEO's way of living has changed, too. It reflects his own realization that his new professional life has shaped his personal life's exposure, travel, and demands on his time and attention, compelling him to live in simpler modules of place and convenience. What is certain, too, is that his being thrust in the limelight will militate for even more privacy and simplicity, but he is likely to get the latter much more easily than the former.

Behind the Facade, the Human Yearning

Why less privacy when the chief executive wants more?

Public suspicion and disenchantment over the pervasive role he plays on their lives will demand more exposure on the part of the nation's CEOs, despite all the changes in their professional and personal style.

In a pluralistic society, where most businessmen think the government largely works against them, many Americans nonetheless believe that business too often has its own way and foists its will on the people.

It seems difficult for most ordinary people to equate an acceptance of the profit principle as a way to a sounder, healthier nation with air and water pollution, constantly rising prices, unsafe products, and economic growth that robs the land of its natural assets.

The inevitable result is that much as the company's chief doesn't like it, his role will become more exposed as pressures require that he personally respond to the public's charges. And those pressures can only grow. A rise in populism, and more aggressive stances by critics and by an ever more adversary press, will roust the CEO from his lair.

But sometimes that press can be dichotomous, too.

On the climactic day of the first commercial flights here of the Concorde, the supersonic transport airplane jointly built by the British and French governments, the *New York Daily News,* the largest American daily newspaper, congratulated Air France and British Airways on a successful flight. This was despite the opposition raised by Long Island residents over the prospect of the Concorde's high decibels and added flights.

But the *News,* long a conservative newspaper, had hired Pete Hamill, a liberal, often-emotional writer, to write a hard-hitting, circulation-building column on public affairs. On November 23, 1977, the same day as the paper's editorial, Hamill deplored the arrival of the Concorde and the businessmen on both sides of the Atlantic who were behind it.

His column, however, was twinned with a news story on the flight and the headlines showed the difference in approach. "We're SSTransported to New Era!" trumpeted the news story. "FLY NOW—PAY LATER FOR 'PROGRESS'" headed Hamill's column.

"Maybe that's the way it always goes," Hamill wrote. "The winners always have the heavy artillery: the big lawyers and the expensive flacks and the people who make deals over dinner tables. The men who run Air France and British Airways have more in common with the men on the Port Authority or some judges than they have with the lonesome Democrats who live in Howard Beach or the Five Towns. None of the people who run the airlines live in such places, and neither do the people who will now be allowed to use them."

Ignoring a victory luncheon press conference at the Waldorf-Astoria, Hamill continued, "Instead I drove out onto the Van Wyck [Expressway] and waved at the handful of protesters, thinking about all those things that had come under the name of progress and how they had helped make life a colder, less human proposition. They had built the Pan Am Building and ruined Park Ave.; carved the Bruckner Expressway through the Bronx and left a hole in the borough's heart; built the East River Drive and deprived us of our river; split the atom and used it to kill people; walked on the moon and destroyed five centuries of poetry."

Writers like Hamill, academics who consistently oppose corporate bigness, activists in Congress, and consumerism advocates give businessmen ulcers. But aside from the fact that Americans are fortunate to have them, even with their occasional exaggerations, they have also been responsible for another trait in the changing profile of American businessmen— a sense of social responsibility, a touch of humility, a desire not to fulfill the charges of arrogance and noblesse oblige.

Unquestionably, it would be simple to overrate this change, because it is only a beginning and hardly universal. But interviews with some of the top American businessmen clearly show it.

"One of the things that stirs me is that there are too many arrogant leaders around who think they know everything—it represents an arrogance of power," said Robert T. Quittmeyer, president and chief executive of Amstar Corporation, formerly the American Sugar Company, the nation's largest sugar refiner. "They try to foist their ideas on your business and the way you do business. I'm referring to government, politicians, the press. They are as arrogant as any of us—and I include myself. . . .

"So many issues are gray, not all white or black in their solution, and expressions of opinion on them often tend to be arrogant," Quittmeyer said. "I have learned that I should try my damndest not to be arrogant—to listen more. I'm a very poor listener. I tell myself, 'Quittmeyer, keep your damn mouth shut and listen.' . . . But sometimes, such as in the sugar crisis in 1974, you can make a big mistake by listening too much to many opinions, many of them arrogant, both in my own company and outside. I did not intuitively act. It was a case where I should perhaps have been a little more arrogant than pluralistically minded. I should have acted on my intuition. Intuition is a reflection of experience—and if you have a broad experience your intuition is not too bad a base on which to make a decision.

"On the other hand, I think a lot of decisions shouldn't be made on the spur of the moment but should be postponed until the situation resolves itself. Executive decisions are mostly in the gray area, and the worst are made when you are uncertain and lose your direction. So they should be made from a combination of intuition and facts, but arrogance, arrogance of power, is a danger and must be carefully watched. It's in all of us, and once we realize that, well, your chances of doing the right things are better."

Implicit in Quittmeyer's words, at least to this interviewer, was an unspoken desire evident most in his earnestness to express the difficulties, the trauma, of making major decisions. It was an evident effort to put the writer—anyone—on his side of the desk. That may be the most important change of all: to appear human, not just a moneymaking, power-building machine devoid of normal instincts.

The hours I spent with John D. deButts, the chairman of AT&T, began in this manner: "Mr. deButts, what I really want to do is put the man at the top of American business in the perspective of the nation's economy and the international economies and to provide some good insights."

"I hope in the process," deButts quickly said, "you'll show that chief executives are human beings. . . . I got a fantastic response to a commercial I did for the company. It ran all during the sporting event. And the reaction I got was, 'Golly, you're human.' It took me back. I said, 'Of course, I'm human—what did you think I was?' And I'm afraid that too many people have the general idea that a chief executive officer is somebody who sits up in an ivory tower and hates to ever come out."

Much more was to come from deButts in our prolonged talks, but his plaintive plea at the outset surprised me.

3

The Web Tightens

In the decade and a half after World War II, the typical American businessman began his day with high hope, conducted his hour-by-hour affairs with pleasure and profit, and ended his day in a flourish of satisfaction.

In the sixties, he started with mixed hope and concern, sweated happily over his capacity to keep up with a big order backlog, and went home with a murmured blessing over how well the stock market had rewarded his efforts.

But in the final quarter of the twentieth century, his situation is very different.

He begins his day by firmly promising himself to keep a grip on things no matter how conflicting and paradoxical they become. During the next eight to ten hours, he often feels himself a captain with largely symbolical braid, the corporate ship often buffeted by winds and squalls through which he and his well-paid top associates can't entirely maneuver. Unpredictably, his own efforts and those of competitors either produce a shower of dollars or rob him of them. And when he calls it a day, he has the bemused look of a man who doesn't really know whether to laugh or cry or throw up his hands.

Nonetheless, as his chauffeured car cuts through the commuter traffic, he is filled with a strangely negative satisfaction. Thank heaven, he tells himself, things didn't get worse and the frustrations that swept him didn't completely immobilize him.

Take, for example, a few incidents involving some of the country's better-known chief executives that occurred virtually in the same month:

Sitting one evening calmly reading *Time* magazine in his living room in Bronxville, New York, Charles F. Luce, the chairman of Consolidated Edison Company, the nation's largest utility and the light-giver to metropolitan New York, didn't stir when his lights flickered slightly. But a few minutes later when his Manhattan office phoned, he bolted out to face the nightmare of three million private and commercial customers suffering through what became a twenty-five-hour power blackout.

Human error, technological foul-up, or management failure—or all three?

He didn't know yet, though he had strong suspicions. But wan, haggard, and exhausted, he realized late the next day that, though the utility's fortune had greatly improved before the blackout, after the blackout he would never again feel he had anything quite under control at Con Ed.

Martin Schwab calmly took a call one Monday morning from the Bankers Trust Company. Chairman of the financially troubled United Merchants & Manufacturers, a large textile company, he had lately felt that he would perhaps succeed in reducing some of his company's disorder. But the next few seconds devastated this hope.

"We are impounding your five million dollars on deposit with us," said the man from Bankers Trust. "We just don't think you can come up with any plan that would work for us or the other creditors."

The next day, the giant firm, which had thought it could gain a new lease on life by folding its highly unprofitable Robert Hall Clothes division, filed for court assistance under the laws of bankruptcy in the year's biggest insolvency.

Charles G. Bluhdorn, the acquisitive chairman of Gulf & Western Industries, was savoring the success of his penultimate effort to take over Madison Square Garden and its various sports and entertainment entities. He had almost forgotten the nagging problem of a former lawyer for G&W telling all to the Securities and Exchange Commission in order to obtain a promise of a lighter sentence on fraud charges against him.

Then, for three traumatic days, Bluhdorn found himself writhing over a front-page, three-part investigative series in the *New York Times* about his and his company's alleged financial "shenanigans," in great part fed by the embattled lawyer's desperate revelations. With all the company building he had done since 1949 and all the employment and economic boon it had generated, he wondered, did he really deserve the *Times'* journalistic bombshells?

Ralph Lazarus, the chairman of Federated Department Stores, the country's largest department-store operator, had just announced an improved second-quarter financial performance and he was feeling pretty well. It reversed the previous unhappy quarters, and behind him, he believed, were also the public memory of price-fixing charges against one of his store divisions and a government consent order on repaying small credit balances, most of which accrued to customers who no longer had any known forwarding addresses.

But a few days later, he had to meekly accept a new consent order from the Consumer Safety Product Commission no longer to "knowingly" sell children's clothes treated with the potentially dangerous chemical "Tris." The commission's act revived the bad publicity that Lazarus hated to have his prestigious organization face. With 150,000 different items in each of his seventy-five stores, a few garments in several stores had trickled through the tight sieve his staff had set up to trap the Tris-treated kids' pajamas. Did anyone really think that he would "knowingly" sell clothes that might produce cancer? he asked himself.

Disappointment and shock were at the core of the spate of top-executive firings that developed in the mid-1970s as the decade progressed. The shove that spun the whirling door began coming as much from incompatibility of personal style as from bottom-line disappointment.

Robert Tyler, Jr., president of Simmons Company, the home-furnishings producer, was summoned one morning by chairman Grant G. Simmons, Jr., and told he had to go. "You're more careful and deliberate than we can afford," Simmons said tersely.

At Kaiser Industries, the steel-mining complex, the reverse sort of incompatibility was cited for another ouster. Fifty-two-year-old William R. Roesch, conspicuous for his brusque, matter-of-fact manner in a company noted for its Kaiser style of paternalistic, decorous relations, was out after three years. Gentlemanly behavior within the firm had always been a source of pride to Edgar F. Kaiser, chairman, and Roesch had riled him once too often. Roesch, however, moved on to a top spot at the United States Steel Corporation.

But perhaps the most unusual example of executive frustration surfaced just before Labor Day, and it involved the continuing energy problem.

In full-page advertisements in the *New York Times, Wall Street Journal, New York Daily News,* and thirty-six other newspapers across the country, thirty-one chief executives from a wide range of American companies addressed "an open letter to the American people" to urge broad-scale action on the energy crisis. "It's an issue of survival," they declared. Everyone—business, individuals, government, and environmentalists—was asked to be ready to sacrifice and help develop new conservation methods in the interests of lowered energy use. And the signers, all standard-bearers of blue-chip companies, pledged cooperation to work with the administration and Congress to formulate a national energy policy.

What was behind the unusual open letter? A spokeswoman for N. W. Ayer, the advertising agency that prepared the ad, said that John deButts of AT&T and other chief executives had been troubled by suspicions that the business community wasn't sufficiently concerned by the nation's continuing energy problem and decided to show their real concern. The $280,000 cost was borne equally by all signers and came out of company funds.

But the life of the typical CEO in the century's final quartile is hardly all frustration or all a matter of looking worriedly over his shoulder. There's another side of it, too, marked by the enjoyment of power, perks, and privilege, recognition from the mighty and the humble, and the rubbing of elbows with the great of the time. These are all part of the day's and night's normal activities.

The head of the powerful E. I. du Pont de Nemours & Company spent a busy week at the end of a recent summer in which all these elements figured. With a smile combining satisfaction and happy resignation, Irving S. Shapiro, Du Pont's chairman, pleasurably recounts the week's activities:

Monday: Coming right after a vacation, that Labor Day weekend bequeaths Shapiro and his wife, Charlotte, an extra day to relax at home in Greenville, Delaware—and, he reminds himself, a chance, too, to savor the absence of urgency for one more precious day.

Tuesday: Into the office at 8:15 A.M. Then a ninety-minute meeting with the Du Pont finance committee. Back to the office the rest of the day to handle routine calls and the mail flow.

Wednesday: Normally he should be at the all-day executive-committee meeting that starts every Wednesday morning at 9:00. But this morning he is in a company airplane heading to the White House. President Carter has invited a variety of government officials and top businessmen to hear his views on the still-pending Panama treaty and to get their opinions. Skips out at 10:30 and flies back to Wilmington, where he takes command of the executive-committee meeting until it concludes at 5:30. Then, back with Charlotte in the plane to Washington and attendance at the White House state dinner for Western Hemisphere heads to ratify the Panama treaty. Lots of chatting with such as Zbigniew Brzezinski, Henry Kissinger, and state heads such as Pierre Trudeau of Canada, Alphonso Michelsen of Colombia, and one Jimmy Carter. And then, when the dancing and entertainment start at about 11:30, Shapiro is back in the plane with Charlotte and happily, wearily to bed at 1:00 A.M.

Thursday: In the office at 8:15 A.M., having canceled a date with Yeshiva University in New York, which wanted to show him the facilities and draw a greater participation from him. Boards plane at noon, tuna-fish sandwich on the way, to debark at New York and chair a meeting of the Business Roundtable. Then, in the late afternoon, a return to the Shapiro New York suite on the fourteenth floor of the Carlton House to dress for dinner, and then on to the River Club, where he and a dozen other guests hear Margaret Thatcher, the head of the British Conservative party, render a report on that country's fermenting economic situation.

Friday: An 8:15 breakfast with a reporter (this one) in the suite. At 10:00, a meeting with Edgar Bronfman, of Seagram's Distillers, to discuss means of raising money for the Hubert H. Humphrey School of Public Service at the University of Minnesota. At 11:30, head for the plane at Teterboro Airport, sandwich on board, and back at the Wilmington office by 1:30 P.M. to catch up on the mail and all that is pending.

Saturday: Reading and relaxing at home. Then host a luncheon at the Hotel Du Pont for a visiting high-level trade delegation from China. Then an appearance at a cocktail party and home to pack for the next day's trip.

Sunday: Departure with Charlotte for San Francisco and three days of international industrial conferences sponsored jointly by the Conference Board and the Stanford Research Institute. He plans to spend much time with Charlotte while in the Bay area. Both, he says, have decided that she will accompany him on as many trips as possible. Why? Shapiro is asked. "I take my wife everywhere," he replies, with a solemn smile. "We've agreed that two thirds of our lives are gone and we had better spend as much time as possible together."

The thrill of power, and the confidence and conviction it exudes, is also a part of the typical CEO's life.

All this seemed to pulse through the veins of David J. Mahoney, to account for his extreme restlessness and his chain-smoking as he engaged in a scatter-gun interview. The fifty-five-year-old chief executive of Norton Simon, the consumer-products conglomerate, had virtually capped his effort to take over Avis, the nation's second-largest auto- and truck-rental service, by beating out two rivals. And only days away from taking the spoils for a round $175 million, he seemed flushed with the juices of victory.

And not just over Avis. Few New Yorkers born in humble circumstances had come as far. A warm personality helped by an easy charm, athletic ability, and a hunger for success had gotten him an athletic scholarship, a first job at a New York advertising agency, and top appointments at three well-known companies. And the jungle skills learned during the Depression and the fiscal conservatism acquired then had helped him build Norton Simon into a major packaged-goods company. To accomplish that, he had edged out one competitor after another, gotten rid of incompatible executives, hired harder-driving ones, disposed of twenty-one divisions, and in eight years spent something like $675 million in advertising. It was obviously a case of a flamboyant CEO running a flamboyant company that he had taken over from a flamboyant entrepreneur.

For a half hour, he kept a reporter waiting beyond the appointed time as he huddled with lawyers. He was used to working with and pushing the legal fraternity. Preparing for the Avis tender offer, he had commandeered twenty-five attorneys and kept them at it for four straight days. Seconds before he finally appeared, his secretary arranged for coffee and deposited two packs of Marlboros at his place. Two packs? She nodded with confidence. He would surely consume them before we were finished.

When the lean, intense Mahoney came in, he apologized for his tardiness with a boyish sincerity. He listened to the introduction and then plunged in, nipping off the ends of questions with his quick replies and resorting to a frantic monologue as he strode around the table.

"I'll tell you, I guess it's true that I'm a maverick in a lot of ways . . . but I'd like to be more psychologically oriented, more sensitive, and more understanding of government. But I'll tell you this—people complain about big government but it's really the government baronies. It is all the bureaucrats. And it's true even in business—two people at a meeting can make a bureaucracy, with fear and insecurity biting at them. . . . This has not been understood—a lot of them are really decent people. Basically, what we all need are better communications—not just delivering messages, but being better understood. . . .

"People say they long for the good old days. When were those days, anyway? And why will the 1980s and 1990s be any different? We've got a higher standard of living, more people employed, everyone wanting a better life-style. . . . Listen, I don't go along with a lot of the complaints by businessmen. They get well paid to cope with problems and what we're facing is just a new set of problems and we should deal with them not in a pessimistic or adversary way but we must delineate them and shouldn't be defensive but positive. . . . The trouble is, dammit, that we in business have withdrawn into a cocoon of our own. Yet compared to the rest of the world, we're in good shape just because of our entrepreneurial system. . . .

"Capitalism is a pejorative—we've been a society of entrepreneurs and they have to be allowed to exist and be encouraged. Consumer-attitude studies show that Americans have a low regard for *businessmen* (repeat, *businessmen*)—but they approve the capitalistic system. When you ask them, Do you want government running things? they say emphatically, No! So, they seem to regard business's running things as a better alternative. But what they are criticizing is the behavior style of businessmen, not the system itself. Personally, I feel more secure about this than if they were upset with the system. . . .

"Let's face it, we've gone into an anti-hero era—the church attendance fall-off, the demonstrations, and all the disenchantment toward business. . . . We're all fallible, right? Nobody walks on water. . . . So, it is foolish to be irked by criticism. . . .

"The trick is, of course, to be decentralized at the same time as you are diversified, but who is really autonomous? The best structure is no structure. As soon as you get things too tightly controlled, it gets out of hand. Look at the American Medical Association, the Catholic church, et cetera. . . .

"Energy, employment, inflation, fractionalization—we've got problems up to our ass. But we do have pragmatism in this country. We have a wealthy system and a constitutional government, otherwise how can we have withstood all our economic ups and downs and Watergate? And we have no caste system—the American dream still lives, doesn't it? Big business should look at all this when their noses are down and realize that it has all worked for them. . . .

"There is a redistribution of wealth going on here today, but it is not as radical as in other countries. And what is even better is that we have seen fit to right the wrongs but we have maintained our right to talk back. . . .

"Am I flushed with success because of Avis? I don't think so. But my feelings of optimism and pragmatism were part of me long before the Avis thing. But—let me tell you this—if I didn't feel that way, I wouldn't have been able to do Avis. . . ."

Mahoney paused, taking a deep breath and puffing on his cigarette. He had, in fact, almost finished the two packs. "We're doing pretty well at Norton Simon. . . . Pretty good for a poor kid from Manhattan, I think." Mahoney had earned $844,444 in 1976. "Listen, next time bring a tape recorder. I'd like to hear how all this sounds played back."

And, of course, pressures, loneliness, and their effects are all part of the chief executive's life, especially in the bigger companies.

The man at the top of the large American corporation is

generally a species different from that of his counterpart in a smaller company. Plunging through the management hierarchy by a process of weaving and dodging to shortcut the human and operating obstacles, he has become what psychologists and psychiatrists call an "adaptive personality." Even if he is brought in from another company, he has the same adaptive trait, probably having already been in anywhere from three to seven companies and zigzagged back and forth from staff to line. In either case, he has had to mold with or "interface" with a variety of personalities in senior management.

And when he gets to the very top, adaptive as he is, he has also evolved into something he never thought he would be: a lonely and very vulnerable person.

"Everyone up there is vulnerable, but they are more vulnerable because all those below them are competing hard to be in his slot," observes Dr. Jonas Kohler, a New York psychiatrist. "So he has to devote an enormous amount of his time to power consolidation. And he has to reinforce his alliances."

Many CEOs and chief operating officers are "very bright, very talented individuals," Dr. Kohler said. "But what happens to them is that some of the talent and creativity is diminished or restricted by their role. Much of their attention and psychic energy are devoted to protecting themselves."

What's psychic energy?

"Well, all of us have only so much energy, the sexual and aggressive energy which are the two basic drives that fuel the human being," he explained. "There is only so much of it, a fixed quantity. A person could distribute it, focus it in such a way that his major role and attention or his energies are devoted to protecting himself. And if he is focusing on maintaining or 'lubricating his interface,' which means nothing more than protecting his position, a lot of his attention is being diverted away from the job and naturally he has less energy available to be creative. The task of maintaining the upper managerial position—the CEO's—is a very delicate task."

And it's depleting. Such a man has "less energy for problem solving and it can reduce his productivity. I don't mean that it's true of every chief executive of every big company—but it's true of a good many, and for the rest it's an ever-present danger," Dr. Kohler said. And there "is virtually no time left for his personal life. It is grabbed on the run. The wife and the kids can go down the tube."

The top executive's intellectual development also becomes stultified because of the same pressures. "As he becomes more sophisticated managerially," the psychiatrist said, "it is more difficult for him to invest his energy elsewhere and so it is more difficult for him to improve his mind. How many of them read books? And how many will claim that they have expanded their knowledge of life and history as they have expanded their corporate role? But then, in all honesty, how can you extract this man from his cultural matrix? You really can't. We are increasingly becoming an illiterate society."

But a New York industrial psychologist who works with large companies claims that today's CEO is more beleaguered than he has been but "he's always been lonely. A recession causes a chief executive to feel more vulnerable," said Dr. Anthony Martin, "and that's certainly understandable. Yet, he retains many satisfactions in his work which sustain him. You will find, too, that there is more tension at levels two and three down from the top. There's more self-induced tension in the upward mobility, perhaps, than when you have actually arrived at the top of the heap."

When the tension does exist, however, there are situations where the pressures can't be withstood and the equilibrium snaps. In 1975, a dramatic event portrayed this to millions of Americans: Eli M. Black, chairman of United Brands Company, threw himself out of his office window in a Manhattan office tower. Black, a former rabbi, had been exposed as the key figure in paying corporate bribes to the Honduran government in order to head off tax increases. For months afterward, Black's and the company's records were scoured for evidence of any other skulduggery that might have caused him to commit suicide. But nothing else was found.

Why did Black take his life?

David W. Wallace, chairman of Bangor Punta Corporation, a director of United Brands during Black's tenure and a longtime friend of the former rabbi, pondered carefully when this writer posed the question.

"You know," he said slowly, "there wasn't one news medium that didn't pillory Black after his suicide. But I think he was one of the most decent people I've ever known. I think the reason he jumped out of the window is because he thought he was saving his company. You know, he was educated as a rabbi, he had decent, strong, ethical standards. But he didn't tell his board anything about those bribes. And the fact that he didn't talk to his board when he paid the money to the president of Honduras is, to me anyway, a basic vindication of his decency. He wouldn't involve the board in this problem and he did it all on his own. He didn't get any money out of it. And I'm not saying that what he did was right. But he jumped out of the window, I think, because he couldn't live with the moral implications of what he had done."

What action did the United board take? "When the directors first found out about the bribes," Wallace said, "their first directive was to contact the State Department and say that the company wasn't paying any more money like this. And, the board said, 'If we can't get the money back, can we have it directed into a hospital or other institution in Honduras where it can do the people some good?' Actually, it didn't help. They were never able to get it out of a Swiss bank account."

But, Wallace was asked, wasn't it true that the really ironic element about Black's final act was that it didn't leave the company or anyone any better off?

"No, it didn't," Wallace conceded. "But it's difficult to say what anyone would have done under those circumstances given that background. You just don't know until you are placed in those circumstances. I'm sure that for Eli Black, with his training, suicide was a very difficult thing, and so I'm convinced that it was a reflection of the terrible pangs of conscience. Yet when you think about what he did, it doesn't jibe with the television image of the completely immoral businessman. If he was that way, he wouldn't have given a goddamn. He would have bluffed it through and carried it out."

4

When the Government Comes Knocking

Fog hangs low over the huge chemical plant. It is the third shift in the sprawling structure hugging the once-fertile valley. The mobility of machines and men should be slower, becalmed. But it isn't. It is the businessman's nightmare, punctuated by the shrieks of tortured equipment and the moans of fractured balance sheets. Glaring, neon-lit signs hang throughout the plant. EPA —$5 million. EEOC—$4 million. FEA—$3 million. OSHA —$10 million. CPSC—$2 million. At the front door a red light blinks over a huge sign reading: "Due to excessive costs of government regulation, this plant will close at the end of the month. Too late to write to your Congressman."

America's top businessmen are dismayed, frustrated, and even frightened by their inability to control some of the major forces that exert a significant influence over their companies. Many are troubled by their inability and failure to stem the drift of the nation's government and political formation to a sort of socialism that in essence will set standards, wages, profits, and policies for much of American business.

Yet, pressed to go beyond that concern which has long been raised by conservative businessmen, CEOs admit that the growing adversary relationship in the United States between big business on one side and government and the many private and public critics on the other is probably no more than the burden they have to bear to function under the American system.

Related to this, too, is the recognition that one of the major problems American business has faced has been its traditional reluctance to speak freely to the public and to the media, seeing journalists as antiestablishment critics.

In two interviews with this writer, John D. deButts, the CEO of American Telephone and Telegraph Company, described his reactions to both the government presence and the need to maintain press contacts:

"Government is becoming more and more a part of the management of the business, I would say—more regulations, more reports, more legislation that affect corporations—and this has required that I spend a great deal more time in that arena, testifying before congressional committees, contacting members of the Congress, contacting members of the Administration in order to be sure that they understand what the facts are with regard to this company.

"There has been more active, if you will, regulation by the normal regulators, which has required a great deal more of my time," he went on. "Testifying, as well as holding meetings here and establishing studies, study groups, in order to give me information that would allow me to make decisions in these areas. We spend a great deal more time on ERISA, OSHA, FCC, SEC—you name it. I would say that I spend a good half of my time on matters involving the government."

The chief executive of AT&T had led into the matter of government's growing hand in business when he described the "externals" that had changed the role of chief executives in recent years. Now he turned to another, "external relations with the media," which he explained as "one that I guess I've undertaken more on my own, that is, so that it's almost a campaign, a crusade."

DeButts said, "I have a very strong feeling that a lot of problems of business today are caused by business. The failure of the chief executive officer to stand up and tell the public what the facts are. The failure to be willing to 'Face the Nation.' (I picked that up because I've been on that show.) Unwillingness to talk to people like yourself or other newspaper reporters. I know quite a few guys who just won't talk to newspaper people."

These questions and answers followed:

Q. Mr. deButts, I ran into a couple of people who won't talk to me on this book. . . . I don't even know them and they don't know me. The basis of their refusal is something I don't understand.

A. I've only turned down one request from the media and I turned that one down because I just know that what he writes is not going to be factual. It's going to be slanted. He wrote about two of my friends and both of them were catastrophes. So I just refused to be interviewed by him. But everybody else I give them my number that comes right in to my desk.

Q. Why are businessmen reluctant to meet the public? Has business too long been considered private even though much of it is public? Is it a matter of just plain attitude?

A. No, I don't think so really. Well, that could be part of it. I don't think that's the key. There are many more demands on business today to disclose, of course. There are some businessmen who resent this. They say it's none of your business. But I think that they're the real minority. Number one, they hadn't had to do it before, so they've had no experience and they're scared of it. And two, they are inhibited by their lawyers and their public-relations people, who are afraid they might say something that will get them in trouble.

Q. So they just crawl back into the shell, so to speak?

A: And yet they're the only people who can do it. I've got a great president, two great vice-chairmen. They appear; they go on television shows; they have had interviews with the press; they make speeches and have press conferences. Just like I do. But really the CEO of a company is the only one who can speak for that company.

Q. He's got total responsibility?

A: What did Harry Truman say? The buck stops here. And so I think that only the CEO has got to be the spokesman for the company, for the industry.

If, as deButts puts it, "government is becoming more and more a part of the management of business," the converse—and the element that irks so many chief executives—is the growing

61

certainty that business is becoming less and less a part of the management of government.

Business discomfiture about government surfaced dramatically at the end of President Jimmy Carter's first year in office. It was partly because the President was a Democrat and most top businessmen are Republicans, partly because Carter was elected as a populist reformer who seemed to concern himself more with people problems than with business problems, and partly because he had failed to come up with an adequate long-term economic policy by the end of that first year. As a result, the Washington-business relationship hardened into mutual distrust and suspicion. And businessmen by the end of 1977 found themselves unable to keep from sniping.

At a meeting of the Business Council, an organization at which blue-chip companies exchange ideas on the economy and legislation, one CEO burst out, "The President ought to reaffirm his faith in the free-enterprise system."

The President's energy program, declared David Packard, chairman of Hewlett-Packard, a California electronics systems producer, "is a disaster." And of James Schlesinger, Carter's energy secretary, Packard said he "doesn't have the brains God granted a goose about the way the economic system is supposed to work."

Walter Wriston, the chairman of Citicorp, the large New York banking holding company, asserted, "The business community is looking for a believable, internally logical economic strategy. . . . That's what the business community hasn't seen yet."

That outburst of resentment may have been triggered early in October 1977 by the President's statement against the oil companies, his lashing out at their "exorbitant" profits as one of the big reasons for the nation's energy problems. For some months before, the troubled murmuring among businessmen had grown to outright muttering among themselves and a long list of grievances privately addressed to Washington. They included not only the fact that the Oval Office appeared to be mostly inaccessible to them and the absence of an economic game plan but also a myriad of indications that the President might, in the face of a slowing economy in 1978, seek temporary stimuli which would only generate new domestic inflationary pressures.

What did business want from Carter? Both the Secretary of the Treasury and the Secretary of Commerce were told in plain terms: a clear economic policy, tax-law changes, and a general change in attitude toward business—all of which would counteract the growing lack of confidence of businesses and investors and shore up the will of companies to invest more in new plants and equipment. Without those, there was a serious question that the economic recovery would continue.

For his part, W. Michael Blumenthal, the Secretary of the Treasury, conceded that American businessmen continued to be wary of the Carter administration, adding, however, "It takes a lot more time for business to feel comfortable with a Democratic administration." Juanita Kreps, the Secretary of Commerce, suggested that the President meet with the nation's business leaders for his first face-to-face discussion. In September 1977, ten CEOs met with Carter in a session arranged by Irving Shapiro.

Hopeful that that session would be the first of many, Shapiro said afterward that the problem of Oval Office access came primarily from the President's work habits, that Mr. Carter "likes to deal with paper rather than people." The President prefers to have businessmen deal with the agency secretaries who have been accessible, Shapiro added.

Although it may be a problem more of style than of substance, businessmen feel that the Carter manner of broad promissory statements followed by hesitant trial-and-error moves has affected confidence. Their reaction, perhaps, has had as much to do with their growing sense of uncertainty as the President's lack of substantive action. If that occurred to many CEOs, they could recall with some self-justification the President's ill-conceived fifty-dollar tax rebate proposal, which he later rescinded, and then his outburst at the oil companies, which he never rescinded. Clearly he was not, at that point, their man.

Looking for Mr. Scapegoat

Are businessmen always looking for a scapegoat?
If not, why the rapid decline in their respect and affection for the new President? Wasn't Carter, after all, an entrepreneur too, who had built a moderate but successful peanut-farming

and distribution business? And wasn't he—a graduate engineer with Navy experience in nuclear submarines and a former Georgia governor with a relatively large staff to supervise and a budget to meet—possessed of at least some of the qualifications of responsibility, logic, mathematics, and stewardship that should have stayed early suspicion and cynicism? And hadn't he agreed with Arthur Burns, the Federal Reserve chairman, during their more harmonious period, that the return on capital investments of the free-enterprise system should be higher?

And besides, hadn't every President's first year shown a loss of confidence by public and businessmen in a traditional letdown of euphoria and early acceptance?

Yes, but—

The but is, simply enough, that stock-market investors, either reflecting their own disaffection or businessmen's own attitudes in more moderate business spending, have given Mr. Carter poorer marks than any of his five predecessors in office. Prompted perhaps by the precipitous 20-percent drop in the Dow Jones average in the first ten months of the Carter administration, analysts began examining how the stock market had behaved in the initial year of the post–Franklin Roosevelt presidents. The Dow rose 12.9 percent under Harry Truman, 18.7 percent under John Kennedy, 10.9 percent under Lyndon Johnson. But under Eisenhower, it declined 3.8 percent in the first year of his initial term and 16.6 percent in the first year of his second term. Under Nixon, it dropped 15.2 percent in 1969 and 16.6 percent in 1973. In Jimmy Carter's case, the 20-percent fall was the worst in thirty years.

Can a President be blamed for the uncertainty that creates gloom in the stock market? Not directly, of course, even his severest critics will admit. But attitudes about an administration's direction make for market reactions. On the other hand, when the head of a government has to choose between business considerations per se and broader issues such as energy conservation, human rights, welfare reform, and the more pregnant international issues, it's difficult to place the blame entirely on the President. Priorities take over.

Yet, business has sulked—and sulked. And it got to Mr. Carter. As he completed his first year in office, he consulted with his economists and then promised a tax-reform package that would include a good measure of business-tax cuts as well as tax reductions for individuals. It was hardly everything, but it was more than a bone.

But if American businessmen aren't just looking for a scapegoat, whom can they blame for their problems? A few point to themselves but most point to government. Is that really warranted?

Given its welter of pressures, the country's economic health is still strong. More jobs are available and government officials proudly cite that some 4 million jobs were added during 1977. Some inroads have been made against the inflation trend. And American economic stability relative to Europe has attracted numerous foreign investments. With 1978's gross national product plunging through the $2-trillion level for the first time, and a $3-trillion level due only a few years hence, the might of our economic force seems undiminished. Added to the 10-plus-percent GNP gain in 1978 are corporate pretax profits estimated at $193 billion, up about 9.5 percent, and plant-and-equipment spending of about $156 billion, up 14 percent.

Do these numbers support fears for a reversal of the three-year-long economic recovery, fears that the nation's business health is being undermined by the lack of a vibrant game plan and fears that the United States will continuously lose ground to other countries where the government-business relationship is more favorable?

Yes, the CEOs say.

Late in 1976, eight hundred major American chief executives who were surveyed said that the most pressing problem they faced was that of government. Of the group, 28.1 percent said government "problems" were their most important and 35.2 percent rated government as the most difficult problem faced by business in general.

Why? Intervention—government interference in the business of business—was the basis for the "problems." Its aim, of course, is reform, reform to dampen the abuses of business, to keep a proliferating marketplace free and to accede to the growing chorus for public rights. In the simplest terms, perhaps, bigness and entrenchment always create opposing forces demanding smallness and less entrenchment. This is the case whether the pressures involve business, government, unionism, education, or any other major element of society. Successful in its efforts or not, reform and intervention have roots deeply embedded in human nature and the nation's history.

From its beginnings, the new country was endowed with the principle of intervention for freedom's sake but limited in order so as not to restrict the nation's "improvement," as Thomas Jefferson expressed it in his inaugural address. By the end of the next century, however, the country "improved" sufficiently to demand curbs against rampant monopolies and abuses of economic power, and the Sherman Antitrust Act was passed in 1890. It was eighty-nine years after Jefferson's inauguration. A broad statute aimed at the jugular of economic abuse, the act prohibited contracts, combinations, and conspiracies that were in restraint of trade and attempts and conspiracies to monopolize.

Difficult for monopolists to swallow, soon judicially restricted to "unreasonable" restraints of trade and later diluted even further, the Sherman Act is nonetheless generally considered the grandfather statute of free enterprise. It has also come to be regarded as the country's economic constitution. But in the manner of the American Constitution, it required amendments or additional statutes to keep it up with changing times. These included the Federal Trade Commission Act (1914), forbidding "unfair" competitive practices; the Clayton Act (also 1914), which restricted discriminatory business practices; and the Celler-Kefauver Amendment to the Clayton Act (1950), which placed a broader ban on monopolistic mergers.

In between came other means for intervention—the Food and Drug Administration, the Securities and Exchange Commission, the Federal Power Commission, the Federal Communications Commission, the Civil Aeronautics Board. These federal agencies, created by an appropriate congressional act, were launched to regulate particular broad-based industries, while the Sherman Act, largely policed by the federal government's chief legal agency, the Justice Department, covers all other industries' trade restraints.

Much as opponents of the regulatory agencies will disagree, the proliferation of new such agencies since then is hardly a new tack for a government hell-bent for intervention. In 1887, the United States had set up its first regulatory agency, the Interstate Commerce Commission, to define rates and service standards for a bloated, discriminatory railway network that fed cutthroat competition, political feuds, rate wars, and stock manipulation.

In the decades that followed, the United States found itself compelled to start yet another series of agencies to administer problems and tackle issues born of a runaway economy and the more populist-oriented era. The newest of these agencies—which have particularly raised the hackles of many American businessmen—are the Environmental Protection Agency, the Equal Employment Opportunity Commission, the Department of Energy, the Occupational Safety and Health Administration, and the Consumer Product Safety Commission.

Too much intervention?

The more direct question is whether business, on its own or without intervention and zealous regulatory lawyers, would give the public what it demands. And the answer to that is no, at least in the perception of the American voter who is convinced that he can ballot the government in or out, once aroused. And the public has been aroused since the 1960s.

In every national and local election starting with the 1960s, the nation's consumers have taken to the ballot to voice their demands. Every presidential candidate, especially those who have moved into 1600 Pennsylvania Avenue, have played to that house. And, as American CEOs learned in his first year in office, Jimmy Carter promised to reduce nonproductive intervention but actually meant to increase productive or "useful" intervention. At the same time that businessmen demanded that the President and his administration help solve the problems of energy, inflation, high corporate taxation, the unemployment rate, pollution, and city erosion, the people want him to simplify government but protect them from the ills that plague their air and their water and threaten their safety, their jobs, and their incomes.

Like every President in recent history, it appeared that Carter would have to use the power of his office to jar the business community into doing things it wouldn't do if left to its own devices.

Most businessmen object to the thesis that the market economy is unable to meet the needs of an aroused consumer body.

This, despite the fact that virtually everyone now admits that consumer activists, led by Ralph Nader, pushed business into pro-consumer actions that it wasn't ready or willing to take until later.

How much is government intervention costing the American economy?

In 1970, eighteen major social and economic regulatory agencies spent a total of $1.56 billion to carry on their activities. Five years later, the group, now expanded to twenty-seven agencies, spent $4.6 billion.

Murray L. Weidenbaum, director of the Center for the Study of American Business at Washington University, estimated that the expenditures of major regulatory agencies jumped from $2 billion in 1974 to $3.8 billion in 1978.

On the business side, or what it costs to comply with the new regulations issued by the agencies, management considers the sum too high and much of it excessive and unnecessary. Dow Chemical U.S.A. Corporation, the nation's most profitable chemical producer, said that it spent $147 million in 1975 for regulatory compliance, "more than a third of it excessive by good business practices."

Paul F. Oreffice, Dow U.S.A.'s president, said that Dow spent about $5 million in salaries and expenses for its staff to testify in Washington. Of this, he said, about 15 percent, or $750,000, was excessive. Special hoists installed by Dow to provide more safety than the cable hoists and forklift trucks it had used were classified by the Occupational Safety and Health Administration as elevators. As a result, Dow was forced to spend $250,000 in each plant to meet the elevator code or return to the old method. Dow also had to spend $60,000 in each plant to lower the railings from forty-two inches to the thirty inches required by OSHA, even though the company's own studies showed that the higher level was safer.

Paperwork burdens caused by intervention also stirred resentment. General Motors Corporation, the largest U.S. company, said that the documents it had to submit to certify its cars for sale in any one year would reach a height of fifteen stories.

As the attacks mounted, they grew broad-based, including not only businessmen and economists but also many others who found hope in President Carter's campaign promises to "clean up the mess in Washington." In little more than two months after the inauguration, Carter told Congress, "Regulation, once designed to serve the public, now stifles competition." Although his words turned out to mean only a push for "useful" instead of nonproductive intervention, they were a spur to businessmen to flail away at all manner of regulation. They based their opposition on the claim that the national economy cannot afford the luxury of waste caused by the indiscriminate use of regulation, even in the best of times—which 1977 wasn't.

In support, they used a relatively new evaluative tool: cost-benefit analysis, which measures the net gain or loss that a company and the public derive from a government regulation. But "C-B analysis," as it is called in economic parlance, isn't foolproof or conclusive. Since it remains one of the few ways with which to deal with sometimes opposing claims from activists, however, findings from C-B analyses have been given some standing.

Among those findings: Government regulation of prices and the entry of new companies in such industries as airlines and trucking generally fail. Unrealistic and uneconomical, the results exact unnecessary costs from the public and provide few market benefits. And where health and safety standards are mandated by regulation, the variance between benefits and costs makes it difficult to determine optimum goals. Studies of costs of air- and water-pollution regulations alone fail to meet normal cost-effective standards, indicating that environmental objectives can be met at costs much lower than those required by regulation.

As esoteric as these conclusions might be to the general public, in both 1977 and 1978 they reinforced businessmen's convictions that too much regulation was probably worse than none.

But the effort, through C-B analysis or otherwise, to put a cost-benefit gauge to safety, health, and life to determine the value of government push and shove may be fruitless. Barring the possibility of agreement on what safety and health are worth, something which government and business will hardly come to in the foreseeable future, the obvious gauge—happier, more contented, more relieved citizens—will do. Many businessmen believe, however, that that is no reason for euphoria, because the consumer pays and pays—as Laurence A. Tisch, chairman of Loews Corporation, the large hotel-theater-insurance conglomerate, emphasized in an interview.

Q: How has running a company changed in the last few years?
A: ... We are spending fortunes on litigation—and the worst part about it is that I see a trend developing in which I see people less willing to invest money. That's the worst thing. The average entrepreneur finds it more and more difficult to be in business.... We won't buy a piece of real estate any more—because that just gives you the privilege to fight for the next five years with the local zoning board, the state zoning board—
Q: What else makes it a problem for free enterprise?
A: Everything. Every place you turn there is some regulatory agency which wants to put its finger in the business. I don't ascribe evil motives to these people, but they don't understand our business. They don't know what we are trying to accomplish. Most of the people who get involved are young, just out of law school. They haven't been in business before and they don't realize that the average businessman is a decent, law-abiding citizen. Business has had such bad publicity in the last ten to fifteen years that we are all ogres, we are all evil, we're all out to cheat the public. Now, I've been on a number of boards and I've never been involved with a company that didn't try to make a better product and sell it at a lower price. But you talk to anyone on the street and they'll tell you that every business is trying to make a worse product and sell it at a higher price. And the public pays for everything. They pay for lawsuits, they pay for government regulation—the public is paying for everything that is happening. And more than anything else, they are going to pay for the lack of investment over the next ten years.

The Score Sheet on Regulation

Against this degree of conviction, how well has regulatory intervention performed in the last decade and a half?

There are definite gains. Automobiles and many other consumer products are safer, if more expensive. Warranties for products and services are stronger. The country's air and water are cleaner, although maybe not purer, than if there had been no regulated standards. Consumers are more informed on the costs of credit and have obtained the right to see their credit records. Food is prepared in a more sanitary manner, and manufacturing standards are better. Minorities and women have a greater number of job opportunities from which to choose, although much more remains to be achieved.

On the minus side, however, are some massive delays and/or foul-ups. The Alaska natural-gas pipeline was held up for five years over a debate on environmental impact. Volkswagen's plans to establish a Pennsylvania plant with a large work force were delayed by the Environmental Protection Agency. Many Americans were sold on saccharin and other products containing the sweetening agent, but the Food and Drug Administration suspended their use. Although the federal government put billions of dollars into new housing projects and urban renewal efforts, city cores are still blighted by slums and industrial decay. The energy-supply problem remains unsolved despite massive efforts to regulate it, while the same impasse has affected much of the nation's railroads, notwithstanding substantial subsidies.

So the scale appears to waver on the boons and ills of intervention. Like the old maxim of regarding the glass as either half empty or half full, government officials cite the social benefits, and businessmen generally point to regulatory costs, problems, and "messes."

Although many CEOs and their top staffs admit the need for new and better standards in the marketplace, which they would prefer to see imposed by the forces of competition, few will forgive the efforts of the Occupational Safety and Health Administration, founded in 1971 to ensure worker protection among some 4 million companies.

Not that any business executive denies the need for worker safety and protection. Seized upon as a prime example of "regulatory overkill," the agency, which represents perhaps the most sweeping effort in recent years to regulate American industry, is criticized for the "arbitrary" standards it imposes and the massive costs it inflicts.

But over a twelve-month period through the spring of 1977, OSHA imposed only $12.4 million in fines, according to the Diebold Group, management consultants. The levies spread over such a large number of companies indicate that the individual fines were paltry. But the economic burdens, businessmen complain bitterly, swamp the costs of violation.

One of OSHA's most controversial regulations—meeting a 90-decibel noise standard in factories—was estimated by one study to cost American industry some $13 billion. The price tag of meeting this standard would be virtually prohibitive in many plants, businessmen claim, whereas nominal hearing protection where needed, such as earmuffs or other means, would be enough. The noise issue has become a rallying point against OSHA.

Charged by Congress with assuring "so far as possible every man and woman in the nation safe and healthful working conditions," OSHA was empowered to impose its own judgment on employers. It was probably too soon a mandate and too massive a job. Opting for existing standards relating to safety and health rules for companies with government contracts and for voluntary guidelines issued by the American National Standards Institute, OSHA stumbled into regulating by using some antiquated rules and by making already-voluntary standards mandatory. The brouhaha that followed was inevitable. In steel, for example, foundries were faced with a load of 5,600 regulations from twenty-seven separate agencies; OSHA alone accounted for 4,000 of the rules.

The agency has since taken steps to issue more realistic and more acceptable standards and tried in the process to offset the increasing chorus urging its dismemberment. Among the steps taken by the agency are improved inspector-training programs, placing an emphasis on health problems as opposed to the predominant stress on safety, weeding out inequitable standards, and attempting to simplify rules to give employers more latitude to meet them.

Overregulation is the last straw, the nation's CEOs say. Especially when added to the many other pressures, arising mainly from a disturbing erosion of some key economic or strategic indicators.

During most of the 1970s, American industry averaged a

real return of only about 3.25 percent on stockholders' investments.

In a fifteen-year period, American productivity growth slipped below that of other major industrial nations. Between 1961 and 1975, the U.S. average annual productivity gain dropped from 3.9 percent to 1.6 percent, behind Japan, West Germany, France, and the United Kingdom.

And despite the $700-billion value of American industrial plants, which represented a 10.4-percent annual growth in the 1967–1977 decade, fewer and fewer dollars have gone into such basic industries as chemicals, steel, aluminum, and textiles. Other industries such as aerospace, airlines, food retailing, and apparel, show a lesser decline but a still-alarming rate of investment. The trend, unless reversed, raises the question of whether these eight basic industries will be able to compete effectively either to get new business or to obtain the financing of new growth.

Yet corporate cash—representing retained earnings and depreciation—in the mid-recovery year of 1976 more than doubled the 1970 level and is expected to grow in the next few years. The total in that pivotal year reached $142 billion. Wasn't the cash in the corporate till more than sufficient for higher capital spending?

But, as pointed out by Loews' Laurence Tisch, American businessmen seriously began pulling back in the 1970s, increasingly so as the decade progressed. The combination of the economic, governmental, and socioeconomic changes required more risk—perhaps gamble is a better term—than most CEOs and their boards of directors were willing to take. And as always happens, the cause soon became effect, an erosion of growth that fed on itself.

It was like a tumbling pile of blocks. The costs of environmental regulation, combined with those created by the multitude of other regulations, dampened investment. The decline in capital expenditures hurt market position both domestically and internationally, particularly in basic industries. This led to heightened competition from abroad. Caught in the squeeze of stiffening rivalry from foreign makers, high corporate taxes, and stubborn inflation, American industry's profits began to slip. A chaotic fall in the stock market's Dow Jones indicator wasn't far behind, descending in little more than one year from 1,000 to the below-800 level which Wall Street thought it had left far behind.

The most dramatic effects were seen among the nation's primary metals producers—steel, aluminum, and copper. More than twenty thousand employees were laid off in 1976 and 1977 as steelmakers shut down old, unproductive facilities made obsolete by the glut of international production and rough foreign competition. The textile industry, which had put virtually no money to speak of into its plants in the most recent years, also closed and consolidated facilities, hoping that attrition among employees would eventually cut its labor costs. In the eleven years between 1965 and 1976, U.S. apparel-textile industry employment plummeted by more than 25 percent.

The real upshot of all this has been to contribute substantially to an unemployment rate in the United States that has mostly hovered for three years at about the 8-percent level, the highest since the Depression of the 1930s. Yet, whether by simple malaise or by diversion to other problems, or because it dropped to about 6 percent in 1978's first half, a high jobless rate shows all the signs of becoming accepted on the principle that a core of unemployables must exist in a free-enterprise society.

As one talks with some of the nation's most prominent businessmen, the feeling grows that many see the economic slowdown of recent years as a clear symptom that high growth must inevitably slacken. In one sense, perhaps, it's like a sprinter who drops back to a jog and then to a walk, warmed, however, by all the prizes he has won and the records he has set.

"If you go back over the two hundred years that this country has existed, excluding the last twenty years, you find that our industrial growth since our founding has averaged just three percent," said GE's Reginald Jones. "This economy, so highly regarded, has had a historic growth rate. And yet when we talk about a three-percent growth rate in recent years, we think we are falling behind. But many of the foreign countries with higher growth rates these years actually started from ground zero."

His confident tone changed drastically, however, when he touched upon the decline in American industrial return on capital investment in the last two decades. "In 1965, the return in real terms was nine point nine percent," he said. "But in 1976, the real return had dropped to slightly over three percent. And it's the decline in the return on investment which has led to the decline in capital investment."

Are CEOs losing their confidence by limiting their risks? he was asked. Is that the problem?

The questions caused him to pause and glance out the window at the neat, flowing acres surrounding GE's modern headquarters complex in Fairfield, Connecticut. Resuming, he said, "Our CEOs today aren't substantial owners of the company. They're professional managers. They see themselves as stewards for the shareowners and employees, and that's what makes them different from the owner-operators of yesteryear, who were almost entirely concerned with the bottom line and the accretion of wealth. Our main job is to concern ourselves with the safety and survival of the company we administer, so that shareowners and employees will not suffer."

Jones, widely considered one of America's most responsible business spokesmen, added, "I must say that our businessmen have neither the confidence nor the motivation they used to have. What seems to be going is the venturesomeness of the American businessman—and this gives me some cause for grave concern. . . .

"But," he went on quickly, "what I do see in the American people is an extraordinary quality of common sense. It's expressed in things like 'Throw the rascal out!' or 'There's no free lunch.' If the productivity decline is really related to the decline in capital investment, then there is a relationship between capital intensity and productivity. Labor has to recognize the direct and close correlation between gains in productivity and gains in real wages. Money gains are only ephemeral if inflation remains high. . . .

"I hate to be a cynic. You don't get to be a chief executive if you are a pessimist. You have to have a fairly good quotient of optimism, faith in people. Given all the facts and the information, I think the people will have to face up to the trade-offs on economic-social issues. All of us are determined to maintain our present system, with all of its frailties, and what we as businessmen have got to do is be so much more articulate that we get our point heard and accepted so that there will be a balanced set of decisions for the people to make."

5

Many Strident Voices

A Heaving Circle

"If you really want to know how I feel," said the businessman with a sigh late one morning, "it's like I'm in the center of a heaving circle.

"The point I sit at should be equidistant from all the exterior points—but it isn't. The top half of the circle presses down, harassing the hell out of me, and there are lots of times I can't even see the lower half, the important half."

He quickly drew a diagram. The upper half resembled a toadstool consisting of three equal parts—economic pressures, government pressures, and constituency pressures. All three pushed at the center—himself. The lower half of the circle, labeled "corporate duties," appeared to be falling away from him. "Because of the turmoil of the pressures in the upper half," he said somberly, "I get less and less time to pay any attention to what's happening in the lower half. That's the hell of what's going on today."

In that visualization, he reflected the general attitude among his peers that all the other demands on their time and attention prevented them from carrying on with their main objective—running a business.

But what if those boiling pressures that make the circle heave weren't there or weren't as overheated? Would he in his business zeal mostly ignore either the fiduciary or social obligations that a modern corporation must meet head on? What are those pressure points that refuse to accept the chief executive's own more ethical sense as a guarantee that he will satisfy his own public and social debts?

Government, for one.

"The basic objectives of business and government, while often complementary, are inherently different," said Juanita M. Kreps, Secretary of Commerce in the Jimmy Carter administration. "Failure to appreciate this difference has contributed to counterproductive, seemingly adversary situations that are not in our nation's best interests."

Speaking to a representative of *Enterprise,* the publication of the National Association of Manufacturers, she added, "The primary objective of any business is to produce profitably; without profits, business does not survive and no other business functions can be performed. On the other hand, the objectives of government extend to broad social issues such as the protection of individual rights, public health and safety, and protection of the environment. . . . Accommodating these different objectives is possible only if government, business, and the public achieve a proper balance of their various objectives."

A second pressure point would be economics. Inflation, in particular.

"The most difficult problem we are going to face is how to deal with inflation," Robert R. Nathan, economist and president of Robert R. Nathan Associates, told a seminar of the Committee for Economic Development. "I happen to think that this problem is not transient in nature. . . . It is probably the nearest thing to a cancer on the body economic of the United States and the world. . . .

"What are the alternatives?" asked Nathan. "In dealing with inflation over time, there will have to be something in the nature of intervention. We must try to improve productivity. I do not think we will have wage and price controls across the board, nor do I think we need them. But we may have to move forward in guidelines, guideposts, freer trade, legislated delays in largest cost and price increases, and things of that nature. But the real hope is that we will take a hard, hard look at the marketplace and see where its strengths and its weaknesses are and what we might conceivably be able to do about the weaknesses."

Stockholders are a third pressure point, particularly in seeking to protect their rights.

"How can one man who is both chairman and chief executive officer evaluate his own performance as president and chief operating officer?" asks Lewis D. Gilbert, the stockholder's advocate and perennial critic of corporate management. "I believe that all corporations should separate the jobs of president and chairman, rather than having both posts vested in one man."

Backed in his contention by Courtney Brown, dean emeritus of the Columbia Graduate School of Business, Gilbert, as a token shareholder of hundreds of American companies, submitted his proposal for stockholder approval to half a dozen of the largest corporations. But he could never summon enough grass-roots backing in the face of opposition by management to get his proposal put on any company's rules of organization.

Stymied in that offensive, Gilbert remained hopeful of winning another. He has asked for a ceiling on executives' retirement pay. Currently, the pension-reform laws put any employee's maximum pension from a tax-favored pension plan (as most of them are) at $75,000 a year, later increased to about $80,000 by a cost-of-living escalator clause. But many corporations are beefing up these pensions with amounts taken out of operating funds. Why should there be no limit to the amount an executive can take in pension, asks Gilbert, when stockholder dividends are limited by board action? Where's the equity?

A fourth source of pressure is consumerism.

Ralph Nader, the most reviled but most successful critic of American business practices, has urged that the seven hundred largest American companies should be put under federal charter, in addition to state chartering, to deal with "the most urgent questions of corporate power."

State chartering, which Nader and his associates equate with "Delaware chartering" (an effort made by states to grant corporation charters so they could receive fees largely without policing the corporations) isn't enough to keep corporations either honest or efficient, they claimed.

The Federal Chartering Act, in Nader's view, should be enforced mostly by the Securities and Exchange Commission, helped by such changes as routing SEC budget requests directly through Congress rather than through the Office of Management and Budget, which has cut the SEC's budget requests regularly since 1972. As part of the proposed act, substantive changes were suggested in the makeup of boards of directors, and tough punitive judgments against errant individuals and firms were to be imposed.

Corporate officers convicted of willful corporate-related violations of the chartering act would be disqualified from serving as corporate officers or directors of any American corporation for five years. Fines under the Nader proposals would be based on the size of the firm and the kind of violation. Penalties should be increased for corporate repeaters that continue to violate the act. No corporation should be permitted to indemnify any executive or director against any liability or penalty of a civil or criminal action. And corporate conflicts of interest should be removed from "the discretion of the boardroom and made the subject of designated civil sanctions in federal district court."

And then come activist groups, fifth, sixth, seventh, eighth. . . .

The Interfaith Center on Corporate Responsibility, acting on behalf of both Protestant and Catholic activist organizations, attempted first to press corporations into more-complete disclosure of activities in the United States and abroad, and then broadened its attack to social and moral issues. The newer thrusts included a demand for a change in corporate policy toward dealing with and granting loans to the apartheid South African government and a push on forcing disclosure by the major television networks of how many minorities and women are employed in various programs. The interfaith group also brought pressure on corporations to curtail the amount of violence in television programs they sponsor and presented proposals for more stringent policies in dealing with totalitarian governments such as that in Chile.

The Arab boycott issue, the subject of a widespread campaign carried on by the American Jewish Congress, won a tacit government supporter when the SEC split within its own members on whether to allow the AJC's corporate disclosure proposal to be included in company proxy statements. Reflecting its belief that the issue exceeded in principle its own statutory authority, the SEC decided it couldn't make a decision. And so hundreds of target companies lost one major defense possibility and were left to deal with the matter in their own ways and to risk the reaction of their stockholders.

The issue of nuclear power has also been raised by church

groups, not appeased by claims from such companies as General Electric that its use of nuclear energy is already closely regulated by the U.S. government. Demands were intended to gain adequate safety precautions and assurances that American companies will not negotiate with any countries that haven't signed the international nuclear nonproliferation pact.

The activists sometimes carried on in tandem or besieged management with their demands. At J. P. Stevens & Company, union pickets marched outside the hotel where the big textile company held an annual meeting. They were protesting the labor policies, while inside both church and union representatives noisily proposed resolutions ordering full disclosure to shareholders of Stevens' efforts to fight off union representation.

Although AT&T may be one of the world's largest companies, its management didn't enjoy the fact that it received the largest number of proposed resolutions to be voted upon by stockholders. There were fourteen in one year alone.

Often akin to a mini-circus, annual stockholders' meetings of major companies provide a magnet for dissident stockholders, as well as needlers, frustrated employees (both present and past), and civil-service employees seeking a few hours off. At such events, the corporate hosts are beleaguered for a while, forced to take the prodding and probing, much of it pointless and nonproductive, in good humor. But the dialogue can, and frequently does, get acrimonious.

What may be even more important, however—as anyone who regularly attends annual meetings knows—stockholders get just about what they deserve. Only a fraction do their homework or ask the right questions or insist on answers. It takes a devoted advocate—a Nader, the brothers Lewis and John Gilbert, a Wilma Soss, an Evelyn Y. Davis—to get the fur flying, and it all takes preparation and planning.

Regardless, it seems certain that management will be pressured even more in the years ahead, as yet newer voices seek to be heard and will not easily be quieted.

Smarter Americans, Less Aversion to Profit?

But the most pervasive voice of all may be the hostility of the American public toward the word "profits." The irony of that, at least in one sense, is well known. Ask a typical American how much the average company makes and he will cite an inflated and unrealistic figure, usually about five times what profits really are. But the greater irony is that corporate profits, however abhorrent to the citizen, have dropped sharply in the share of the nation's gross national product, even though the total amount of earnings in dollars has multiplied since the early 1950s.

As a share of the GNP, after-tax earnings dropped from about 9 percent in 1950 to under 5 percent in the mid-1970s. But wages and other employee compensation rose from 54 percent to 62 percent.

Why do Americans show an aversion to the profit concept?

James Davant, chairman and CEO of Paine, Webber, Jackson and Curtis, one of the major stock brokerages, observed, "Our educational process hasn't been very good in that regard. It raises some strong suspicion that many people wind up as economic illiterates. But unfortunately, part of the blame must fall on the businessman. He seems to talk mostly to the other businessmen. He hasn't addressed himself enough to outsiders. We must get across to the average man that profits are good for business and for him. My own feeling, too, is that before anyone can vote he ought to have the equivalent of a high-school knowledge of economics."

On the other hand, it isn't at all certain that people would cease criticizing profits even if they were more educated and informed about the benefits.

At a two-day conference held at Harvard University early in 1977 to study the future of the profit system, a number of business leaders and economists concluded that resentment against profits is endemic and chronic because it is in the nature of the democratic system for various levels of society to complain about one another's prerogatives. Profits, the participants agreed, will continue to be controlled by the government, be challenged by the people, and be reduced by inflation, regardless of the public's degree of education. That was the way of the system, they rationalized, and it would continue to survive, if in some changed form, because it "worked."

Yet in that system, the conflict between free enterprise and occasional but dramatic examples of the unproductivity of profits continues to stir hostility. While the vast majority of Americans will rally behind the system as "the best there is, faults or not," they will simultaneously question how well profits work to use physical or scarce resources to the greatest general advantage.

While on a visit some years ago to a major Texas city, for example, an out-of-towner was taken on a tour by a leading real-estate promoter, who proudly pointed to a collection of gleaming mid-city office towers and said, "We put all those up in the last few years." Then he added, "The problem is, I guess, that we put up too damn many. They're all less than fifty percent rented." The problem is indigenous not just to Texas but to New York, Chicago, and Los Angeles as well.

As the Harvard meeting brought out, the public attitude has traditionally displayed a certain amount of moral discomfiture about income that is earned by money as opposed to perspiration. And the profit system, despite its ability to finance economic growth, hasn't precluded occasional high unemployment.

But the conferees didn't leave before raising the question of whether companies shouldn't balance their priorities between a quest for profits and a quest for social boon. But, they decided, in order to do good, one must have the cash to finance good works. Otherwise, what would be the source? And the prospects of many American companies agonizingly trying to juggle the need for profits and the need to raise charity to a major corporate goal raised a vision of fantasy, government strictures, and loss of productivity and direction that might make the head spin.

The solution, as always, seemed to work down to a simple principle: make a reasonable profit and use part of it to help cure society's ills, a greater proportion surely than has been allocated in the past. But the complexities of the problem and the frustrations of a simple solution weren't lost on those present or on those who seriously considered the discussions.

The FTC: Waxing Weak, Waxing Tough

Although many do, not all chief executives single out the SEC as the major government culprit in giving them a hard time or a bad name. For some, the reawakened aggressiveness of the Federal Trade Commission is the biggest irritant and the most unpleasant voice to emerge in recent years in the nation's capital.

Under its various chairmen since the 1950s, the FTC has waxed tough and it has waxed weak. But when President Carter selected activist Michael Pertschuk over other candidates, more amenable to business, to be his FTC chairman, a new era of enforcement seemed to dawn for the agency that functions as the nation's watchdog over business practices.

Gearing up for a stronger enforcement of both its trade practice and its free-competition efforts, Pertschuk freed the agency's twelve regional offices to investigate and develop cases. They were also invited to seek out in their own areas issues and violations that were national in scope. No longer kept on a short leash, the regional offices quickly began to unearth their own micro-to-macro issues, helped by shifts in regional directors either displaced or energized by Pertschuk.

Somewhat like talking back to the traffic cop, businessmen in the wake of the Pertschuk push began openly complaining that the FTC was engaged in a process of harassment and was using the media to declare them guilty before they were even tried.

What makes the FTC especially galling to them is the open-endedness of its authority. With broad but vague powers, the agency has greater authority than other regulatory agencies. Its custom in recent years of tackling traditional business practices so as to bring about legal precedents that would have the effect of law seemed to abridge regulatory and legal behavior. Its enforcement energies also appeared to fluctuate with the change in its staff personnel. And its drawn-out procedures involving consent decrees on business practices of years earlier irked chief executives who were quite willing to drop controversial practices and get on with others that weren't so moot.

More and more, in the latter 1970s, companies began to cease their practice of accepting cease-and-desist orders without admitting guilt because they no longer wanted to fight. No matter how they tried to avert a fight or short-cut it, they lost, anyway. This increased their frustration, and it wasn't helped by the recollection that in 1970 the FTC came to the brink of being discontinued. Criticisms of inconsistent, even petty investigations brought increasing pressure on then-President Richard Nixon to impanel a task force to study how the agency might improve its effectiveness or whether it was really needed. Under the chairmanship of Miles W. Kirkpatrick, an antitrust lawyer, a group was assembled by the American Bar Association to review the FTC's operations. The conclusion was that unless changes were effected no substantial purpose would be served by the FTC's continued existence.

And Kirkpatrick himself was tapped by the President to be the FTC's chairman. But, surprisingly, Kirkpatrick opted for activism. He quickly added to the staff a number of young, idealistic lawyers who struck out into such uncharted directions as finding real-life business practices to fit legalistic issues never tested outside professional journals. For example: Should an oligopoly—a market situation in which a few producers control the needs of many buyers—be curbed or controlled in the manner of a monopoly, where one producer fully dominates a market? And should a company which has practiced deceptive advertising be compelled to erase the effects of that practice by sponsoring advertising that renounces its statements of the past?

By pursuing the oligopoly issue in bringing a case against the four major producers of cereals, and by enforcing the advertising-recanting issue against the Hi-C fruit drink produced by Coca-Cola Company, the revitalized FTC won the support of leading members of Congress. Evidence came in increasing congressional appropriations for the agency since Kirkpatrick's tenure.

Kirkpatrick resigned in 1973 and was succeeded by Calvin J. Collier, whose administration was considered more middle of the road. But the advent of Pertschuk rubbed new salt into the wound. This was the case not only with businessmen who became new targets but also with some of FTC's regional directors who had attempted to create a bridge between their roles and the businessmen's classic resentment of enforcement agencies.

Such FTC career men found themselves promptly invited to find new jobs.

Do the media favor the FTC's side at the expense of target companies? As newspapermen have learned, a company cited by the FTC will often not officially learn of it until the press announcement is made and will be caught short without any prepared statement. The story citing the company is prominently displayed, while the next day's rebuttal by the company receives the lesser treatment normally accorded second-day stories.

Not all reporters or magazine or other journalists take the trouble to call for company comment when FTC charges are released. But then the FTC is also one of the few regulatory agencies that informs reporters in advance to be prepared for the release of a major story and is also one of the few to hold press conferences on significant cases. In each such instance, it conditions the media to prepare for a "big story," which will be patently of a negative nature as far as the target business is concerned. The agency, after all, doesn't mention a company for "good behavior."

With the FTC's new aggressive stance and the recent administrations' expressed enthusiasm for consumer protection, two signs are clear. Businessmen will find more developments emanating from the watchdog agency to complain about. And more businessmen will complain. The syndrome will be self-expansionary.

The SEC: Good Marks but, Oh, So Costly

Whether it's the FTC or the SEC that troubles corporate chiefs more, there's little doubt they have more respect for and more fear of the agency which polices the nation's securities markets.

On at least one level, the greater prestige that the SEC carries may be due to the fact that its sister agency, the FTC, has such a broad mandate and frequently attempts to develop legal precedents which expand the original law, that it often seems to flounder, especially when confronted by complex situations. But the SEC, perhaps because of its much more restricted mandate, pursues a hard, straight line to its objectives, although it took almost forty years before the agency finally freed commission rates on stock transactions and allowed competition to set them. This move alone has saved investors an estimated $300 million a year, although it's likely that big investors have gained more by it than small investors.

Yet the SEC's move to allow the marketplace to solve an ethical issue—commissions were low on small transactions and large on big ones, an open invitation to bribes and special payments—rather than act to regulate commissions itself spread an aura of great accomplishment over the often-berated agency, especially when many dire predictions of individual and general brokerage disasters to come from the decision simply didn't materialize. And after years of experience with the competitive forces acting to bring down commissions, all the criticisms and trepidations melted away and shifted to begrudged approval. Despite the fact that it was carved up into four separate steps culminating in May 1975 when the SEC fully eliminated fixed commissions, the SEC's move also demonstrated something else—something that few business chiefs or heads of brokerages elected to mention until the results were all in. It showed that a regulatory agency can push reform through the natural forces of the marketplace perhaps more easily than it can by adopting a strong regulatory stance.

Not that the SEC isn't criticized and cursed at times—and for some very pertinent reasons from the businessman's standpoint.

An internal SEC memorandum late in 1977 revealed that the agency's reporting requirements cost the typical company seeking to sell securities an additional $93,000 to $182,000. The cost of periodic corporate disclosure fell more heavily percentage-wise on the smaller companies than on the larger ones, but the cost hit every business, size notwithstanding. The 10-K form, required annually from all publicly owned companies, costs $13,000. A proxy form, solicitations to stockholders referring important corporate matters to them, costs $15,200. An S-1 form, required for the registration of securities, costs anywhere from $28,000 to $203,000. And an S-7, the registration form submitted by larger companies, costs between $21,200 and $299,000.

The inescapable conclusion is that the SEC's reporting

rules add to company costs, especially the extra overhead paid by the company to prepare the various forms required. (This was not included in the memo's calculation.)

Should one shed any tears over the businessman's added costs in meeting SEC requirements? Not necessarily. But those costs represent an added irritant to what most chief executives consider increasing, often unwarranted regulation of their businesses.

As James Davant of Paine Webber put it: "There are too many regulators and too much regulation. You need a policeman, that's for sure, but the result of a lot of what the regulators do is the reverse of what they profess they want. I'm told by my peers that the SEC is probably the best—but the costs of abiding by it are very high. In 1975, for example, our costs of ensuring that we abided by the SEC amounted to about seventeen million dollars. And that's quite a lot of additional cost."

Underlying much of the concern has been not only a more militant approach from some of the prime regulators to stiffen penalties but a team approach to pin violators to the mat and press criminal proceedings against them and their top executives.

The Justice Department, for example, teamed up with the SEC on corporate bribery cases to bring criminal proceedings, in contrast to the previous practice in which the SEC itself would have resolved such cases merely with consent agreements.

The Internal Revenue Service has begun working closely with the SEC to seek back taxes from companies being investigated by another agency. This followed a ruling by the U.S. tax court that the IRS could collect back taxes in a civil case on evidence furnished by a taxpayer, even if the tax agency could not criminally prosecute the company.

A Lobbying Overkill?

Needless to say, the baying and snapping at the heels of the average American chief executive has complicated his days and his nights. But in the 1970s he snapped back. Irked by the diversion of his primary attentions from his own business, by the apparent overcompensation of many critics and regulators who he believes are asking for the stars but really are willing to settle for the moon, the CEO has added specialists in government relations, financial relations, and consumer relations and expanded his Washington and state-capital offices.

In fact, so intense has been the retaliatory effort that, unless it is better controlled, it can get out of hand and defeat its own purpose.

Busy legislators in Washington, for example, are hard pressed to give audience to the representatives of the many trade associations and corporate lobbyists and lawyers who are constantly seeking their ears.

Only two legislators attended a recent dinner meeting with the top management of a large chemical company, despite the fact that nineteen new Congressmen had been invited by the corporation from districts in which it operated plants. Was it a bad turnout? Not really, in view of the proliferation of corporate lobbyists and the many invitations that flood Capitol Hill.

The Washington press corps—and that in Albany, Sacramento, Springfield, Illinois, and other state capitals—are likewise inundated with calls, invitations, and literature from lobbyists.

But the center of the potential lobbying overkill remains in Washington, where the lobbying and public-policy-molding activity may be one of the nation's fastest-growing industries. More than 80 percent of the nation's largest corporations either have their own offices in the capital or are represented there by resident lawyers, consultants, or public-relations people. The oil industry alone has about 300 registered lobbyists in Washington. And there are also 29 law firms and PR firms there registered as representatives of some 60 oil and gas companies, as well as 19 trade associations servicing them, the most prominent of which is the American Petroleum Institute, which has 400 employees and a $25-million budget.

The oil industry, for one, has generated such a barrage of propaganda that some of its attempts to influence public and governmental opinion have apparently been misdirected. One of the campaign's aims has been channeled toward fighting corporate divestiture of such oil giants as Exxon Corporation. Another has been directed against rampant regulation. But both have already lost their thrust, at least in terms of the oil industry, in favor of an all-out program to solve the energy problem. Yet by keeping the issues alive, a vast advertising and lobbying campaign by Mobil Corporation may not only have the backlash effect of reviving the dormant issues but also compel legislators to feel they must take a stand, even if negative, against Mobil.

Other efforts are so patently self-serving that they amount to an insult to employees, stockholders, and the public. Standard Oil of California, for example, has engaged in mass corporate mailings to about 262,000 stockholders and 40,000 employees, pressing for "more positive support of the efforts of Arab nations toward peace in the Middle East." Can anyone really question whether SoCal wants Mideast peace or a smoother flow of oil?

Much as top business executives rail against the stridency of their opposition, their defensive efforts also give the impression of working to the public's disadvantage. But it isn't industry alone. The legal community has multiplied in the nation's capital cities, pushing litigation, entangling the courts, and causing judicial figures such as Chief Justice Warren Burger to express dismay over the complexities of the legal machinery in the United States.

Increasingly the butt of jokes and criticisms that they work only for each other, certainly not for their clients, attorneys dominate Congress and have inordinate representation in federal agencies, committees, councils, boards, and commissions. Of 535 seats in Congress, more than 300 are held by attorneys. Washington has more lawyers per capita than any city in the world. Many gravitate toward lobbying and corporate law there and in other major American cities—where the money is, in other words—and more than a few have wound up as chief executives of large American companies.

While a legal decision is frequently awarded to the client with the largest legal funds, those cases that do not easily lend themselves to a decision may last for months and even years as the company plaintiff pours more and more money into the litigation. A prime example is IBM Corporation, which has defended itself with fifteen lawyers deployed by a major law firm to fight the Justice Department's suit on monopoly grounds. Begun on May 19, 1975, the antitrust suit has dragged on for three and a half years. IBM never specified what it spent in the court battle, but estimates are that costs have been many times Justice's $7 million in what, before a similar antimonopoly suit filed against AT&T, represented the biggest and most expensive antitrust suit ever lodged against an American company.

IBM may not exactly be fighting for its life, notwithstanding the government's compilation of some 50 million documents and court transcripts totaling more than 60,000 pages. But, even if it is ever divested of some of its key divisions, which would reduce its proportions but scarcely end its existence, IBM has been acting as though its very survival depended upon its defense. AT&T's trial may go on even longer, since it is a regulated monopoly, founded under government decree, and its divestiture would involve seismic changes in the traditional federal relationship with other regulated industries, such as railroads and public utilities.

Yet, with all the public-relations forces it has put into play, all the mechanisms of defense it has generated, business has been unable to stem the tide of anti-business sentiment that has become a principal trait in the perception of Americans. The challenge falls directly upon the chief executive in corporate America, whose role, whether he likes it or not, has become in great part a communications one. All the strident voices must be dealt with. While each may not individually jar a company out of its position of strength, collectively the chorus can inflict damage that could sap that strength.

"In the next five years, the requirements for recruiting senior and chief executive officers will change dramatically," said Lester B. Korn, president of Korn/Ferry International, a leading executive-recruiting firm. "The executive's ability to fulfill and effectively communicate the company's commitments to its corporate social responsibilities will become second in importance only to protecting earnings capability."

Korn added, "Chief executives and senior executives must come out of their executive isolation booths and listen to and communicate to these publics just how their producers and services contribute to the quality of their lives. This failure, I think, can be laid directly to the top executives of many corporations. They are still communicating in the same old ways which are no longer effective in today's changing society."

6

Multinationals, Dollars, Payments, Oil, and All

There is a vision . . .

A swashbuckler bearing the banner of a company that is a household word in the United States, his teeth clenching a rose, his pockets crammed with money, and his eyes awash in goodwill. With abandon, he strides across the lands and oceans of the world, bestowing flowers, largess, or love—often all three. He is admired more for his zest for adventure than for his dollars or goodwill. Cries ring out for his presence everywhere.

Who is he? The smiling, dashing, irresistible American in a three-piece suit with slash pockets, of course.

The vision fades, however. And under the puff of reality it completely disperses.

Multinational companies, the totally United States–owned foreign subsidiaries, or the joint ventures with foreign partners were the pride of American chief executives during the decade bridging the 1960s and 1970s. Foreign investments through American presence were a great force for human progress, they boasted, and also, incidentally, added a good increment to the corporate bottom line. But increasingly in the 1970s, the typical CEO spoke less of the multinational and more of other things.

The reason was obvious. The multinational company of American origin has slipped badly. Between 1971 and 1975, Americans were divesting their foreign subsidiaries with almost the same zest they exhibited when they launched them. In those five years, 1,350 were sold or disposed of out of some 3,000 American foreign businesses extant.

The exodus from Europe, Asia, Africa, and Latin America, especially Europe, grew from Americans' inability to profitably compete with local concerns. The multinationals' profits declined because the need for American business and know-how fell off, helped in great part by what the nationals learned and adopted from the Americans. And when nationalistic movements cast a shadow of "ugly American" or just plain "foreigner" over the U.S. outpost, it seemed time to go—especially when things were getting sticky in the home economy, too.

But there were still a good many American companies that continued to do well abroad, selling a combination of products of their own and of their host countries, their own particular brand of U.S. expertise and marketing services that remained highly competitive. Among them are IBM Corporation, Sears, Roebuck & Company, Xerox Corporation, and Texas Instruments. Swashbucklers they weren't, but in regions of the world that are more and more looking askance at intruders and worrying about their own economies, the successful U.S. multinationals still prospered because they filled a vacuum.

Nonetheless, the eclipse of many U.S. foreign subsidiaries, especially in the mid-1970s, came during an intense flux on the world economic scene in which the chief executive of almost every large American corporation found himself embroiled and, in many ways, helpless.

It was again a case where causes swelled into effects leading to further effects that exploded into more complex problems:

With the United States remaining the world's largest user of energy, some 35 percent of its oil needs being imported, its mounting balance of payments deficit soared to $30 billion in 1977 and continued to mount in the succeeding quarters. As traditionally when the U.S. trade deficit goes through the stratosphere, foreign governments again urged the Americans not to resume efforts to impose new trade protectionism in order to reduce the deficit. But, U.S. officials retorted, if other countries would move together to stimulate their economies, American goods would enjoy a demand resurgence, exports would shrink the deficit, and the fears of new trade protections could be erased.

Such was not to be the case, however. Except for West Germany, Switzerland, and the Netherlands, every other Western European country chose a course for moderation and adopted conservative fiscal and economic policies. Inflation and payment deficits remained high. Capital investments were low. Unemployment continued to grow, rapidly in some cases. And Europe's leaders seemed especially troubled by pervasive pessimism over the Continent's political drift leftward and by the lack of motivation and hope that had descended like a cloud over many of their people in the late 1970s.

European businessmen, too, appeared to be hugging the status quo for dear life.

And what of Japan, which, along with West Germany, was acknowledged to be making the strongest economic strides? Japanese businessmen and the government, however, remained poised for higher oil prices and a slower economic growth. Thus, they too took a gloomy view of the benefits of economic stimulation. And consumer spending seemed to have fallen into the same lull that had infected the United States in late 1974 and much of 1975. The Japanese, also, continued to be sensitive to becoming the butt of new moves in the United States toward trade protectionism. The result was that the typical Japanese businessman decided to be cautious, to invest no more than 2 to 3 percent of his funds in updating his company.

Difficult as it all was of itself, the international malaise couldn't have come at a worse time.

Farewell to Leverage

Whether it was in the no-longer-so-insulated top executive suites of American corporations, at the International Monetary Fund, at the White House, or in the quietly troubled principal business offices of Frankfurt, Paris, London, or Zurich, the truth had hit home. Five years after the international energy crisis had radically changed the world concept of reciprocal supply and demand, there was no longer any doubt about what had happened:

The global recession, which many diehards thought really affected only the less-developed countries, was actually worldwide and would only intensify through the 1970s and the early 1980s.

In the industrialized countries, unemployment had climbed to a momentous level of about 16 million persons. And in the less-developed countries, it was estimated to be at least a dozen times that number.

Desperate to feed their people and to obtain fuel for their vehicles and factories, ninety of the poorest countries in Africa, Asia, and Latin America had accumulated debts of as much as $250 billion. At least $50 billion had come from American banks, with the remainder borrowed from international agencies such as the IMF and the World Bank as well as from other developed countries.

Would that debt ever be repaid? The question soon became abstract, even silly. The answer was not slow in coming from the borrowers: The lenders should from a moral standpoint absorb the debt to make good in some measure for their exploitation of the less-developed countries over the years.

"The quadrupling of the price of oil in 1973 and 1974 severely shook the economies of the oil importing countries and was a major factor in the world recession of 1974–1976 and produced enormous payments deficits in the oil consuming countries," reported briefing papers left by retiring Treasury Secretary William Simon to the incoming Carter administration.

But, the Simon papers stressed, the hardest hit were the less-developed countries. "These have suffered greatly because of oil price increases," which they had to pay at a time when the world economic recession withered their markets for exports.

Yet, if the Western countries could still savor any possible leverage in the role of creditors of such insolvent debtors, it was largely illusory. The members of the Organization of Petroleum Exporting Countries had by accumulating some $150 billion since 1972 accomplished the greatest transfer of wealth in the history of the world. The balance of economic power clearly had passed from the West to the East, and so had the leverage.

If Western businessmen still retained any doubt about that, it was soon dispelled by a report from the International Monetary Fund. "The central problem of the world economy is the dramatic shift of the oil cartel into a current account surplus of about $40 billion annually—the result of a five-fold price increase since 1972," the IMF said.

Of course, the reverse side of that coin was that the oil-importing countries, or the rest of the world, were forced to cope with that degree of deficit.

The next move—the developments came too quickly to allow anyone to adjust—was the decline of world currencies, especially the erosion in the dollar, the value of which most of the other countries depend upon as a benchmark of financial stability. The lira was quickly devalued, as was the pound sterling, which later, however, showed some signs of viability. But the burden of the dollar decline especially hurt, resulting in falling profits for American firms with a substantial stake in foreign countries.

Yet chief executives of major American companies weren't permitted to feel sorry that their earnings were carved by the weak dollar. On a late-1977 trip through the Middle East and Western Europe, Simon's successor, W. Michael Blumenthal, was dogged by complaints that the United States had not acted to support the dollar and may in fact have set out to lower it to stunt the flow of goods entering his country.

And when Blumenthal attempted to soften suspicions about the dollar decline by asserting that the American economy remained strong and would continue to expand, although at a slower rate in the latter half of 1978, it didn't quite play. Even when he stressed the basic qualities of the U.S. economy—its innovativeness, its resiliency, and its high agricultural productivity—his credibility was only hurt by the realities of a precipitous drop in the stock market, the high inflation in the United States, and the turbulence in the international monetary market.

If Blumenthal or any American business chief executive bristled at the obligations to the world community that foreign statesmen or businessmen saddled him with, he had only to recall the warning that President Carter had given his own staff shortly after he took office. The best road to world peace, Carter had said in effect, wasn't better relations with Russia and China, harmony in the Middle East, peace in South Africa, a disarmament settlement, or even the resumption of diplomatic relations with Fidel Castro. The greatest threat to world peace, he declared, would be an economic collapse of the Western countries. It would lead to the fragmentation of the Western alliance, he believed, and probably the political collapse of the free world.

Avoiding the Problem for the Solution

So, in effect, all the Western world and all the less-developed countries, too, turned an anxious eye on the United States, the President directly, and the American CEOs indirectly. Did the chiefs of American business still have the capacity to turn the trick, to show the way for the rest of them in management skill, foresight, and courage? Could they act to avoid an economic collapse in the West and even in most of the East?

But perhaps the real question was how long it would take to find out. No one, outside of the most desperate and frustrated, assumed that the answer would come soon. And it didn't.

Yet, if the challenges were too massive and too deep to be quickly met by a simple touch of the button, as everyone realized, nevertheless the latent doubts also began to surface. Hadn't the Americans, especially the big businessmen, lost at least some of their much-envied superiority? The evidence was certainly there to make the question valid. Consider their own economic slowdown, et al. Those CEOs who were more internationally minded were mindful of those doubts. They heard it in international forums, at the IMF, and in the American embassies. Blumenthal himself sent back word. And those business chiefs who weren't as aware of the doubts read the challenge in the press. Some of the media were sympathetic, as shown by an October 1977 editorial in the *New York Times:*

> Not only are [American] profits down but profits of any size are much less certain today than a decade ago. Economists talk of a rise in "risk premiums." In a world where a powerful oil cartel can quadruple fuel prices or cut off critical supplies at will, business planning is extremely difficult. In an international monetary system still groping to cope with the huge transfer of funds caused by the oil crisis, the future must be worrisome. In an economy where inflation and unemployment defy the old rules and rise together, other goblins are bound to haunt business. In a world where international competition has intensified, it's tougher for American business to envision new markets.

Some major chief executives responded. Increasingly a spokesman for the big diversified corporations, General Electric's Reginald Jones told a San Francisco outlook conference in January 1977 that General Electric was still optimistic about the world economy and the tremendous business opportunity it represents.

Nevertheless, Jones stated, the period immediately ahead "is going to be a troubled one—a period of transition and adjustment—which could, if mistakes are made, cause serious social and political problems in many nations of the world."

What should be done? For those who may have still entertained thoughts that businessmen set economic policy, Jones's program came as strong medicine. Most of his proposals sought vital changes in Administration policy, although by implication he asked his peers to stiffen their backbones.

The United States should set a good example for the other economies of the world, Jones said, to make sure "that we are part of the solution, not part of the problem." The United States, after all, is still the premiere economy of the world. In view of our role as a trader nation—the United States imports 13 percent of the manufactured exports of all other nations combined, imports nearly 10 percent of all commodities, and absorbs over 15 percent of all the fuels—a U.S. recession can become a world recession.

Americans should pursue "vigorous and expansive" economic, energy, and trade policies for reasons both international and domestic. The world needs a healthy U.S. economy.

When the United States experiences a slow recovery pace while maintaining a low ceiling price on domestic fuels, thus encouraging consumption and substantially raising oil imports, "we thereby confront our trading partners with the worst of all possible conditions, namely, weak export markets for their manufactured goods and high import prices for the oil they need so desperately. For nations whose employment and price levels are highly dependent on foreign trade, this is a very severe test indeed. And these nations include our most important allies and customers."

Congress should enact a program of permanent tax reductions both for individuals and for business, coupled with tight restraints. "And to stimulate capital investment, which is lagging badly," Jones suggested a $3-billion tax cut for business in the form of a permanent increase in the investment tax credit from 10 to 13 percent.

Special programs are needed to solve such specific unemployment areas as those of minorities and teenagers—"social dynamite that has to be defused." Such programs should include a $5-billion increase over the next two years in public service jobs and training programs. Jones said that a program of that type "would not be unduly inflationary in today's slack economy." But it would assure "a healthier and more productive U.S. economy this year, next year, and into the 1980s."

The United States must provide incentives, "not disincentives," to develop its own indigenous energy resources—coal, oil, gas, and nuclear energy. These would include removing the regulatory tangle that slows up the increase of energy. It was also vital to move ahead forcefully on tomorrow's energy technologies—solar, geothermal, synthetic fuels, and so on.

Wrapping up, Jones said that, as the world's primary economy, "we have certain responsibilities that fortunately coincide with our domestic interests. The world looks to us for a measure of stability and a maturity that recognizes the needs of other nations as well as our own."

The Herculean Prerogative

Where did it leave the American CEO? Was he, in the midst of the onrush of all his other problems, obligated to take the world on his back, too?

But he hadn't acted as if he had wanted to bear the burdens of the world on his back, even if he was still looked upon as a Hercules by a good many foreigners and occasionally by himself. Super-aggressive but self-aggrandizing, his behavior over the last few decades had indicated that if he performed well in his own company, the world, too, would benefit. To do otherwise would be to reverse priorities, foolishly.

He had already given much. By his own skills, he had reached the summit of international attainment and repute as businessman. Despite all the pinpricks of doubt, everyone said so, so it must be.

What he had done, in the most basic terms, was turn business into a quasi-science. What had been for many decades in America, Europe, and Asia no more than mere peddling was transformed into a series of progressive logistics that had first stunned and then delighted European and other businessmen. No longer acceptable was the concept that all one needed to do business was a monkey with a hat. Americans changed that after World War II with their research, production, selling, and financial techniques. If they hadn't totally originated them, they had certainly developed them all into an art-science: marketing (the technique of producing goods and distributing them based on actual socioeconomic needs); advertising (the exploitation of media to sell goods and build corporate image); public relations (the building of perceptions to create demand and acceptance); cybernetics (the automatic-control and computer systems to create a cross-fertilization of information); and industrial relations (the building of employer-employee rapport to assure a harmonious working relationship).

All that had worked very well for the American businessman, and much of it eventually was adapted by enlightened foreign businessmen who found ways to tailor it to serve their own nationals. But, swayed by his great accomplishments and rarely taking his eye off his domestic competition, the American CEO operated abroad with his left arm, so to speak. There was business to be had, but the real arena was the United States. And that was his main priority.

"Up until the oil crisis changed everything," declared Robert Coppenrath, president and general manager of Agfa-Gevaert, Inc., "the American businessman didn't really need to build up his foreign business. Since exports pay for imports, he needed only to export ten percent of his production because he and others like him imported about ten percent of their needs. But European businessmen were in an entirely different situation. The Continent needed to export fifty percent of its production because there was no surplus of consumer income to absorb production."

Coppenrath, who heads the American subsidiary of the Belgian photography complex, believes that the American production-consumption system worked because it created increasing affluence. The low-income and middle-income classes gradually became better and better consumers, he added, "whereas in Europe the middle class was much smaller and the lower class had nothing."

Despite its slowly increasing investments abroad, America's business community put its dollars primarily where it was convinced it should—in its own business in its own country. "America got rich," said Coppenrath, "but Europe didn't. But Europe got America to invest at least one hundred thirty billion dollars since World War Two."

That financial involvement in Europe, however, as well as billions of dollars invested in Asia and Africa, accumulated into a vast stake in the world economy. A study by Hay Associates, a Philadelphia-based management-consulting firm, found a "massive" international involvement of the U.S. business community representing more than 16 percent of the gross national product, or a total of $226 billion. About 8.5 million jobs in the United States are export related, and over 3,000 American companies have direct investment abroad. "International sales now represent nearly one dollar in every five of all [American] business revenues," Hay said.

Yet much of it had all been accomplished offhandedly. "The typical American businessman," Coppenrath observed, "is much less internationally oriented, and it is a big weakness on his part."

Since the oil crisis, the need for a change in the U.S. business attitude toward its relationship with the rest of the world became painfully clear. Inflated by a $40-billion oil bill in 1977 and by an imbalance in its imports and exports, the United States trade deficit had soared. To many the record deficit seemed to signal a severe loss in Americans' ability to supply their own needs and especially to compete in world markets.

In the view of Treasury Secretary Blumenthal, the deficit had mushroomed because the American economy was expanding faster than the economies of Western Europe, Japan, Canada, Mexico, Brazil, and other countries that represent large export markets for the United States. This market erosion reduced sales of American goods but increased the U.S. need for imports, especially oil.

Blumenthal contended, however, that the trade imbalance had a stimulating effect on international trade which would help invigorate the sluggish world economy. Much of the money the United States spends to buy imports comes back to it in investments. But, said the Treasury Secretary, no doubt echoing what many American businessmen believe, the United States can't stimulate the world economy alone. The other countries were scarcely of a mind or in a position to reciprocate, however. The big malaise settled in and the outlook augured for little change.

What he individually and collectively could do to get the situation off dead center undoubtedly occupied more time of the American CEO in the late 1970s than he normally would have given his company's involvement abroad. The President had stated the issue. Blumenthal was grappling with it. And Henry Reuss, the Wisconsin Democrat who chaired the House Banking Committee, criticized Treasury's sanguine viewpoint about the deficit by saying that Blumenthal's staff "was singing a happy song while the ship was sinking."

But was the typical CEO also singing as he stood navel-deep in water?

The Export of Morality

As if to haunt the CEO and his minions abroad, next came the big noise about illegal foreign payments and bribes paid by American companies.

Climaxing dramatic disclosures that began several years earlier, the Securities and Exchange Commission announced in 1977 that it was opening its files dealing with its investigations of corporate payments. Approximately 385 American companies that had foreign dealings involving the "greasing of palms," had paid bribes, or had given gratuities would now have their actions fully exposed to the public. Reporters began lining up more than two hours before SEC opened its doors in Washington that fine day in May.

Everyone heaved a big sigh, not of relief but of expectation, that appetite and digestion would not be equal to the exhaustive fare. So much had been served already.

Bribes are as old as human nature. This phase, however, began three years earlier, in the summer of 1974, when United Brands Company decided to make a simple competitive move. When several Central American countries imposed substantial export taxes on bananas, United Brands, operating in Honduras, found that it would suffer the main burden since the tax in that country was stiffer than that in the neighboring countries. United Brands had three options. It could pass on the tax to its customers and lose sales to its prime competitors, Del Monte Corporation and Castle & Cooke, Inc. Or it could swallow the tax increase and suffer a loss. Or it could bribe José Abraham Bennaton Ramos, the Honduran economics minister. Electing to do the latter, United Brands passed $2.5 million to Ramos to cut Honduras' proposed tax from 50 cents to 25 cents a box the first year and to allow the tax to rise only 5 cents a year afterward.

The decision and the disclosure of it later began a chain reaction that led to the suicide of Eli M. Black, United Brands' chairman of the board, and the ouster of Oswaldo Lopez Arellano, president of Honduras, as well as the filing of the first suit on foreign-bribe charges by the SEC. The traumatic announcement of its act by United Brands also set off a series of events that involved allegations of general immorality by many heads of American business and angry claims by foreign governments that the United States was attempting to regulate laws within their borders.

The SEC action was followed by twenty-four others, frightening a host of American companies into making voluntary disclosures of questionable or illegal payments in the media. By year's end, more than 250 American companies had "confessed," admitting bribes totaling more than $300 million.

One chief executive, Bob R. Dorsey of Gulf Oil Corporation, resigned his post, along with three other top executives, primarily because of the stigma attached to a combination of payments, both to politicians in the United States and as favors abroad. Gulf had passed $4 million to the party in power in South Korea, in one case, as well as a total of $5.4 million within the United States to political candidates.

But the harshest spotlight fell upon the Lockheed Corporation in 1976, when it was disclosed that Lockheed paid more than $25 million in bribes to sell its aircraft in Japan, the Netherlands, and Italy.

What was illegal about such payments, which were common enough and fully accepted as business practices in many foreign countries? Most American firms that made them failed to disclose them in their financial statements as required by the SEC Act, and the agency charged them with nondisclosure violations.

Although it made no difference at all to the SEC, there were two types of payments. The more serious one aimed to affect governmental policy decisions in foreign countries. Since such payments help the bribe-payers attract business on the basis of the bribe rather than because they are able to offer either a better or a lower-priced product, both the country involved and the nonbribe-paying competition lose out.

In the other type of payment, in which money is passed to facilitate action, the bribes are smaller, more widely passed on, and do not necessarily foist inferior products on the foreign citizenry or affect the nonbribe-paying competition. But in the aggregate, such bribes amount to millions paid by some companies to functionaries in customs, tax, port, security, licensing, and other foreign-government and quasi-government activities.

Nervous under the intense media coverage, every company and its chief executive promptly renounced foreign bribery. Some went so far as to prepare codes of behavior, which they furnished the press to show they were serious in curbing the practice. Others said they would continue the facilitating payments in order to cut red tape in foreign bureaucracy. They took the precaution, however, of restricting each payment to a maximum of one hundred dollars and made the payment subject to prior authorization by senior management.

Other companies that figured prominently in the disclosures of foreign payments included some of the big-big blue chips. Among them and the amounts they paid were: Trans World Airlines, $1 million; AMF, Inc., $3.4 million; Ogilvy & Mather International, Inc., $789,000; Gulf Oil Corporation, $4.9 million; Ashland Oil, Inc., $500,000; and Allied Chemical Corporation, $3 million.

In addition to the two types of foreign payments, there was a third transaction that drew punitive action. It involved the Bank Secrecy Act, which requires anyone transporting more than $5,000 between the United States and a foreign country to file a report with the government. Gulf Oil became involved when a study prepared for its directors found that the huge oil company had "laundered" or kept hidden millions of dollars in illegal political contributions through a Bahamian subsidiary. The money was transferred back to the United States, the study discovered, and doled out to various candidates, including the then-President Richard Nixon.

The upshot of the disclosure was a $229,000 civil penalty imposed against Gulf by the Treasury Department. The amount represented 90 percent of the funds brought into the United States after the Bank Secrecy Act became effective in July 1972.

The penalty was the largest ever levied under the statute.

But there was another dimension to the issue, one that underlies the sense of the old saying "When in Rome, do as the Romans do." It was raised in large type when Dresser Industries, Inc., the Dallas company that supplies products and services to the international energy and natural resources industries, took a full two-page advertisement in the *Wall Street Journal.* The headline read, "As Washington regulates American business overseas, it endangers jobs and trade." Under the headline was a large cartoon, captioned "The Race for World Trade." Four runners from England, Germany, Japan, and the United States were poised to sprint. The American, however, had a ball and chain attached to each ankle, reading "Regulation" and "Legislation."

Interviews with prominent American CEOs on the government scrutiny of foreign payments elicited that the subject was a bitter pill for most to swallow.

"This whole overseas payment thing," said Laurence Tisch, chairman of Loews Corporation, "suddenly became wrong. It's been going on for a hundred years. People went to the economic counselors of the U.S. embassies around the world to find out whom you should pay. This is nothing new—the question is whom do you pay? Look, we're not going to change the world overnight.

"The big question is how much business is America losing overseas because of discontinuing payments overseas," Tisch continued. "How is it affecting our balance of payments? How many jobs have been lost? I think we've lost a tremendous amount of business, because if certain machinery makers or airplane producers can't pay off overseas, they are not going to do the business. The French, the English, the Germans, and everybody else other than the Americans are still paying off. If it's American policy to change the system for American businessmen, okay. We will abide by the law of the land. But people should understand that there is a cost involved.... Anything the government says I should do, I will do. But don't fool the public and tell them you are getting this for free.

"It's going to cost a fortune. There are certain companies that are unique. Maybe only General Electric can build a nuclear reactor. But the other thing is it's very good to be high and mighty and say we're not going to pay off any more, but who knows how much a company is paying indirectly to sell their merchandise? I could call a lawyer in Washington and give him a two-hundred-thousand-dollar fee and accomplish something that maybe if you tried to give a guy a weekend you would go to jail for. So at what point do you separate right from wrong? No one is facing that—the legal profession wouldn't like to face that. You have more lawyers per square foot in Washington than anyplace else in the world using influence, not legal services."

Concluding his obviously impassioned feelings about the entire matter, Tisch added, "All I know is one thing—if we don't sell the foreigners, the Germans will be only too happy. The French, the Swiss, the Canadians—everybody over there must be laughing up their sleeves at the Americans. And it's all not illegal under American law as long as you disclose it. It's not illegal—it never was."

"I have strong views on the subject of so-called illegal payments," asserted Michel C. Bergerac, who had been responsible for IBM's international operations before becoming chief executive of Revlon, Incorporated. "We are trying to reconcile an unreconcilable situation. It is not possible for the U.S. government to take upon itself to define what is morality here and everywhere in the world and to impose a code of conduct on U.S. companies operating in countries where such a code is impractical."

He added, "Japanese, German, and other foreign businesses will do well, but if the U.S. government continues to impose its code on American companies operating abroad, it must lead to loss of jobs, loss in the balance of payments, and inevitably to the continual loss of the dollar's value."

Bergerac urged American regulatory agencies to "recognize the world for what it is. American companies should be given freedom to compete—that's what American enterprise is all about." Yet, as a realist, he said, "I don't expect that to happen for political reasons. But I believe that water will find its own level when it becomes clear that the punishment can become so great."

The same point was expressed by Arthur M. Wood, who retired in January 1978 as chairman and CEO of Sears, Roebuck & Company, which has substantial operations abroad. "Unless we have an international acceptance of new mores in buyer-seller relationships, this country must lose out," he said. "Some of these payments not reported were made by a foreign-based subsidiary and weren't really bribes. They are really extortions in a sense. These sums are paid to get customs clearance for people reassigned or to obtain similar favors to facilitate entry or life in a foreign country. We have from the beginning had an ironclad rule not to do this, but it remains an accepted form of life abroad."

As the debate grew, the question inevitably emerged about the quality of the executives dispatched by large American companies to manage their foreign ventures. Most chief executives interviewed defended their resident managers in Europe, Latin America, and the Far East and Middle East as equivalent in skills to those who remain in the United States. But one company head, who requested anonymity so he could speak candidly without riling his peers, asserted, "With all their big stake in other countries, the hard fact is that most American companies keep their best managers at home because that's where the real action is.

"The guys they ship abroad are like displaced persons. They get paid well but live in a golden ghetto in the foreign country. And most don't get recycled back into the U.S.," he said. "The exceptions maybe are in the big airlines, like TWA or Pan Am, where they rise to the top after serving abroad. Or in journalism or the U.S. Army, where a foreign hitch gives a man's career a big shot upward." He shrugged, adding, "The top businessmen in America come from a domestic background. So there's a reverse natural selection in terms of people sent overseas. But don't expect anyone to confirm that."

Tackling the Global Village

Confronted by all these factors—the challenge from Washington that he had an obligation to bolster not only the American economy but international economies as well, the decline of the American multinational effort, the descent of the dollar, the debatable morality of his foreign payments, and even some question about the worth of the people he employed abroad—what could the American chief executive do about them all?

Even before any answers seemed to be at hand, another problem surfaced that made international operations even more complex—the Arab boycott of American companies doing business with Israel. The issue was the reverse of the charge that the United States was attempting to regulate the laws of a foreign country by frowning on U.S. business payments to their nationals. In this case, foreign countries were in principle and in reality attempting to tell American companies where they could do business.

The boycott question came down to a standoff after several years of debate when separate bills drafted by the Senate and the House aroused fears among many American businessmen that any legislation would seriously disrupt trade with the Middle East. Compromise efforts by the Business Roundtable and by the Anti-Defamation League of B'nai B'rith had not been reflected in the proposed bills, charged the Chamber of Commerce of the United States.

Because of "ambiguous" language, the bit was thrust back into the teeth of American business. "Corporations being what they are," said a Chamber spokesman, "they will play it safe" and suspend questionable trade, thus threatening the loss of jobs and income in this country.

So it was another of those international pressures that mitigated against concentration on the home scene. What could be done about it and all the rest of the international pressures? As the head of an individual company, what can one chief executive do?

Perhaps the most pragmatic answer to these frequently posed questions in my interviewing came from John L. Hanigan, chairman of Genesco, who had come out of retirement in 1976 at the age of sixty-six after a successful career as CEO of the Brunswick Corporation.

"Yes, I've had a lot of these problems and I've worked on them," he replied. "And it does appear that all of us live and work not just in our hometown but in a sort of global village. Just the same, it seems to me that all you can really do is keep your eyes and ears open and make sure you do the best job in your own company that you can. If enough of us do those things it may not solve all the world's problems, but it sure as hell won't make them any worse."

7

How Good Are American CEOs?

The Best in the Midwest? . . . And All the Rest

There is a claim in business circles—semi-serious, semi-jesting in intent, but probably only a myth—that a disproportionately large number of the best American corporate chief executives come from the Midwest. The rationale goes something like this:

The Midwesterner comes from a poor or middle-class background and for years worked part-time in a nearby farm, store, or factory. Firm-boned, corn-fed, and with a liking for potatoes with his breakfast, he represents the finest, clearest-eyed, sturdiest stock. He knows from his early days that he has to dedicate himself to every task, because the soil only yields up the sweat that is put into it. He goes to a state college, like Ohio State or Michigan State, and supports himself in part by working nights and summers. "Pa," he says in his manly way, "I've got to leave the farm and make something of myself 'cause I can't let you support me all my life." So he grows up with an unaffected manner, acquires a direct way of thinking, and develops a humble but winning charm. Open with everyone, he makes people feel comfortable, and his simple integrity wins trust. His values are basically rural, uncluttered, and organically sound.

The Easterner is a totally different sort. Living in confined quarters, pushing others for space, his ways are calculated and he tries to outsmart everyone. Often, he outsmarts himself. "I can manipulate the next guy and outthink him, too," he says. A bit lazy from overconfidence, he doesn't quite trust his own natural talents—if he has any, which is a good question—but seeks to make his way by bravado. And it works. The laws of averages and self-propulsion work whether on a crowded pavement or a tight table of organization. In his upward thrust, however, the Easterner is mistrusted, and he never quite surmounts it. Somehow he is also personally blamed for being too self-involved because he hasn't curbed the bankruptcy of the eastern cities and the high crime rate, especially muggings.

The Southerner is made of different grits. The old-school ties are strong in him, and his roots are sunk deep in the rich clay. He is reluctant to be transferred out of his hometown even if it means a good kick upward. His values are irrevocably small-town and blindly homogeneous. "My family's been here for generations and that's where I'll stay," he is prone to insist. But the economic wheel has happily turned in the direction of the good old boys. The Sun Belt, that wide swatch from Florida across Texas and enveloping Georgia, Kentucky, Arizona, and New Mexico, includes his hometown, too, and all of it, as everyone knows, has been swept by the nation's fastest-growing prosperity.

The Westerner has that faraway look, but he is probably just sun-drenched. He has, it seems, an unfortunate lack of depth. Why? Because California, the biggest and the farthest west (forget Hawaii and Alaska; they haven't been evaluated yet), consists of residents from just about every other state. Yet because of the area's low per-capita population and the many business opportunities that come from it, the Westerner is both more entrepreneurial than most other regionals and less disciplined. Inclined to accept a new trend quickly, he drops it just as quickly. After all, isn't everything plastic and spastic in the Far West? Living in those wide open spaces amid the wealth of natural resources tends to stifle one's initiative and application since, let's be candid, those are some sunsets!

In this slightly mad appraisal, which is certain to make everyone angry, there are some kernels that apply to the bigger, more serious question of whether American business chiefs aren't losing much of their steam to the foreigners.

For example, if American businessmen, however different their regional backgrounds and native influences, are affected by them, do they lack the overview and long-term instincts that a nation's economy needs in order to grow?

Or is it that we are not yet a cohesive nation, are still divided by area differences, even within a region, by taste, income, and vocational gaps, by deepening ideological cracks, by the shifts of economic power away from the older cities to the newer ones and from eroding ghetto cores to the reborn rural plains?

And, perhaps more basically, do all of us—and especially our corporate elite—insist on believing that American dynamism is a God-given trait and will carry us through despite the growing scope of our economic and national problems?

Or is it all much more simple in nature—that after two hundred years the dynamism of the nation must slow down and its businessmen take a deep breath, in order to enter a more mature era in which our forces can then be deployed more effectively with the wisdom of experience? Most businessmen think so.

But something seems out of sync with this consensus.

Whether it reflects more cautious policies taken because of smaller economic growth, or the latter because of the former, there is much evidence that American economic dynamism has been stunted.

In the fifteen years between 1960 and 1975, American economic productivity has dropped precipitously. Explaining it, Americans cite too much government, the burden of environmental costs, the growing dependence on foreign oil, high inflation, and the country's transference from a predominantly manufacturing economy to more of a service-marketing economy that has a lesser growth rate.

American corporate profits—running in the late 1970s to about $104 billion annually—have not shown any notable progress. On a conventional basis, they averaged about 10 percent of corporate income in 1977, down slightly from the 10.5 percent of the last two decades. However, on a more realistic basis —that is, minus the "phantom" profits representing marked-up inventories and depreciation based on book value rather than on replacement cost—1977 profits ran at about 6.5 percent or one fourth below the 9 percent long-term average.

"This low and unimproving level of profit margins is not an encouraging sign for general economic prospects," observed Edgar R. Fiedler, vice-president of economic research for the Conference Board in New York.

"Given the reasonably comfortable liquidity position of most corporations, maintenance of the present level of margins, which implies gradually rising dollar profits, does not appear to threaten the ongoing steady increase in business spending for new plants and equipment. But unless and until a better profit picture comes in sight, the much-desired and much-needed acceleration in the trend of capital spending is unlikely to emerge," Fiedler said.

There are other worrisome factors to be considered, too:

The balance-of-trade deficit of the United States catapulted to an all-time record of $30 billion in 1977, fed by growing oil imports and rising fuel costs. No short-term, or for that matter long-term, solution appears to be in prospect for what an increasing number of businessmen term "our biggest national headache."

Although the traditional U.S. executive position is that it is difficult to compete with foreign countries because of lower wage rates, those foreign labor rates are also being forced up by inflation. Yet in the last decade, the United States has virtually given entire industries to other countries. Electronics to Japan, Hong Kong, and Taiwan. Shipbuilding to Russia. Steel to Japan and Europe. Footwear to Italy and Spain. Toys to Europe and the Far East. Sweaters to Italy and the United Kingdom. Even the Soviet republics have successfully entered the tough U.S. market with cheap watches.

Despite an intermittently tough antitrust policy by the federal authorities, corporate giantism has continued to grow. Yet the expansion of such super-giants as General Motors, AT&T, and General Electric hasn't worked to reduce inflation, raising doubt that lower prices result from the "economy of scale." In fact, it is the element of competition, often touched off by the zealous hunger of a small operator, which has given consumers the opportunity to buy goods at lower prices.

And possibly as revealing as any single other factor is the heavy turnover of chief executives in recent years. Between 1970 and 1975, about one half of eight hundred American companies had changed their CEOs. By the end of 1976, about two thirds of all large American companies were headed by chief executives or presidents who had been in office less than seven years. The turnover trend continued into 1977 and hardly seems due to abate in 1978. The companies in which heads rolled included

RCA, Singer, Pillsbury, Bulova Watch, Johns-Manville, National Broadcasting, Lockheed, Gulf Oil, and many others.

And Now for the Big Question

Given all that, how good is the American CEO?

The obvious answer is: Not as good as he used to be. But in what may be a case of comparing apples with oranges, almost all the chief executives this writer interviewed insist that the comparison is not a valid one. In 1950, they said, the concept of the CEO's job was a lot simpler than it was in 1960. Since 1970, the job has grown infinitely more difficult and complex, and it will grow even more so in the years to follow. In other words, the job is vastly different from what it used to be.

"The role of supervising a business has been changing for some time," said John Diebold, chairman of the Diebold Group, an international management-consulting firm. "Outside environmental changes, mostly due to value changes in American society, are so great that they must weigh more on the chief executive's time than ever before and he has to devote much of his time to them," he said.

Once solely evaluated for his performance at the bottom line, today's corporate chief is now graded on the basis of how he recognizes and deals with value changes which inevitably impact that bottom line, Diebold said. "As a result, there is a terrible conflict among many CEOs between short-term and long-term responsibilities. Their job, in effect, is very much larger than it was in years past," he added.

One of the best-known American management consultants, an adviser to Presidents and a member over the years of many corporate boards, Diebold is one who thinks that American businessmen tend to feel that the vaunted American dynamism is a guarantee of success. "That is a real mistake," Diebold said. "It's the kind of thinking that isn't realistic in today's world. It is very important that the heads of our businesses be terribly alive to changing values and not live in the past. We're in a pickle today because of that type of syndrome, and it's essential that private-sector leaders address themselves to the changes in our society."

The irony of such a situation is that America's business community demonstrates the technological capability to manage complex responsibilities, he continued, but "yet we can't seem to handle simple tasks. We put great stress on short-term problems—and we are ruled by a tyranny of small decisions. We make decisions, which individually seem of modest significance, without fully understanding their implications. After a series of these small decisions, we find we are locked into disastrous patterns that defy our capacity to break."

Diebold said that coupled with the alienation from authority and regimentation that characterizes current changing values, "the productivity of our economy is declining." He went on, "Attitudes toward work and personal value systems have changed radically, but few large corporations have altered their systems for managing, promoting, and paying people.

"We need large organizations," he said, "and we also need our creative younger people. Yet the way we handle people in business and government agencies has not kept up with the changes in their values. Imaginative innovation in adapting job hours and pay to today's realities could go a long way to unleashing the energies and creativity of many members of our society who are turned off by yesterday's organization concepts and practices."

Pierre Rinfret, the bouncy, ebullient economist, is convinced that the American chief executive is in serious trouble because of government pressures, his lack of understanding of and slow response to social changes, and the increasing control exerted over him by the legal profession. "The CEO's ability to run a company is hemmed in by lawyers who put one fear after another into him," Rinfret said. "I know—I'm on five boards."

Rinfret, an adviser to several Presidents, including Richard Nixon, is sometimes criticized by more conventional businessmen who claim his natural liking for controversy makes him as much a public-relations man as a qualified economist. But others respect him for his candidness and shrug off the considerable personal publicity he gets.

"I think the situation will get worse," Rinfret told me. "American industry is losing its drive, its guts, and its venturesome spirit. It has lost its entrepreneurial courage. And its CEOs have become cautious, careful managers of businesses that continue to grow only on sheer momentum."

He added, "One reason for the chief executives' malaise is that they really don't have much of a stake in the business. They don't own much stock, like their predecessors used to, and their stock options have turned out to be a bomb because of the severe decline in the stock market. One CEO I know borrowed heavily to take advantage of his company's stock option and bought a lot of stock at fifty. Now, it's down to sixteen, and he still owes lots of money to the bank that gave him the loan.

"The chief executive's salary may seem large in dollars but it's only so on a gross basis. He doesn't really get enough money for the responsibility that he has. If you compare him to his predecessor of a decade ago, the present tax bite is so big that he isn't doing as well financially as the other ones did. Inflation and taxes mean that the job isn't paying as well in real terms as it did ten years ago. And boards of directors are getting chintzy with him."

He cited one recent example of a board on which he served recommending a $5,000-a-year increase for a CEO earning $120,000 a year. "I raised strong objections," Rinfret said. "I asked the other directors whether they thought that a four-percent increase, which is about what that raise would amount to, would give the CEO any sense of recognition. They eventually increased the amount—but that is typical of what is happening on lots of boards these days. So what's happening? Too many CEOs are telling themselves or saying out loud, 'I'm not going to bust my ass if that's all my work means.'"

And what of chief executive officers in other countries. How do they behave and how do they compare?

Executives who frequently travel abroad to do business in other economies and have met often with their counterparts gave these impressions of them:

Many Europeans and Japanese businessmen display a greater worldliness and educational background than Americans. As a result, they are more articulate on worldwide aspects both economic and social. But the Americans say they aren't as aggressive as the U.S. CEOs, probably because the latter concentrate on short-run goals, tying one to another as they come up so that there is a greater tendency in American financial performance to attempt to show unbroken quarterly rises in sales and earnings. But the foreign genre, the Americans admit, have a longer-term view, thinking of five- and ten-year goals, and take a longer perspective on immediate problems.

Work habits are different, too. "Our CEOs are more flexible in their daily working lives," observed Henry Shapiro, president of Maryland Cup Corporation in Owings Mills, Maryland. "We frequently change appointments to accommodate sudden developments or even the unexpected arrival of foreign businessmen. But many foreign chief executives live by their daily diary and are reluctant to change appointments. Maybe it's because they are more used to being catered to rather than catering to others."

Diebold cited innovative approaches to manpower used abroad that have proved highly successful, the key of which seems to be the effective identification of the employees' interests with that of industry. In Japan, employees see themselves as part of a vital, working community. In Germany, workers feel as great an economic stake in productivity and profitability as management does.

"We should be able to combine the possibility of self-fulfillment with the fact of working in large organizations," said Diebold, "building on our own traditions of individual initiative and the recognition of talent."

But despite national differences, Shapiro said (and his sentiment was repeated by others), both American and foreign businessmen are being forced to spend much more time on external matters, particularly social changes, than ever before.

"If the typical American business head tried these days to personally do as much as his predecessor of a decade or two ago, he would quickly find that he was out of his own element of expertise," observes John D. Arnold, president of Applied Synergetics, Inc., of Waltham, Massachusetts.

Arnold, an executive counselor, added, "The U.S. CEO has such a breadth of challenge that its scope is unparalleled anywhere. As it is, rather than involve himself too much into the many aspects of the business, both internal and external, he has to know enough to ask the right questions of the people in the organization who have the functional expertise. And that's a lot in itself."

So the CEO has to be a catalyst or set up a process that

performs a catalytic role, Arnold said. "If he can't get his team hooked up on his wavelength and get their support, he will not be able to get a handle on all the facets that bear heavily on his role and he'll also lose their support and trust, not to mention their commitment."

The business chief can no longer work on a "one-to-one basis with anyone else in the company, although some still do and it limits their effectiveness." More and more, Arnold said, the chief executive is compelled to use his talent to develop a constant input from the major executives in his company. "What he ends up with is a list that no one man, even including himself, could have developed through the use of his own brain or experience," Arnold added.

But this exacts a price. The effort to orchestrate his players while at the same time viewing the score through his own growing perception puts constraints on the chief executive that are infinitely greater than his predecessors' of earlier years, Arnold and others observe. And it leaves him lonely in the midst of a crowd and beleaguered in spite of all the assistance and cooperation from his team of functional experts.

The CEO's Face Is an Interface

What do others say?

"Power in corporate America is shifting in response to outside pressures. There is a new chairman of the board emerging, and the fate of major business organizations—and ultimately of our economic system—rests with his ability to cope with an often hostile social and political environment," asserted Dr. Eugene Jennings, professor of management in the Graduate School of Business Administration at Michigan State University.

In an introduction to the once-in-five-year profile studies of business leadership trends by Heidrick and Struggles, one of the leading American executive recruiting firms in Chicago and New York, Dr. Jennings added, "Embattled, bewildered, and often defensive in the face of a quantum increase in constraints and uncertainties during the first half of this decade, big business now evidences a more realistic view of what is required to survive, let alone prosper, in a radically different world. . . .

"While the president is charged with managing day-to-day operations, it is the chairman and CEO who has developed as primary interface with outside groups in both the public and private sectors. This is a natural consequence of the scrutiny boards increasingly have been undergoing.

"Granted, some chairmen have yet to conceptualize this new role, holding to the tradition that strategical planning involves only acquiring and maximizing return on employment of hard assets. In the most progressive organizations, however, the chairman has already assumed his new duties with the clear understanding that today's most pressing concern is not short-run profits but long-term viability. He must be willing to bring about changes which may adversely impact the corporation in the near term in order to achieve a more favorable environment over time.

"This power shift at the top of the corporate pyramid," added Dr. Jennings, "calls for a different type of executive: bold, not bland. In the past, the chairman's position often has been regarded as a reward rather than as the supreme test of competency. Indeed, holders of the title rarely interfaced with or needed to concern themselves with individuals outside the senior management group.

"Today, the chairman as CEO increasingly is involved personally in promoting his company's cause in the arena of public opinion. His ability to persuade dissident stockholders, consumer activists and even disgruntled employees of his worthiness to maintain his position of power will determine his degree of effectiveness and ultimately his tenure in office," Dr. Jennings said.

Sounds familiar by now, doesn't it? But the Michigan State professor articulated it all well, although he saved until the last his best observation and perhaps the most cogent argument that it's difficult to compare today's CEO with his predecessors.

"In conclusion," he said, "corporate America is experiencing the changing of the guard, but this change runs deeper than titles might suggest. No designation can adequately identify the incredible demands confronting the chief executive officer in his struggles to retain options for his firm in the conduct of its business. The glamour is gone; truly, the work of the CEO has just begun."

Carl W. Menk, president of Boyden Associates, the largest recruiting agency for businesses, is convinced that American CEOs generally are still the top men around the world, but takes exception to a certain type.

"The worst chief executives are the overachievers," he said. "They live by their wits. They call themselves professional managers and know how to put their act together, somewhat in the manner of a stage performer. They come into a company and are good for maybe three years. They shake the tree well, use acceptable objectives, but demonstrate a lack of follow-through. A year after they are there, they start revving up the public relations in preparation for the second and third years. Then some hard, original thinking is needed, and that's the tough part.

"But they are good communicators," Menk said, "and attractive physically and have good charisma. They will make it for a short span of years, not in the biggest companies but in those with sales of between two hundred million dollars and six hundred million. In time, their spotty record of success and inconsistent background emerges, but in today's tough business scene there are situations that appear to demand the charismatic, hard-hitting guy.

"And they are surprised when they run into objections. And how do most of them react? They say, 'Sure, if I never made any decisions, I wouldn't have any enemies.' It's a reaction, of course, that covers many sins."

But the "good" American CEO, Menk added, "is a very effective guy. He reduces the problem to its simplest terms and then often makes a decision without having all the facts to save time. Why? Because he may never have all the facts and there's no point in waiting endlessly to make a decision. Is it possible for him to know how Washington will behave six months from now? Of course not, and so he moves based on a combination of facts, instinct, and lots of hope."

"When I became a CEO, the total responsibility of it elated me," said Peter S. Redfield, president of Itel Corporation, a San Francisco computer-leasing company. "But the power associated with signing something and knowing that was it hit me and scared me. I got very concerned because I had to depend upon other people. And what was the biggest shock of all was that I had to communicate with the financial world and I know I have no charisma. I am a decent-enough public speaker, but I am not clever on my feet. I mean that in response to questions from the floor I am not tactically clever. And I don't want to develop a public personality. I therefore resolved to do it by performance and by my efforts. As it is, I spend more time with analysts, four times as much as with any other group. . . .

"Now that I have been a CEO for several years," he went on, "I get invited to fancy dinners with other chief executives and listen to them sitting around and bitching about government. But that's not the biggest problem by any means. Since World War Two, there has been a vast technological change in which the work can be done with fewer people operating systems. So we don't really need one hundred million workers any more, probably only fifty million. But then thirty million women have entered the work force, and American industry can't cope with it. So we'll always have high unemployment and we'll have to create artificial jobs. Government will be a growth industry."

Impaling the CEO

"The Midwest continues to produce more corporate leaders (40.7 percent) than any other region," reported the Heidrick and Struggles study of 1977, profiling the chief executives in 342 companies out of 500 of the nation's largest companies. "Midwestern headquarters of many organizations account for this phenomenon in part, though the region is still disproportionately represented," the study found. "Among industrials under $500 million in sales, nearly six out of ten CEOs are natives of America's heartland."

So, there's that canard again.

But almost every one of the chief executives interviewed by this writer scoffed at the superiority of the Midwesterner. Most said the origin of this contention was the existence of many company headquarters in Illinois, Ohio, and Michigan and the growth of many capital industries in that tier of states. One such chief executive, William M. Agee, chairman of Bendix Corporation, Southfield, Michigan, quipped, "Thanks for the compliment. The only problem is that I come from California."

Other findings in the Heidrick and Struggles study include the following:

In choosing their most important responsibilities, six out of ten CEOs cite planning and the selection and development of key personnel. Financial decisions ranked next, then policy making, maintaining morale, and finally meeting government regulation and relations requirements. Personnel development and selection was the crucial area of concern that cannot be delegated, according to one third of the respondents.

"It is surprising then that most CEOs have not determined their successor. Though half have two or more candidates in mind, only one third have narrowed the field to one individual," according to Heidrick and Struggles.

The strongest lure attracting CEOs to their current jobs was personal contact, in six out of every ten, the study found. And one out of ten was related to an influential executive, stockholder, or director. Most frequently, the CEO had a father who was chairman, president, or chief executive of the company or of another company.

The typical chief executive began his career at age twenty-three and assumed supervisory responsibilities before he reached twenty-seven. He set his sights on becoming chief executive of a major corporation long before he reached that objective. Although the break into supervisory ranks took longer within banking, financial, and utility companies, Heidrick and Struggles said, the lag had little impact on the career goals of the future CEO. "The probability that current chief executives aspired to top positions declines with the size of the industrial. This trend reflects the tendency of executives within large organizations to rely on sophisticated management development programs to assure their steady upward progress," the study reported.

The CEO of today is typically fifty-seven years old, seven years older than the functional heads reporting to him, according to the findings. This compares with presidents surveyed in the 1972 sampling who averaged fifty-three years of age. And a shift of the CEO status to the chairman from the president has moved the average age upward. As complexities of management continue to escalate, "the wisdom of experience frequently outweighs the vigor of youth. Moreover, chronological age no longer delimits vitality, with medical care becoming an entrenched priority in benefit programs and management-development schemes."

How hard does the CEO work? The typical CEO puts in more than sixty hours a week. For every one who takes care of his business affairs in less than fifty hours, another works seventy. And though CEOs of the largest industrials work longer than heads of the smallest firms, the difference amounts to just three hours a week.

Who is the most effective chief executive in America? About one third of the responding executives answered the question and the majority agreed. It was Reginald H. Jones, chief executive of GE. He made the lists of six of seven utility executives who gave their opinions, and he was just as popular among chiefs of industrial companies with a billion or more dollars in sales. Seven of the eleven bankers chose Walter Wriston, chairman of Citicorp (New York) as the most effective chief executive of the time.

Bunting's Way

Controversial among bankers, but admired by many younger executives, John R. Bunting, Jr., the chairman and chief executive of First Pennsylvania Corporation, the holding company of the First Pennsylvania Bank, is one of a new breed of American CEOs who quite possibly may break up some of the country's business stagnation.

In addition to some of the nonconformist actions he took to shake up Philadelphia's largest bank and startle the nation's banking establishment, Bunting has some personal attributes and quirks that also rock critics but please his admirers.

Slim, natty, handsome, he demonstrates an easy, smiling graciousness, flavored somewhat by the hyperbole of the salesman, which makes him an atypical banker.

Often he will do things for effect and admit it. In 1972, early in his tenure as CEO, he appointed a black and a college student to First Pennsy's board and confessed that the moves were symbolic. A non-Jew, he also publicly criticized a Philadelphia club for restricting Jews.

A slightly twisted grin lets one through to an impish boredom with traditional approaches. An economist by education and vocation, Bunting insists quite seriously that companies of all kinds, including banks, need not only economists but anthropologists, too, "to see beyond the economist's disciplines." Top executives have to be good listeners, he claims, and he is, but he never passes judgment on a man's suggestion at the time it is made. "I listen, I participate, and I think it over afterward," Bunting explains. "Later, I'll decide if the idea has merit. That's all people really want—the chance to be listened to with an open mind. They know that the final decision isn't theirs."

And so, Bunting is convinced, a chief executive has to be a sort of master of ceremonies. "Ceremonial, yes. But your people want you to project a certain image of leadership, even aplomb, and they want you to be important. But do it as a sham and it will be ineffective. Do it as real and you will keep things going. And the more interesting and alive you are, the more you will inspire others. Decisions, of course, evolve, but beyond that, the corporate chief executive has to have charisma, and if he has he is lucky."

At lunch with an interviewer in the bank's modernistic Penn Tower in downtown Philadelphia, Bunting displayed a breezy confidence, taking occasional calls, ordering food, making interesting asides to ease the strangeness of a first meeting. At no time in the more-than-two-hour discussion, however, did he refer to the problems he had encountered at the bank-holding company since his dramatic, initial success in his first two years as chief executive. It was all past him but no doubt not forgotten.

By 1973, or five years after he was named to First Pennsy's top job, Bunting skillfully blended aggressive acquisitions and lending policies to push the holding company into the first tier among all United States banking enterprises in terms of profit on stockholder's equity. So dramatic was his success in jogging the corporation, although it was only the twenty-first in size of its type, that the same year Harvard Business School students in a poll rated a job at First Pennsylvania as equal to berths at IBM and Xerox.

But in the next two years, the oil-related recession brought dark days to many banks and even darker ones to First Pennsy.

Saddled by heavy loan losses and earnings declines, Bunting reluctantly called a halt to a corporate acquisition campaign that had already included consumer-finance companies, a mortgage-banking house, and a real-estate investment trust. A loss was actually recorded in one fiscal quarter, and in 1976 First Pennsy ignominiously fell from its top perch all the way to forty-first in the country on profit on stockholder's equity. In 1977, earnings began to show improved performance again. Yet Bunting, who had given many bankers a sour stomach, reaped the overflow of their bile and to some extent still does.

At one point in the midst of First Pennsy's biggest problems under his tenure, rumors mounted that he would be dumped. But the holding company's directors remained confident that he could master the situation. It took lots of doing. In a two-year period, some 650 employees at both the holding company and the bank headquarters were let go. Key executives were changed. More stringent controls were enforced on lending policies. And Bunting, who became a more conservative banker, now bears a few more lines under his eyes and nose than he had when a financial publication hailed him as "the golden boy of banking."

Yet with his more austere approach to creative stewardship, Bunting's management efforts still remain noteworthy. If he brought a public-relations man's instincts and even something of a hustler's methods to the restricted air of American banking, they were undoubtedly needed.

The son of a manager of a branch savings bank, he absorbed the feel of a bank early. But he grew up in Philadelphia's Tacony section, an industrial-residential area of tiny homes far from the city's Main Line, which is usually associated with Philadelphia's bankers. While he attended the well-regarded Hill School in his senior year of high school on an athletic scholarship, he received a bachelor's degree in business administration and a master's degree in economics from Temple University in Philadelphia. Like City University of New York, the sprawling, inner-city university was hardly considered in the Ivy League camp.

As an economist at the Federal Reserve Bank of Philadelphia, the slight, bouncy young banking executive developed a dislike of the rhetoric of the "dull science" and became a popular luncheon and after-dinner speaker by often making light of its ponderousness. "After perusing the Fed's latest report of two hundred forty-three thrill-packed pages," he would begin, "I'd like to digest them in the following sentence...." Small member banks of the Philly Fed scrambled for his appearance. After shifting impatiently in his chair through some "terrible, terrible meetings," Bunting would come on refreshingly brash and untraditional.

With fourteen years at the Fed behind him, Bunting was offered a job by William Kelly, chairman of the First Pennsylvania Bank and president of the American Bankers Association, as the Pennsy's vice-president and chief economist. Kelly, who evidently liked to get his money's worth, also wanted Bunting to be his assistant and write speeches for him. And although Bunting had been told he might eventually have a crack at the presidency of the Philadelphia Fed, he decided to take the nongovernment post.

What happened then was totally unexpected. The genial bank president, long the First Pennsy's mainstay, developed terminal cancer shortly after Bunting's arrival and lapsed into a coma. For the ambitious Bunting, it meant the immediate loss of a sponsor and the imminent death of a friend. For the bank, Kelly's demise in 1966 left it not only bereft of its top man but without the spokesman it had depended upon to put it into the savings-account arena, a controversial move since it operated as a correspondent bank with others, including savings banks, and kept substantial deposits with them.

The problem that loomed was that the concept would have to be sold to the correspondent banks. Kelly, with his strong local and national standing, could have put over the advantages of offering time savings accounts even though it meant competing with his own customers. After pondering who could best articulate it in Kelly's absence, the bank's directors decided to throw the strategic assignment to Bunting even though he himself was not even a director. He was given all of five minutes to make his pitch, but whether it was an ability to express sincerity cut to the bone or his characteristic light touch, he sold the idea.

What was more important, however, was that the move proved to be an excellent one. First Pennsy's 5-percent certificates of deposits sold like Philadelphia scrapple used to. Two years later, the economist now recognized as marketer was named to succeed Kelly. But his accession to the bank presidency and later to the CEO's role didn't convince Bunting to adopt a low-key approach traditional for a principal banker. Shortly afterward, he got the other Philadelphia banks hopping mad by introducing free checking accounts. Although checks are costly to process, the other banks were forced to follow First Pennsy's lead. The trend didn't prove to be successful in Philadelphia, though it did in other cities, and most banks in that city have dropped the service. But the incident didn't leave Bunting any more popular.

When the bank-holding-company trend began, First Pennsy had already been considering its own way of diversifying to nonbanking activities and so quickly joined the movement. Three years later, in 1973, Bunting became chairman of the First Pennsylvania Corporation, the new holding company, and again proceeded to shake up the Union League Club. He broke the long-accepted practice of allowing the bigger West Coast and New York City banks to be the first to announce changes in the prime or basic commercial lending rate. And he pushed his acquisition program, although he was forced to scale it down under the pressure of declined earnings. But even when the income curve went up again, Bunting came under criticism for some of the elements in First Pennsy's profits. One such component was revenue from a one-time sale of an asset. Another was a high proportion of earnings from trading in government securities. Bunting's rejoinder, accompanied by his slightly twisted grin: "Income, after all, is income."

While casting off the stodgy image of First Pennsy as the nation's oldest and one of its most conservative trust companies, and achieving national recognition in the process, Bunting believes he has learned a few things.

"I became a chief executive when I was forty-three. As a younger CEO, I was inclined to do more myself. And when it worked, I withdrew a bit and let the organization go to work. But when the 1974 depression, the worst since the 1930s, hurt Philadelphia, I had to come back and put my own stamp on things again. . . .

"The chief executive can't communicate with everyone. First, there are some matters of strategy which are inappropriate to put on paper. But that works two ways, I guess. There are people I communicate with who aren't terribly confident of their stature, so quite naturally they withhold full information. And some of those people are so insecure that they even withhold information from subordinates so they can have an edge over them. . . .

"I have an advantage, self-imposed, maybe, but it has helped me because I suppose I used it. I was in the Federal Reserve System and it has a lot of mystique. . . . I was completely convinced that I knew more of economics and banking than anyone else, and it helped to make me pretty brash. . . .

"I no longer think of building the size of our business but of making more money out of it. The 1974-1975 recession knocked the bejesus out of all of us and it could happen again. The world economy isn't working well, I'm afraid, and we'll have to be more conservative than our competitors."

Although it is true that bankers have a particularly difficult role—in tough times they are damned if they are generous and damned if they aren't—Bunting developed into an unusual banker, demonstrating at least one capacity for which both critics and admirers haven't fully credited him. It was the ability to learn on the job and to use the knowledge productively.

How Good Is Great? Tracking Harold Geneen vs. Reginald Jones

If Harold S. Geneen, the flinty, spare, hot-cold chief of the giant International Telephone and Telegraph Corporation, who retired at the end of 1977, was long considered the master chief executive in American business, it's reasonable to assume that the crown has passed to Reginald Jones of General Electric.

Between the two there are superficial similarities but deep, drastic, and subtle differences. Oddly enough, both are English-born but came to the United States as children. Both are the products of big business, nurtured and trained by its disciplines and politics and hardened by its heat processes. Both emerged as enormously skilled corporate tacticians.

Geneen, however, was the classic hands-on manager. Jones is perhaps the contemporary prototype hands-off manager. And that makes for a world of difference. The ITT boss believed in confrontations, acrid, difficult, and bloody, among his executives and between them and himself.

But the GE chief took a completely reverse tack. He believed that everyone did better if given authority and that once they demonstrated skills and management poise they could well be left alone.

The two men, each considered the best of his time, could not have had more different personal and professional styles.

Both Geneen and Jones have been among the nation's highest-paid corporate executives. In his final year, the ITT chief earned $934,564; Jones earned $620,000 the same year. But both came to their high earnings via entirely different routes.

Geneen, the offspring of divorced parents, worked as a page in the New York Stock Exchange and studied accounting at night at New York University. He was employed by an accounting firm and held various jobs in industry until he achieved strong success at the Raytheon Corporation.

In 1959, when he was forty-nine years old, Geneen came to ITT, where he promptly changed the content and image from a motley collection of rather unstable foreign holdings to a conglomerate owning such plums as Avis auto rentals, Levitt and Sons (the builders), and Sheraton Corporation (the hotel chain). Tight operating controls, strong acquisitions, and a tough management policy gave ITT a long profit run unduplicated by any other major American corporation.

After an abortive effort to acquire the American Broadcasting Company, which aroused animosity, Geneen settled for the Hartford Fire Insurance Company, one of the largest, more diversified insurance companies, but was compelled to divest ITT of several major companies, such as Levitt, in order to hold on to Hartford Fire.

Always controversial and probably proud of it, Geneen ran into his most severe hassles over strongly based charges that the company had offered the Republican party a large contribution for a favorable settlement of the federal antitrust suit. The pot almost boiled on two other incidents. One was the 1970 disclosure that ITT had plotted the overthrow of the Chilean government after the Allende regime had nationalized an ITT subsidiary. Another involved evidence that ITT had attempted to lure the Securities and Exchange Commission into an arrangement that would permit the company to acquire Hartford Fire. Geneen, who liked action, also seemed to breathe confrontation.

Jones, on the other hand, has been pure as rain in terms of controversy and had a simpler, more straight-line career. On the surface, life has been much more serene for him.

A graduate of the Wharton School of the University of Pennsylvania, he joined GE's business training course in 1939 and became a company career man. For eight years a traveling auditor, learning many aspects of the business, he was appointed to a number of operating jobs. Sober, adaptive, premeditated, he moved up and through the ranks in what appeared to be well-measured steps. But after becoming group executive of the GE construction industries group in January 1968, he was unaccountably named vice-president for finance five months later. It seemed to be a kick upstairs, but it wasn't. "I wanted to refuse it because I enjoyed operations more," he recalled, "but I soon found that I enjoyed that job so much that for a time I refused the next promotion."

Then, between 1970 and 1972 he was promoted four times, until at fifty-five years of age he found himself sitting, more sober than ever but not yet as adaptive as he was to be later, in the chairman's seat. But he quickly showed that he viewed the CEO's role as a catalytic one.

Geneen instead gave his managers duties and functions that deliberately overlapped, creating a rein on each either through sheer competition or confusion or both. Because the technique was actually intended to dredge up a rich silt of information, research, and opinion, Geneen hoped that the participants would not be oversensitive when their efforts were frustrated or their pride battered. It was all in the nature of protecting the company, of course, but Geneen, himself a peculiar mixture of hauteur and often self-effacing zeal, was at times baffled when he detected the pain of disappointment and shame on executives who found themselves often flailing away at assignments that had been also handed out to others.

The apostle of conflict, Geneen also trusted no one, commanding that tides of data and information flow to him personally. Weekly reports followed by more detailed monthly reports were compelled from more than one hundred managers. He read everything, often more than 2,500 pages a month. And he loved to gather his staff at marathon meetings, lasting from 8:00 A.M. through midnight, and scarcely breaking except for eating or natural functions. Not infrequently, the meetings would explode into shouting matches in which he would grill his men and caustically throw their words back at them. It was no less than the old Marine Corps basic-training system—fight back or die!—and the fall-outs were many. But conversely, ITT executives turned out to be in great demand by other companies. Once through that survival course, in other words, you were a man—or an animal—or perhaps it was an animalistic man.

Controversial as the means were, the ends in terms of bottom line proved enviable. Nothing in American corporate profit performance, perhaps, was as admired as ITT's fifty-eight consecutive fiscal quarters of improved earnings through 1973. The 1974–75 recession trapped the big conglomerate as it did many others. But earnings improved once more and continued to support the Geneen style through his retirement after forty-nine battle-scarred years in business.

What he bequeathed to his successors, 400,000 employees, and thousands of stockholders was a company with $12 billion in sales, a net income of $490 million, businesses in half the countries of the world, and 250 divisions. Much of ITT was put together by one of American business's most dazzling acquisition campaigns (many of its products and services sold overseas, which aroused considerable criticism by those who saw it all as the most arrant example of corporate greed and wheeling-dealing) and despite government action aimed at preventing monopoly and stifled competition.

For his part, Jones, a straightforward but somewhat starched individual, inherited a role at GE that had been clearly charted by several predecessors along decentralized, carefully planned lines. One of the world's biggest producers of power equipment, industrial products, and consumer goods, GE maintained a policy of vesting major segment or division authority in its group chiefs. It pioneered delegated responsibility in the 1950s and 1960s and, under Jones's advent as chief executive in 1972, pushed strategic planning, the concentration of efforts on long-range growth. The big electronics concern also was one of the first major American companies to establish an "executive office," a top-management team to broadly administer the business, and it effectively refined that function despite growing criticism of the concept in American business.

As 1977 rang out, Jones carried the decentralization one step further. Recognizing the rapidly growing pressures from such external matters as government regulation and taxation, he created in his first major executive reshuffling a new tier of top executives just under the three-man chairman's office. The new management layer, which he termed "sector executives," consisted of five former group vice-presidents, to be known as senior vice-presidents and sector chiefs, each directing a multi-billion-dollar group of company units. Each was to represent a clearly defined "Mr. General Electric" in one or more industries served by GE and, in effect, to assume chief-executive duties in them.

In addition, Jones and the other two men in the chairman's office, vice-chairmen Jack S. Parker and Walter D. Dance, singled out four other staff men and said that from the nine would emerge Jones's successor. So, in one combined move Jones had fulfilled three objectives: freed himself one step more from direct supervision of the massive GE operating entities to give time and attention to the externals that would increasingly occupy the remainder of his tenure; increased the recognition and opportunity for nine talented men; and created a vehicle for selection of his successor.

In essence, it was also a reversal from the Geneen style. Direct reporting was curbed. After formerly reporting to the chairman's office, group heads were now directed to answer to a sector chief who reported to one of the vice-chairmen. Strategic business units, some fifty entities on which GE based its corporate planning, normally reported to the chairman's office but were now answerable to the sector heads.

Explained Jones, "If we had not made this change, our direct reports would have grown quite substantially, and by 1980 we would have been faced with a really unmanageable situation." What it all amounted to was a reduction in top management's control, while at the same time enhancing the company's manageability, Jones said. And by elevating departments to divisions and divisions to groups, "it will still permit us to recognize the growth in component areas of the company," he said, "and without increasing the span of control at the top."

For the company that had been widely recognized as the country's pacesetting management, the latest move stirred wide attention. Was GE overdecentralizing, even for a company with $18 billion in sales? Hadn't the same thing happened with Westinghouse Corporation, once a GE arch competitor? In the 1970s, Westinghouse was bogged down by a huge gamble in uranium contracts, the high costs of which had robbed the big company of virtually its entire $2-billion book value, and by erratic performance from its diversified divisions, over which minimal controls had been exercised.

But the betting seemed to be on Jones. Under the wiry, brusque executive, GE, while not yet avoiding the cost-overruns of building nuclear plants, had taken the stand of no longer writing contracts for such facilities without including escalation costs, even if it lost business because of it. GE had also taken care to have good financial controls and earnings strategies. And while GE's earnings had wavered, unlike ITT's long-sustained profit record through the early 1970s, the trend line has been good.

In my talk with him, Jones admitted that GE's high degree of delegation made it a subject of high interest to many other executives, but he added, "Not all of us here have the same style —some are more hands-on than off. But it really comes down to a rather simple point—when you have an area of management in place for an extended period of time, you tend to leave the people alone. And when you find you can rely upon them, you also tend to do more of it. It's really that simple."

If there is any validity to claims that some of America's major businessmen have reached the status of businessmen-statesmen, it's likely that the group includes Jones, who has already spurned two Cabinet posts, along with John D. deButts of AT&T and Irving Shapiro of Du Pont. All three spend between one third to one half of their time in Washington, covering a triangle from the White House to the Hill to the agencies.

If his retirement at age sixty-eight hadn't interfered, Geneen probably wouldn't have wanted to join a government that had so harried him in the courts and pressed him in the corporate office. But Jones, continuing in his private-sector job at this writing, still may.

The comparison of Geneen with Jones, while demonstrating the clear divergence in style, also inevitably leaves one with the feeling that each followed his style in response to the needs of the time. ITT was really going nowhere until Geneen was plucked from Raytheon to give it some more substantive basis and he responded in his own, characteristic way. Jones, the product of a corporate hatching process of a large, stable company, surmounted it to become its paternalistic head, separating jobs and duties to keep it afloat not unlike a vast ocean liner with hundreds of air-tight, bulwarked compartments.

And that, perhaps, is the real answer to the pregnant question, "How good is the American CEO?"

On a superficial basis, compared to his predecessor of a decade or two or three ago, he isn't as dynamic, as creative, or patently as much of a leader. But on a more realistic basis, the role has changed so drastically that today's American CEO can't reasonably be measured against his corporate forebear. It would be much like comparing today's pollution-controlled, seat-belted, unleaded-gas automotive guzzler with the simple transport-intended autos of the 1950s and early 1960s, or today's globe-hopping jets with the piston-prop planes of thirty years ago.

If the need changed, it seems, so did the role. And as the role changed, so did the man.

8

The 80/20 Syndrome
(*Or Methuselah's Law,*
It's as Old as Human Activity)

In many an American company, there's a by-product that doesn't come out of the smokestacks, assembly lines, or computers. It's waste. Not waste of materials but something much more precious—waste of time, people, and priorities.

Broadly viewed, it can be called the 80/20 syndrome. That's because it involves concentration not on the most vital elements but on those that are pressing for the moment, that ruffle the interior facade, or that must be solved promptly to save corporate face. The seeming urgency is so great, so sensitive, that more important considerations are either pushed aside or entirely forgotten. So, 80 percent of the time, attention or energy is devoted to matters of convenience or matters that have short-term effects or are narrow in scope. But only 20 percent is given to more vital requirements.

The syndrome works its destructive effects in a variety of ways:

Temporal priorities. At virtually every level of management, not just on the executive-committee level, the bulk of discussion is about momentary matters, with the depth and breadth of thinking directly related to the subject's urgency. One of the big problems here is not just the excessive amount of time devoted to lightweight considerations. By the time the agenda has progressed to long-term or qualitative matters, the meeting hasn't only passed its prime but thinking has dulled and the gray cells have lost vitality. Everyone is already meditating on lunch or on how heavy the homeward traffic will be.

History just might repeat itself. Planning and strategy based on past performance just aren't realistic. When it comes to planning, budget allocations, and policy change, every division and every element of a business are almost universally considered from the standpoint of previous years' results, investment, and strategies. But in the face of rapid change, this invites a preponderance of judgment based on previous, not existing or developing, market conditions.

What's going on in D.C. and other pressure points north and south? Too much concern with externals and not enough with internal matters can become self-defeating. "As long as the majority of businessmen wail and complain how tough things are in this economy," observed the head of a large consumer-goods manufacturer, "the better it's going to be for us. It will keep their eye off the ball while we're batting the hell out of it." Externals are proliferating government intervention, consumer advocacy, stockholder champions, and encroaching labor demands—none of them, incidentally, unimportant. But major internal matters, such as communication, motivation, employee productivity, and morale can be more important in maintaining or losing a share of the market.

We've been around a long time, so that means we've learned to survive change. Conversely, strategic analysis that is too internal or too narrow and doesn't involve questioning of cultural patterns can be even worse. Question: Is the company there simply because it always has been a raison d'être that has perhaps become an operating policy and maybe even a credo? If so, will the business continue to exist, especially if it doesn't examine and act upon major socioeconomic trends? Penn Central Transportation, W. T. Grant, and REA Express, to name just a few, were in business a long time, too, but failure to adapt to change fatally exposed the jugular.

Ultra-fine channels emit the best frequencies. Undue concentration on communications, human needs, and favored treatment to a relatively small percentage of employees results in malaise, low spirits, and declining productivity on the part of the majority. There is scarcely a company in which 20 percent of the employees or even less do not enjoy close contacts with and favored benefits from management, while the majority of employees are relatively ignored. Is it likely that 80 percent don't merit a greater degree of such consideration, or is it really a reward for the real achievers? Or is it more likely a reflection of cronyism, a preference for the complaisant, a desire for convenience and the easy way? Do the same people keep talking to each other all the time?

Or Is 80/20 Just the System?

Admittedly, a numerical symbol of these corporate mores such as 80/20, may be arbitrary and even capricious. But it puts a measure on the waste of time, people, and priorities, a loss which may have serious consequences for American business, both domestic and international.

Wasteful in both quantitative and qualitative ways, the 80/20 syndrome can be rationalized as "part of the system," the checks and balances in a democratic society that at least in principle keep each major element from becoming predominant. But the heartbeat of that system is the individual who calls the shots in every company, the chief executive, who for better or worse sets the tone, the style, and the policy of his business. And if his company languishes from the existence of the 80/20 problem—and many do—he's the culprit.

"You can broadly classify top executives into two categories —maintainers and builders. The maintainers are more prevalent," observed Marvin Schiller, vice-president of A. T. Kearney, Inc., the Chicago-based management-consulting firm. "The reason for their greater numbers is that by the time a man has reached the highest responsibility, he's interested primarily in a holding action. He wants to maintain the momentum already established in the business and to assure the positive trends that are in evidence."

Such a CEO tends to swat "the gnats that provide a periodic disturbing element" and seeks to avoid innovation or assertive, aggressive, controversial action. "Those approaches," Schiller says, "aren't typically part of their management style."

Too many heads of major corporations fall into this category and are sustained, because companies, like people, go through various life phases, adds Schiller. Many need "the stable influence." They have been running fast, he says, need to slow down, retrench, solidify, and catch up—but frequently that process lasts too long and becomes counterproductive.

"Who selects this guy? Nobody, really," asserts Schiller. "Such CEOs have come up through the ranks and are politically astute." His rise through the ranks, Schiller says, is not unlike the politician who has come up in his party from precinct captain and moved up with each election. "A guy like that needs a friendly board (i.e., party captains) and the party generals (i.e., the company's directors) need him. But when the system is to be changed," Schiller notes, "he just can't do it. He is the system."

If CEOs *are* the system, what should their bedrock priority be?

"Most people—CEOs and their staffs—don't like to face up to the truth," says Laurence Tisch. "This is your big problem in business," adds the chairman and chief executive officer of Loews Corporation, the highly diversified company with interests in tobacco, insurance, real estate, hotels, and movie theaters. Tisch and his brother, P. Robert Tisch, Loews' president, joined in a discussion involving internal decision-making and divestiture of less profitable divisions.

"People get a vested interest in old decisions that they made, and try to prove ten years later that they were right in making those moves," said Larry Tisch. "So when, let's say, you are considering selling or making an acquisition of a candy company by a tobacco business like ours, they have to prove that they were right. Now, in proving that they were right, they don't want to face the fact that our tobacco salesman, perhaps, is spending an inordinate amount of time selling candy which is yielding no profit. We have orders around here for our people —we don't mind if you make mistakes but just don't compound the error by throwing good money after bad money or good time after bad time."

Added Robert Tisch, "Our people were wasting their time selling candy for six million dollars gross when they were also selling cigarettes at that time for about five hundred fifty million and so they were wasting about ten percent of their time." Two years earlier, he went on, "we sold our pipe tobacco business to U.S. Tobacco Company because we did a study among one thousand two hundred forty people in sales and we found that the amount of time needed to sell three million dollars in pipe tobacco could be better spent selling cigarettes."

The phrases "avoiding innovation or aggressive, controversial action," "keeping their eye off the ball," or "don't like facing up to the truth" may well be another way of describing the 80/20 syndrome. But businessmen, traditionally spurning stating their case before an unfriendly audience, have a way of attacking an apparent problem by making an adversary a friend and then finding it won't play.

At a recent meeting of the Conference Board, for example, forty chief executives discussed the future of the American free-enterprise system, seeing growing government intervention as the prime threat. But one of the more independent, freer-thinking participants remonstrated, "When we find out that intervention hurts us, what do we do? We appeal to Washington for help and that means in effect only more intervention. So, we're at fault ourselves, aren't we?"

And, at least in the view of some businessmen, the reluctance to grapple with the truth has led to a flurry of rule bending.

"What seems to be going on now is that people are changing the rules instead of trying to live up to them," says Russell Banks, president of Grow Chemical Company, a New York–based chemicals producer. "When inflation seems to be more and more difficult to deal with, we say, 'Let's start inflation accounting'—you don't have to have real profits because the built-in inflation factor robs you of them. So the problem becomes the excuse," Banks said.

Not unrelated is the increasing use of zero-based budgeting, a cost system that ignores past criteria for expenses and allots them as if previous budgets didn't exist. In a time of constant rises in cost and of shifting market conditions, casting aside previous expense criteria makes good sense, its advocates say. A moot but infiltrating practice, the advantages of ignoring past allocations in expense budgeting haven't yet been fully proven. But its sponsors are articulate, even vociferous, in their claims that the practice represents realistic, hard-nosed thinking.

Although not as prevalent, there is another "zero-based" practice—zero-based strategic planning—which offers an intriguing reverse of the 80/20 syndrome. One of its most enthusiastic advocates, Reuben Gutoff, the president of Standard

Brands, Inc., a major packaged-goods firm, described it in this manner:

"There's been a lot of talk, but probably much less understanding, about zero-based strategic planning. Don't confuse it with the recently popular term 'zero-based budgeting,' which is primarily overhead cost-oriented. Our thesis is that we will be able to outperform our peer companies by a rigorous discipline of different allocation of resources to high-potential market and competitive opportunities.

"This is very difficult to do because each strategic business unit has its own historical momentum and traditional view of its activities. These factors normally can only be modestly modified year by year because each year's new budget and plan almost invariably take as a given fact that the starting point is last year's result and the businesses' accumulated investments and strategy."

Added Standard Brands' president, "In zero-based strategic planning, the starting point is to examine each business as if it were completely new and competing for funds based on a Garden-of-Eden view of the external environment and the businesses' competitive strengths and weaknesses. We feel that eighty percent of the strategies being followed in our company may be right, but to find out the incorrect twenty percent we will review, on a zero-based planning basis, one hundred percent of our activities."

Standard Brands (sales of $2 billion, with such food brands as Chase and Sanborn Coffee, Planter's nuts, Fleischmann's Yeast, Dry Sack sherry) began the process in 1976 and found it a "painful but rewarding process," Gutoff reported. "The willingness to question many things that are already well accepted can be traumatic as hell."

Once it is started, "the chief executive must remain committed to it and know that the divisional heads will resent the searching process. 'Get your ass out of here,' the divisionals will yell at your aides who carry out the probe. But it can only work if the top man sticks to his guns."

All those changes, their total effects, are nothing more than "the dynamics of business." Changes seen as problems make people pull in their horns, but changes seen as potential advantages can be helpful, Gutoff said.

He agreed that too many top businessmen and their associates worry more about the externals—government, social responsibility, advocacy pressure—than they do about internal matters.

The 80/20 syndrome seems to be pervasive in American business, albeit the forms it takes vary in a dazzling array of misjudgment, soft thinking, laziness, and simple procrastination. But it also has a positive side.

In the retail field, the 80/20 problem has begun to hit home in recent years. Merchants clobbered by downtown erosion and population shifts outwardly have decided that while 80 percent of their items produce almost 100 percent of sales, only 20 percent yield 80 percent of volume. So, they have launched a feverish merchandising and promotion effort on those 20 percent. And better profits have come through a resulting improved sales productivity.

Yet, many store buyers too close to their supplier contacts continue to buy many products (80 percent probably isn't an exaggeration) that don't sell well. The net effect is high markdowns and unsatisfactory departmental profits. Chief executives and merchandising chiefs who don't watch this practice or who tend to ignore the fact of life that retailing, like manufacturing, is dependent upon what the consumer wants (marketing, after all, is based on consumer needs and desires, not the producer's or the seller's) soon find the ground slipping from under them.

But perhaps what makes the 80/20 factor more noteworthy and more intriguing is its natural force in contemporary life.

In any given office in any company, 20 percent of the staff appears to do 80 percent of the work. Or, put another way, most of the dynamics or brilliance in any business or institutional performance seems to be accomplished by 20 percent of the force. Axiomatically, in any sales force, 20 percent of the salesmen bring in 80 percent of the business. In most product markets, 80 percent of sales are accounted for by 20 percent of the producers.

The list could probably go on and on, involving almost every area of human endeavor, including government, professional or amateur sports, fund raising, church volunteer work, and so on. Woven through the fabric of American life, the dominance of achievement accruing from the efforts of the more motivated, the more creative, and the more energetic is too easily accepted.

Some 20/20 Vision on the 80/20 Problem

If the irking, nonproductive effects of the 80/20 syndrome are to be removed, how can it be done?

The big challenge has to be tossed into the lap of the CEO, most sources agree. If the "maintainer" type of CEO is the drag, he should be replaced by the "builder." And in more recent years, the trend has in fact moved to the builder, according to Marvin Schiller of A. T. Kearney. "It's gone the other way, once directors and important stockholders began to realize that black ink is a powerful sedative. Once it turned red, the spotlight fell on the maintainer and he was in trouble," he says.

Charted against the rise and fall of the American economy, the increasing move to the builder appears to follow the return of the economic facts of life to a more real, more normal pattern, Schiller says. "I think that the U.S. economy has been greatly affected since World War Two by the maintainer," he observes. "In the 1950s and 1960s, we were primarily interested in getting back to a safe, nonwar way of life, and that's the kind of chief executive who was voted into authority. But that type of man and his 'safe' way of operating has hampered us since."

What's the builder like? Not the most palatable or pleasant of personalities, he is a man who subscribes to change, to risk management, to solving problems as opposed to fighting fires. In Schiller's words, "he's a hip-shooter." But he's creative and has an emotional and intellectual capacity to solve problems and expand his company. He's also abrasive, ultimately demanding, and rarely satisfied.

Harold Geneen, the former chairman of International Telephone & Telegraph Corporation, is a strong example of both those attributes and pressures on people. Omnivorous in demands and in pushing growth, he built ITT into a super-giant. But there are others who have accomplished a similar high degree of growth without being a body wrecker. One such a CEO is J. Peter Grace, Jr., president and chief executive of W. R. Grace & Co., a conglomerate that has divested itself of its shipping mainstay and become an important factor in chemicals, consumer goods, and natural resources. "A man with a mission," Grace changed a staid, family-dominated (his own family) business into a diversified empire. Impulsive and filled with nervous energy, Grace prefers to hire outstanding executives, often without a clear assignment, and keeps them busy until he figures out where they can best fit in. In most cases he allows them to show him what they can do for the company.

Eager and endlessly ambitious, Peter Grace is a good listener, too, a quality not all CEOs possess, and W. R. Grace's improved fortunes and scope reflect it. But, like Geneen, although to a much lesser degree, Grace is controversial. His effect on people is much less bruising, but some wonder, as they do about many builders, if he can keep his disciplines or lack of them in check.

There are, however, cases where a builder was brought in to "maintain" a super-builder's company to consolidate its far-flung, international operations without stunting its growth.

Michel Bergerac, the head of IBM Corporation's international operations, was tapped by Charles Revson when the aggressive founder of the Revlon cosmetics empire learned that he had a terminal illness and decided that no one within his own company had the capability to succeed him. A skilled administrator and marketer, Bergerac installed a more leisurely but more professional style in Revlon even before Revson died in 1976, and since then he has surprised many critics. Revlon's sales and profits continued to soar, and product innovation, perhaps Revson's prime forte, hasn't waned under Bergerac's tenure.

What's Bergerac's system of management? He responded to the question in an interview by first answering how he felt about stepping into Revson's shoes. "I did not feel dismayed by it. I felt I understood the company and even though its sales were quickly heading to the one-billion-dollar level, I felt I had the background. I had already managed five billion dollars' worth of ITT's foreign business."

Speaking in a heavily accented French English, he said, "As far as Mr. Revson's so-called one-man rule, it really wasn't quite that. He had good people making good input into policy and operations. But I don't think that anything can replace the individual decisions. Joint decision-making reflects the growing size of corporations, but it represents the erosion of the chief executive's role, in my opinion. One should not let the number of zeros in your dollar sales scare you. A one-billion-dollar company is more than a one-hundred-million-dollar company multiplied ten times—and most of the big ones usually lose what made them successful in the first place. But size makes a difference, of course; you need a strong central staff.

"The larger a company gets, the magnitude of its problems increase and the more input it needs. And that is broadly my management credo—a strong central staff to help the management analyze and strategize its operations, and strong operating people. But I think that final decisions should be made by the head of the company, after strong input by staff and line executives."

Queries among Revlon's executives indicate, however, that things have changed considerably within the country's largest cosmetics producer. Division heads are given more authority, allowed not merely to suggest but to introduce new products as well. In a great sense they are being given their heads. As opposed to Revson's "dictatorial" presence, Bergerac's style is paternal, but profit achievement remains paramount in evaluating divisional performance.

The freeing of senior- and mid-executive shackles (suggested by the Bergerac approach) appears to be one of the major roads away from the 80/20 syndrome. Challenges, increased delegation of responsibilities, and a more open attitude about direction drifting upward, instead of always downward, would have a salutary effect on the removal of waste of time and effort and on the setting of major priorities. But in a business community at least partly traumatized by its external problems and by the prevalence of chief executives who are devoted to maintaining the status quo until things clear up (the question of when remains unanswered), a change of this type will not come easily. As a result, the following seems indicated, based on a consensus of business chiefs, consultants, academics, and just plain observers:

Chief executives should consider retiring earlier. In most American companies, retirement at age sixty-five is mandatory for chief executives. But age sixty as a new general rule makes sense, with the reservation that in cases of exceptional performance the rule might be waived a year or two or three or even longer.

Such a decision puts the bit in the teeth of directors, especially those from the outside. Few inside directors, nominally loyally subservient to the CEO, their boss, would have the courage—or foolhardiness—to push him out before he is ready. But the outside director—the Wall Streeter, college professor, head of another company, or economist—has the opportunity to be more objective. Individual evaluation of a CEO's worth should be hard, independent, and intelligent. Too often—even after a series of corporate disasters at least partially created by directors' malaise or negligence—the outside director still operates on the buddy system.

Corporate aristocracy should be "democratized." The executive strata in many concerns is so ossified that rigidity of thinking, behavior, and independence is virtually paralyzed by fear and protocol. What, for example, would be so wrong if a CEO occasionally asked an assistant divisional or department head to breakfast or lunch and invited him to speak freely about the company, his role in it, and his criticisms of its operations, without the junior's getting embroiled in condescension or fear? The CEO might learn a thing or two that higher-ups won't tell him. And the word that the boss is letting his hair down a bit might sweep through the entire organization like a breath of fresh air.

Going that far, the chief executive could easily go one step further. To open the crack to freedom a bit more, he could generate a program of allowing many more senior, middle, and junior executives to take a week or two off to engage in some vital outside expeditions—attendance at a university seminar on the humanities, a tour of a geographical area in which the company's products or services are sold, or a short sabbatical just to talk to a cross section of people about the company or business in general.

The goal would be not merely written reports about the findings but impressions presented at various corporate levels of the perception of various levels of society about (1) the company and its products; (2) what people are saying and thinking in general; (3) the executive's own perception about where the company is going in terms of his own experiences during his expedition. A waste of time, people, and money? Hardly. The average employee will respond both constructively and productively to such an assignment.

How many American companies circulate questionnaires to

their staffs to ascertain how executives—and even the rank and file—visualize the company's growth pattern in the years ahead? Its social responsibilities, its personnel policies, its production, marketing, and advertising performance? Not many. It's too democratic or unprogrammed or untraditional.

Use of outside consultants—management, financial, marketing, and public relations—shouldn't be postponed until a crisis of some sort hovers over the company.

It's axiomatic that in most cases the corporate fire fighter has been called when much of the damage has already been done. And then, again, how many consultant reports are seriously considered? Too many, consultants say, are promptly thrown into the boss's bottom drawer. Too radical, too sweeping, too ambitious are some of the criticisms applied by the CEO (or the executive he has consigned the report to). Not all consultants' findings are applicable, that's certain. Yet, most consultants confide that their biggest frustration is their inability to carry out vital reforms while there is still time, because of their being outsiders.

Meeting agendas might well be assigned to someone other than the CEO for preparation. Naturally, the boss will have the final say in it, but drafting by another member of the group working with the CEO and others could produce a more comprehensive, less restricted listing of matters to be taken up. But perhaps most important would be the CEO's invitation to suggest that others offer suggestions to be worked into the agenda.

Such an agenda, incidentally, should be broken down between externals and internals, and both of these further broken down into "present" and "future." Simplistic? Of course. But what an opportunity to cover terrain!

With these and similar steps, the 80/20 syndrome might be eased, even broken. One may carp, argue, cast aside the concept, and perhaps ridicule the ratio of the numbers, but who can really rebut the charge of waste of time, people, and priorities?

The alternative might easily be an interesting new variation or reversal in the 80/20 rule. Eighty percent of the current CEOs might have to be eased out and only 20 percent remain. But then time and age will take care of that, anyway.

9

Only So Far and No Further

Women and Blacks: Irritants to the Comfort Index

Caressed, soothed, cooed over, overpraised, and underpraised, the woman executive should have come into her own in recent years. That seemed to be the indication of the rosy promises of senior management and of the twin thrusts of feminism and affirmative action. Yet the attitude toward her advancement up the executive ladder of American business has been singularly coy.

She's been treated like a kitten. She has been dangled by a protective hand, observed as though a curiosity, cuddled with downright goodwill, given her own warm, clean corner with the blinds carefully arranged so that she could bask in the sun while on public view. Of course, she was closely studied for her reaction, and if she didn't exactly purr with delight it was understood. How many years had she been on the outside looking in, right?

Wrong. The reason she couldn't purr even if she wanted to was that she was too busy gagging.

Black executives, too, have been treated with the same duplicitous movement of the hand—the welcoming pat on the back followed by a slap on the head.

In the frantic rush of the 1960s to counter criticism of discrimination and to accede to the tenets of affirmative action, many American companies hired black executives, put them on display, invited them to public meetings, and then soon forgot them. This was partly owing to the recession that pared corporate profits, so that the stress was on recovery rather than on use of human assets. But, that aside, most chief executives felt they had taken pains to meet the need, although the minority-group skills and talents weren't that plentiful. The charges that it was all a token effort stung, but these were brushed off as mostly qualitative interpretation.

In the 1970s, however, the blacks who had a place in corporate America appeared to find that they had gone as far as they could go. One way or another, "the blacks had reached an invisible ceiling," as Richard Clarke, a prominent New York minorities recruiter, put it. "It usually occurred at the department-head level or slightly under it. An assistant district manager or assistant brands manager was likely to stay that way, rather than move in on the district or brands manager," he said.

Was the resistance to women and blacks respectively sexism and racism?

Yes—but not totally. The prejudices against upward movement for both types of executives had other roots, common to both blacks and women.

Companies have their own "comfort index." This is nothing more than the friendly, warm, accepted ambience created by the chief executive and his top associates who otherwise set the corporate style for the firm. So the comfort index involves the assembling of a team with which the CEO (and the other brass) is at ease and upon which they can depend for not only loyalty but also a generally smooth one-to-one relationship without any traumatic difficulties. For women and blacks to fit into that index isn't impossible. It just isn't very possible. Are there any exceptions? Of course, but not many.

The most important, the most devious, and the biggest cop-out of all is the senior-management claim (often muttered into one's palm rather than openly expressed) that there just aren't enough women, blacks, Hispanics, and so on with the proper professional qualifications—at least not to the degree and scope necessary to give them a greater representation in management.

They lack the criteria, it's claimed, that better jobs demand. But even if one ignores the cliché about where you can obtain the qualifications if no one will give you the chance to earn them, the claim just doesn't hold up. In any corporation, it is an accepted fact of life that many promotions are given to and key jobs held by white males whose prime qualifications are that they fit their superiors' team concept in age, religion, sex, race, school, social outlook, recreational preferences, and general chemistry. Any combination of any of these adding up to four, even three, makes you acceptable—and any larger combination makes you a shoo-in. In other words, qualifications are often a matter of the boss's interpretation. The best, however, are rooted in experience.

All this is not to ignore the strides that women and blacks have already made in getting better jobs. But the gains are small compared to what they should be. This is especially so in view of the rapidly growing need for many companies to raise their productivity, to improve their employee motivation, and to increase their capacity to grow.

If it is true that women have been treated like kittens in their corporate advancement, then it appears that blacks have been treated like clowns. They have been allowed to "perform," to show their bag of tricks, one of which is to behave like a real white executive and by their presence demonstrate the truly liberal inclination of their employer and also his obedience to the laws of the land, Clowns are fine, of course, like fun and games. But you wouldn't invite one to sit in the boxes with you or take one home.

Harsh words? Perhaps.

Traditional Attitudes, Male Platitudes

Women may be the bosses in the home, but in business they are a discriminated-against minority. A dramatic exception herself to the inability of women to climb high, Juanita M. Kreps, U.S. Secretary of Commerce, recently cited a trend by a significant number of women to become entrepreneurs "and to take their chances in the free-enterprise system." But their rate of success was not encouraging, she reported in an article in the *New York Times*. "Women's problems include those faced by any small businessmen: lack of capital, lack of management and technical assistance, and lack of marketing and procurement opportunities.

"But these problems," Mrs. Kreps stressed, "often are compounded by traditional attitudes that prejudice their chances of success in a male-oriented business world."

Whether in corporate advancement or in entrepreneurism, holding the capable, ambitious woman at arm's length has long prevailed in American business, despite the claims of chief executives that corporate attitudes about the problem have improved.

In 1977, approximately 87 women occupied executive-officer posts out of the nation's leading 1,300 companies. As to directorships, the 50 leading companies had 780 board seats but only 14 women held them. In all, about 1 percent of America's top management are women—a deplorably small segment.

In entrepreneurism, the typical woman-owned company accounted for only 4.6 percent, or 402,025 of the total 8.73 million businesses in the United States, according to the latest findings of the Census Bureau. The average such company was small, too, employing fewer than five people. Total receipts of all companies were nearly $2.4 trillion, but firms owned by women accounted for only 0.3 percent of that amount.

Why?

Despite all the clamor and flurry of media coverage, the top-executive suites in American business and all the other suites surrounding it still remain a male preserve. Power flows from them in a widening pattern over all the company's physical and human assets. It won't be said publicly, but privately the corporate brass don't consider women strong enough, judicious enough, or objective enough to exert that power with the disciplines required. The prejudice that creates the problem has three ingredients: women are too emotional to handle pressure; women have difficulty supervising men; women disturb rather than soothe the team environment (comfort index) that is so vital to corporate success.

It's generalizing, of course, of the most flagrant kind. The fact that many male executives have deep problems handling pressure, have difficulty supervising other men, and don't mesh easily with the team is often overlooked. No matter how rationally one looks at that prejudicial attitude, it's hard not to view it as a remnant of the feudal mentality. But then the attitude at its core isn't much different from senior management's traditional reluctance to try new things, fit square pegs into round holes, or take a gamble on a promising candidate or new project that doesn't quite fit the mold.

But while women have succeeded more than blacks in penetrating the executive ranks, their numbers after a decade of feminist aggressiveness still aren't encouraging. Estimates are that about 2 million women hold executive jobs of one sort or another in American business. That doesn't sound bad, except for the fact that the 36 million women working today account for about 40 percent of the nation's work force. So their representation among executives is not only slim but far below their sex's proportion of working adults.

Salaries also are below proportion. In 1977, more than 60 percent of all men earned more than $10,000 but only 18 percent of women commanded that level of salary. Among college-educated males, the median salary was about $20,000. Among women college graduates, it was $12,000. The salary discrimination, too, seems to have a strange life of its own, entirely separate from that prejudicing women's executive advancement.

A woman in a large New York–based company was promoted to succeed a man as section head in a large department. She performed well, in part because she had been promised a second salary step-up after six months to bring her close to the earnings of her predecessor. After eighteen months of waiting, she asked formally for the delayed increase. Much as the management professed to be anxious to promote women, she was not only refused but told she was being "well paid" in relation to others. She resigned in anger.

What she lost, of course, were the fifteen years she had worked for the firm, although her experience there helped her land another post outside. But what the company lost may be more damaging: the contribution of an astute, sophisticated executive and another in its fading pile of credits marking its status as an equal-opportunity employer. The incident, supported by an almost identical one some weeks earlier, indicated that the company's interest in promoting women was basically tokenism.

Not all critics decry tokenism, however. "I believe in tokenism," observed Pearl Meyer, executive vice-president of Handy Associates, Inc., the New York management consultants and executive recruiters. "I believe that today's tokenism is tomorrow's practice and I recommend that women take 'showcase' jobs because once they are in and management realizes that they are not so bad to have around and that the women should be retained, more will be let in."

Mrs. Meyer, who has placed many executives of both sexes in the last decade, rebutted in an interview the contention that women who succeed in reaching the top rungs of business must behave like men. "I don't believe that the intelligent American woman is able or wants or cares to live like a man," she said. "We want to lead the lives of women and yet be people with equal opportunity and equal pay for our efforts. The old homily 'Do a good job and the rest will take care of itself' doesn't work. Also another one—'Work your way up the ladder.'

"Perhaps this is why I find bias by top executives more prevalent, or perhaps more freely expressed, against women than any other minority group. That's because the old homilies don't pertain—to women, that is."

In spite of industry's highly vocal insistence that it can't find talented women managers, Mrs. Meyer said, the fact is that there are many. But due to years of unequal opportunity, they have languished in supportive staff or subordinate roles rather than in more productive and more visible executive posts. In any company, she added, "you probably will find high-caliber female buyers but not merchandise managers, analysts but not research directors, tellers but not treasurers, assistants to presidents but not vice-presidents."

The situation isn't bad only for women, she said, it is worse for industry. The reason is that American business is faced by a "curious paradox." She added, "U.S. business numerically is staffed with the smallest management generation in modern history. Executives between the ages of thirty-five and forty-five are depression babies, born when the birthrate fell to its lowest point in some time." But at the same time, recessionary business conditions have compelled companies to be less tolerant of poor executive performance, Mrs. Meyer said. "Managers who do not shape up are being shipped out." But these realities of executive recruitment, higher standards, and increasing need and tight supply are working directly against each other in the executive market.

Once women take a job in a company, she said, "there is a problem of communication." Why? "Women are severely disadvantaged since we lack the same basic experiences and background as men. There is a language barrier; in many instances, a common frame of reference is missing."

Women talk in different patterns of speech, she said. They have different values. "And we don't know how to listen. We hear, yes, but we're not listening." For example, Mrs. Meyer said, in a mixed group of product managers at a meeting the women are likely to get lost over the men's jargon, like, 'Why don't we adopt a shotgun approach this time?' Or from another end of the table, 'What's Tom Seaver's ERA these days?' Believe me, that doesn't mean the Equal Rights Amendment!"

So women tend to feel left out. They're uncomfortable at being excluded and many feel it's intentional. "But they've got to learn the rules," Mrs. Meyer said. "Women need to learn how to interact on the same friendly basis and be comfortable with it so that they can establish an important rapport. At each level of management, women must learn a different language so that men will be more inclined to want to hear them out."

Mostly, even today, senior management regards the corporation's internal life still pretty much as a locker room, a male sanctum that would offend and be offended by the presence of women. This is much more true of heavy industry and utilities, chemicals, and the durables industries than it is of retailing, manufacturing, and the consumer-goods fields, where the number of women entering has been much greater.

Toughness, firmness of fiber, and an unflappable demeanor tend to keep the hidebound male at bay when women demonstrate their self-confidence in those ways. Katharine Graham, the publisher of the *Washington Post,* listened carefully when a top executive of *Newsweek* magazine, a *Post* subsidiary, cautioned her against inviting women to meetings. After listening, she hurled an ashtray at him.

And when Muriel Siebert, New York State's superintendent of banking, became the first woman member of the New York Stock Exchange, probably the world's biggest club of wealthy men, rumors started by nettled stockbrokers indicated that she had agreed as a condition to joining not to appear on the stock-exchange floor for two years. It was not true, of course, and she unemotionally denied it.

It took Evelyn Berezin eighteen years to become an entrepreneur after she ran out of money in 1951 before she could acquire a Ph.D. in cosmic-ray physics. Already a skilled engineer, she took a job designing computers. Attending outside professional meetings and fruitlessly reporting back to the company's management, she found herself facing the kind of frustration that many business and professional women do. "Nobody ever listened," she recalled. "I felt completely impotent. I guess the worst thing in the world is to have no effect."

And when she later was told that she would never become the firm's engineering vice-president, she decided it was time to start her own business. Prevailing on a dozen friends to put up about $1 million, she then recruited a team of eager but also frustrated male colleagues and, with two partners, launched the Redactron Corporation to produce technically advanced typewriters in Hauppauge, Long Island. In 1975, the sale of the firm to Burroughs Corporation personally netted her $250,000. She still heads the company, which, while small, is today under Burroughs' ownership the American concern second-largest to IBM Corporation in the production of automated word-processing systems.

Summing up the moral of her business experience, she said, "That's the history of company start-ups—people who aren't listened to."

Being listened to. It seems a very small obligation for senior management, but more women—and men, for that matter—have severed their company ties over that than any other factor outside of, perhaps, salary disputes.

Yet the reverse—listening to and imbuing a woman's job with an entrepreneurial responsibility—has been responsible for women's making it in American business, says Beatrice Fitzpatrick, executive director of the American Woman's Economic Development Corporation, a nonprofit group formed to help women advance in the nation's economy. "But women mostly aren't being given such opportunity," Miss Fitzpatrick said. "And many are looking to their own businesses because of it."

One Chance for Blacks, Two, Three . . .

More than a decade ago, Joseph Wilson, the chairman of Xerox Corporation, paused in his push to make the copier company the giant he wanted it to be and announced to his top staff a new social objective. He wanted Xerox to become a leader in employing blacks and women.

Within two years, the Rochester, New York, concern became just that. As Xerox moved past the $1-billion and then the $2-billion mark in annual sales, more blacks and women rose to posts earning $30,000 and $35,000 a year.

But a year before his retirement in 1971, Wilson was dismayed as he saw the ranks of black executives thinning at Xerox. "What's happening?" he demanded. His personnel staff was contrite. As Xerox's minority executives advanced and acquired management skills and sophistication, their worth rose in the marketplace and other companies dangled more attractions. Much like the outflow of WASP executives at IBM and ITT, Xerox's talented blacks were being pirated away.

"That's our fault!" Wilson snapped. "We shouldn't let them be stolen away under our nose. Let's do our own pirating. Bring in qualified blacks and pay them $35,000 and above at the executive stock-option level."

Wilson's dilemma wasn't unique. Other companies, too, were grappling at that time with a loss of investment in black professionals and specialists who appeared to be moving eagerly from large companies to smaller ones. Coming in at the narrowing point of the corporate pyramid, they were finding that life in the big corporation was something of a rat race. After emerging from routine junior-management posts and being tapped for bigger things, they were dismayed by the heat of the competitive pressures and were never certain that they wouldn't be victims of some subtle racism.

"Those blacks felt that they didn't need that kind of hassle," said Richard Clarke, the recruiter, "and soon left for smaller companies or for a division position in another large company. There was more security there, and maybe more satisfaction."

That retreat from big-company turmoil to smaller-company tranquillity may well represent the strategic challenge in the black executive's confrontation with corporate America. Having come that high on the executive rungs, the qualified black concluded that he didn't especially like life at that altitude with its constricting air. Was the withdrawal a matter of the black's inability to handle pressure or a matter of his resignation to the certainty of discrimination at high-pressure levels? Whatever the reason, the problem is even today as vital for corporate America as for those young blacks who still hope to break through.

Since then, the hiring and the advancement of blacks have leveled off to what some liken to a sort of détente. Fewer blacks are getting there, but those who make it are being regarded more seriously by senior management. "The time is gone when a company said, 'I want to hire a black—any black,' " asserted Richard Clarke. "Now the more qualified black is wanted, the one with more potential. At the same time, black aspirants won't settle for jobs of little substance. They've become sophisticated and want to know what the career trend line will be from ground zero. And that's true of whites, too."

Yet within the context of those changes—the more pragmatic attitude on the parts of senior management and the black hopeful—much has happened to point both to progress and to the lack of progress.

Even at the height of the late-1960s surge in black-executive hiring, many companies settled for the single "corporate black." All related projects and activities were thrown at him, regardless of their diversity. "Now," observes Arch Whitehead, who operates an executive-recruiting firm in New York, "you find minority specialists for most major functions—marketing, sales, engineering, special projects, and so on. It works much better, gives the company the results it wants, and motivates the people involved."

But, as the black proves more valuable and moves up the ladder, Whitehead said, he comes smack up against stiffer criteria. The social aspect, which is an important qualification for advancement, tends to work against him and frustration sets in. "The successful black executive of between thirty-five and forty-two years old, earning between thirty and forty thousand a year, finds himself bottled up, and even if he's a fast tracker he can't do much to dislodge himself from the hard mold," says Whitehead.

If, for example, he becomes a vice-president, the ability of the black to move up another rung is limited because of the social community or environment in which the company lives. "Membership in the country club and the tennis club and the habit of the executives' wives of going shopping together are some of the otherwise indefinable criteria that go into the decision of whether a guy advances or doesn't," Whitehead said.

On the other hand, there is a rising demand for pragmatism in the selection of executives to the vice-presidential level and above. "What it all comes down to," Whitehead went on, "is the plain fact that corporations are built on two foundations—capital and contacts—and these support each other. Are lenders, whether bankers or insurance companies, confident of the people they meet in the corporation that will sooner or later make financial demands from them? Will the banks be comfortable with the black executives who come calling on them? These are questions that senior management asks itself, often irrespective of the social aspect, and that all too often determine who moves up the executive scale."

What that produces, of course, is a burgeoning sense of reality by senior management, Whitehead said, if not a heightened challenge. If personal contact is that vital, there's no point in building up false hopes on the part of the qualified black. If it isn't, the aspirant should be judged on his own merits.

"I guess it amounts to a realization on both sides that you just can't buy short and sell long," Whitehead said. "You can't build a long-term relationship on something that will be only of short interest or value when it comes to promoting the black executive. It's a big challenge for the chief executive to resolve that, and the resolution will mean a great deal to business and to the minority executive.

"In life, things don't seem to work unless someone is committed to a policy or principle," Whitehead asserted. "As far as minority equity in our society is concerned, the time is long past for halfhearted commitment."

For those who still assume that American chief executives have already met the test, surveys conducted by Whitehead over the years indicate that this is far from the case.

In a February 1976 to January 1977 sampling of college-educated females employed in one thousand of the top U.S. companies, the breakdown was females: 272 black, 53 Spanish, 49 Oriental, 14 Indian, and 2,727 white.

In a May 1977 survey of 1,500 college-graduate executives, in a sales unit of a large firm, Whitehead found 83 white females,

1 Spanish female, and 1 black female. And in a September 1977 sampling of a staff of 57 in a research laboratory, there were 44 white males, 1 Spanish female, 9 white females, 2 Spanish males, 1 Oriental male—and no black females or males.

Citing an especially glaring case, Whitehead said that one of the country's best-known cosmetics producers, with its national offices only a "subway ride" from the largest black population bloc in the United States, had 23 white females, 1 black male, 1 Oriental female, and no black females at all.

But that company, viewed in the context of urban-based, consumer-goods businesses, is hardly typical. Since the mid-1950s, packaged-goods and consumer-products companies have increasingly added minority-group executives, sales managers, and salespeople. Primary among them are liquor, beer, food, candy, drug, and cosmetics-toiletries firms, as well as certain branches of banks and insurance companies and oil companies with local gas-station chains. The reason is obvious. Much of their sales are to minorities, and for competition's sake the companies have placed appropriate executives and salesmen —not to mention such minority celebrities as athletes and entertainers—in a direct line to meet customers. It is, in the business vernacular, an "interface" with people of their own kind.

"It didn't make sense after a while to send a blue-eyed, blond WASP salesman to sell beer in the East Bronx or Spanish Harlem," Whitehead said.

What is needed, say experienced minorities recruiters like Whitehead and Clarke, is to go beyond the "ethnic interface." The person-to-person solution may have pushed more than one company into lowering the barriers, but it may only prove the fallacy of buying short and selling long, as Whitehead put it. Blacks—like everyone else—want to be evaluated as individuals and recognized as such. And they want to advance as individuals in competition with others who are also viewed as individuals, not classes.

Perhaps a prime reason for this yearning to be treated as an individual with his own unique warts is that the black executive knows his easy entry doesn't guarantee permanency. Goodwill, even if backed by senior management's commitment, will only go so far. Richard Clarke, a twenty-one-year veteran in the executive recruiter field who spent many of those years working with qualified minorities, observed, "Sometimes a guy gets burned out on a job, black or white. Or he makes mistakes. Or the latest boss doesn't like him. Maybe, if he's black and he gets a second chance, he may do better, because of the paucity of blacks. But he most likely won't get a third chance."

And Then—There's Reverse Discrimination

Despite male-dominated attitudes and subtle racisms—which create the framework for the comfort index—an insidiously growing evil in recent years has been the rise of a reverse discrimination against white males in favor of women and black executives.

It appears to work in this manner: A post opens that in the normal course of departmental or divisional advancement should go to an assistant manager or qualified specialist. But either because of outward pressure or court-imposed hiring standards, the likely white male is overlooked. Instead, the post goes to a woman or a black. And the frustrated white male who might well be liberally inclined to minorities grows bitter, equally toward the woman and the black but most toward the senior management that blocked him.

One white male who found himself in such a position was especially frustrated. The division head who had interviewed him and told him he was one of three being seriously considered for the post had also confided that one of the candidates was a woman whose work he did not particularly respect. Six weeks later, the man learned that the woman had been appointed. Later, he received a letter from the boss advising him what had disqualified him was the fact that he was a man. But, the superior confided, "I consider you so well qualified that I want to continue to have your input into the job. Please let me have any suggestions you have—and keep them coming."

Contacts with mid-management executives in a number of companies indicate that instances of reverse discrimination are growing. The irony is that this is going on at a time when advocates of women's, blacks', and Hispanics' advancement are convinced that the door has been left ajar for their people only slightly. Much more remains to be done, they insist, and they are right.

But must this be at the expense of the still-ambitious white male who has already paid his dues by devoted effort and skillful performance? Probably, and it means that he is in for much more frustration, unless he is one of those rare individuals who rationalizes that he will just have to wait his turn, perhaps always.

The dilemma, of course, falls into the lap of the senior manager and ultimately into that of the chief executive. If much more remains to be done to recognize the ambitions and skills of minorities, those of the white male should not be forgotten either. The same principles of selection and criteria applied to women, blacks, Hispanics, Orientals, and so on should be extended to the white male, within the context of the company's personnel policies and needs. Righting one wrong and creating another, even if it means resorting to a cliché, is no solution. White males, like women and blacks and other minorities, should be viewed as individuals. For that matter, so should everyone in business.

10

How Honest Are They?

A Matter of Principle, Not Principal

The misuse of business funds and services for private purposes by executives, always a pimple under the surface, has swelled in recent years into an ugly boil on the neck of corporate America.

The disclosures and the notoriety have led not only to management embarrassment and discomfort at some of the country's better-known corporations but to ousters of CEOs and other top executives, to lawsuits, and to federal and state grand-jury indictments.

Several cases are typical, all having drawn the attention of the Justice Department, the Securities and Exchange Commission, and the Internal Revenue Service. While most cases have been uncovered because of income-tax evasion, some resulted from stricter corporate disclosure policies and the appointment of tougher audit committees.

"The executive perpetrators arrogate to themselves a sense of righteousness, no doubt on the basis that the king can do no wrong," declared Herbert Robinson, a New York attorney specializing in representing companies that have been victimized by white-collar crime. "But the illegal or immoral perks they take cost the company money, reduced the gross and net profits, and stole from the stockholders and public," he said.

The cases vary in their circumstances, but they contain a common thread—an apparent flagrant abuse of responsibility, according to the charges laid against those individuals involved mostly by their own companies.

In one instance, Thomas L. Brook, who retired in 1977 as chairman and chief executive of Asamera Oil Corporation, accumulated at least $1 million in company funds in a Bermuda bank account, according to company documents filed with the SEC. Only Brook knew of the bank account. But he agreed to return about $846,000 to Asamera in exchange for a promise by a company subsidiary and its two partners in an Indonesian joint venture that they wouldn't sue him.

In another case, John T. Potter, chairman and the largest stockholder of Potter Instrument Company, was accused in a complaint filed by the SEC of receiving substantial undisclosed benefits from the Long Island company. These included $100,000 a year from 1970 through 1974 to maintain his palatial, French-colonial home located on a ten-acre site and his personal racing yacht and to pay the salaries of servants and yacht crew. The company, which had been compelled to file for bankruptcy status, successfully emerged from it and made a settlement with its creditors. But Potter insisted he was personally bankrupt.

In New Jersey, a state grand jury indicted Charles and William Pritchard, principals of Pritchard & Baird, a bankrupt reinsurance brokerage, for allegedly stealing more than $8 million in insurance premiums. The Pritchards were accused of siphoning to themselves funds from four subsidiary companies by depositing checks into their personal checking accounts. It was the largest fraud case ever brought in the Garden State.

About $1 million allegedly went to refurbish Charles Pritchard's 126-room mansion in Bedminster Township and to construct paddocks for horses used in fox hunts. And thousands of dollars were said in the indictment to have been spent for paintings and jewelry.

William A. Baxter, an executive vice-president and director of Frank B. Hall, Inc., an international insurance brokerage in Briarcliff Manor, New York, resigned following an audit-committee investigation. The company said that certain personal and other expenses, mostly, according to a spokesman, "in the area of travel and entertainment," totaling about $400,000 had been incurred by Baxter and several other employees in a subsidiary. Those expenditures during 1973–1976 did not satisfy its standards for payment of employee expenses or reimbursement, the company said. Baxter repaid $86,276, or all the expenses accrued by him, and the company got back more than $300,000 from all the employees and said it hoped to recover the rest.

In yet another case, Jack Lansing resigned as president of the Pacific Power and Light Company, following the disclosure by the Internal Revenue and the Portland, Oregon, utility that he had made improper use of a company-leased Cessna aircraft. Terming it a "misunderstanding" with Western Skyways Service, the airline lessor, Lansing agreed to repay $15,000 over a three-year period.

The issue of moral responsibility or the lack of it by those in high authority is an old one, frequently cited with shock or ridicule or with some tolerance in books, musicals, and plays. But the legal attitude is stern and uncompromising.

"Many forms of conduct permissible in a workaday world for those acting at arm's length are forbidden to those bound by fiduciary ties," declared Associate Supreme Court Justice Benjamin Cardozo in a famous 1930s brief accompanying a high-court decision. "A trustee is held to something stricter than the morals of the marketplace. Not honesty alone, but the punctilio of an honor most sensitive is then the standard of behavior."

Some of the subtleties of the issue of corporate versus personal conflict surfaced in a celebrated court case involving charges of misused company funds in the late 1950s. Solomon E. Shahmoon, chairman of Shahmoon Industries, Inc., was accused of spending $10,700 annually for five years on gifts, travel, and entertainment. In addition, flowers grown in his private garden were installed in his office at company expense. He and his wife used a company automobile for personal needs and operated it at company expense. And travel expenses involved in taking his wife to conventions were also billed to the company.

The use of these company funds weren't accounted for on the company's books. But Shahmoon's defense counsel argued that the expenditure of $10,700 a year was "petty, even miniscule, compared with the $13-million average annual sales of the corporation over the five-year period."

The prosecutor, however, countered: "While the amount in question here is certainly not large in comparison to the company's volume of business, the duty of a fiduciary does not extend only to major matters or substantial amounts over which he has control. It extends to the last penny with which he is entrusted. . . . This is not a matter of principal but of principle."

Attorneys who deal with white-collar crime point out that while misuse of funds periodically crops up in regulatory-agency citations and on court dockets, it took the Watergate break-in episode and the subsequent related disclosures to generate new heat under such practices.

"Watergate was the ultimate catalyst," said Charles A. Stillman, a former member of the U.S. Attorney's office in New York and now a practicing attorney in Manhattan. "What Watergate has done is announce to the public that law enforcement will take a harder look at the legitimate citizen who has stepped across the line," Stillman said. "Now it is all surfacing from more aggressive enforcement by the SEC, the Internal Revenue Service's harder look at foreign and domestic payoffs, closer scrutiny by audit committees, and so on."

The IRS's "Eleven Questions," a questionnaire directed at companies and their executives to ferret out illegal payments, has been generally hailed in legal circles as an extraordinary new audit technique. Its use has also been criticized as equivalent to forcing self-incrimination. But lawyers claim that it has brought out an increasing number of instances of kickbacks or unaccounted-for misuse of company funds.

Later extended by the tax agency, the questionnaire and its circulation allows the IRS to probe several sides of the potential violation—the taker's and the giver's and the corporation's tax returns. "There are still lots of violations to be uncovered," one attorney said. "The IRS should be busy for some time."

As the executive climbs the corporate ladder, the perks that often increase in scope and degree along with his advancement have a way at times of exceeding his own desires and leading him astray.

With a rueful smile, the former chief executive of one of the Fortune 500 companies related how this had worked in his case and almost presented him with a problem. After asking one of the company's in-house attorneys to help him prepare his income-tax return, the executive waited for a bill from the lawyer to cover the personal service. The attorney repeatedly promised to deliver one but it never came. Finally, the chief executive insisted on it. To his surprise, he got a bill for only $300, much below the normal fee for tax-returns on an income of his level. Sternly, he told the lawyer to give him a new bill befitting the work done and it was finally delivered.

Because of such perks and the increasing complexity of business operations requiring senior managers to spend more time on their responsibilities both at home and away, the line between professional and personal expenses seems to grow fainter all the time. Yet even in cases where on the surface it appears that company funds have been misappropriated, lawyers point out that corporate executives involved often insist that a large measure of those expenditures was for company purposes.

If, for example, a vice-president entertains suppliers or service contractors at his home, expenses should rightfully be paid by the company, lawyers say. But, they admit, the question of what is professionally social or strictly social continues to nag at the issue, often falling into a sort of never-never area.

"Many businesses maintain yachts for entertainment, hunting lodges, country-club memberships, boxes at the Metropolitan Opera or the New York Philharmonic concerts or the sports stadium," one New York attorney said. "Are they always used for entertaining customers? Or for friends and family occasionally, too?"

But Gary F. Naftalis, also a former member of the U.S. Attorney's office and now practicing law, believes it is important to make a distinction between acts of quasi- or actual criminality in the misuse of company funds and simple "indiscretions." In the former case, he said, "it's a matter of civil or federal violations or embezzlement. Too many corporate executives forget that they are working for public companies. But those who indulge in indiscretions are hardly criminals. What they do isn't praiseworthy, but it's certainly no reason to disqualify them for their positions."

Some lawyers, like Herbert Robinson or Gary Naftalis, believe that the increased climate of moral insensitivity will lead to more prosecutions and deter executives from looting corporations. "But," adds Naftalis, "what we shouldn't have is too puritanical an approach, which leads to continuous niggling criticisms so that a good man just can't perform his job."

It's likely that this issue will continue to generate debate as the trend of investigation mounts in regard to the misuse of company funds. Not many months ago, a Justice Department official disclosed that there are one hundred antitrust grand juries sitting on cases of statutory violations, so that the cases which have surfaced on the misuse of company funds may well turn out to be only that tip of the iceberg.

$40 Billion in White-Collar Crime

Yet, all the foregoing notwithstanding, the unbiased observer, if not the jaded critic, too, cannot pin the black tag on most businessmen. If nothing else, immorality, shabby ethics, and downright dishonesty are risky, and few chief executives will practice them if they value their professional survival. At best, however, chief executives are no more dishonest than anyone else, although their temptations and opportunities are often considerably greater.

Despite this, observers and critics alike would agree that the mind boggles at the vast sum of money which has passed in overseas bribes, payments, and kickbacks, a total admitted by American corporations to be more than $412 million.

But even that figure is ridiculously puny compared to the extent of white-collar crime in America—$40 billion, as estimated by the U.S. Chamber of Commerce. And that organization, a traditional spokesman for American business, also estimates that of that amount, domestic bribery and kickbacks amount to almost $7 billion. But the cost of business crime could be much higher, too.

In an interview with *Dun's Review,* Jack Kroll, head of Kroll Associates, a consulting firm specializing in procurement controls and security, declared, "Assuming that the average company nets a 5% profit on sales, $20 in goods must be sold to earn back each $1 lost in shady deals. So the $7 billion balloons to $140 billion." This, as *Dun's* pointed out, is nearly half again greater than the national defense budget.

Who's responsible? And why?

Men and circumstances. Power and the disease of corruption. Sales aggressiveness and the inevitable temptation. But perhaps most of all, a pervading attitude that no matter what, human nature will never change. Another contributing factor, which tends to convince the public there is a complicity between top management and mid-management perpetrators, is the corporate habit of wanting to bottle up or contain disclosures of abuses from the press and public until the company is ready to announce it, if ever. And given its own preference, business would rather ferret out, judge, and sentence—or not sentence—its own perpetrators instead of announcing the abuse to the detriment of its public image.

Contacts with company chief executives for over three decades, in my own experience, has convinced this writer, for one, that the vast bulk of them are honest and want to be ethical and moral in their professional and personal lives. But some fall into two varieties of traps.

One, set up when boards of directors fail to do their jobs properly, is the trap created by the abuse of power that inevitably leads to loose ethics and then to corruption. Though it may be a venerable cliché, Lord Acton's 1904 comment in a letter to a friend, "Power tends to corrupt and absolute power corrupts absolutely," accurately describes the inexorable effect of men in total control.

The other trap is built from the defensive nature of corporate chiefs in their desire to keep the affairs of the company they supervise entirely under their own control. It is not merely a simple matter of stockholder and public be damned—although a few company heads still tend to feel that way—as much as it is a matter of strong proprietary inclinations. In a great sense, it's arrantly patriarchal—the head of the family has total power over and responsibility for its members. Outsiders and their beliefs aren't wanted. But the problem is that that sort of trap also snaps shut on itself. Few companies today are states within themselves. They have not only employee rights but stockholder, customer, and public rights, too. And much the same, except for more-than-minimal stockholder rights, can be said of privately held companies.

Caught in either of those traps—the corruption of power and the myth of proprietariness—company heads sometimes condone or create an internal atmosphere of loose ethics or improper moral behavior. Whether these involve themselves or those who work for them isn't really important. The rigid governance that would in the abstract build a moral environment has done the opposite because it has few independent curbs or checks and balances built into it.

The instances in which otherwise clean-living Americans turn corrupt because of the efforts of overeager salesmen are legion, temptation growing under the blandishments of initially small "gifts" that quickly increase in number and value. The question isn't so much a matter of numbers, in other words, how many succumb to the bribes. What's more important, more likely, is the issue of why and how the trend of offering business customers sweeteners that are inevitably built into the price of goods continues to mount in American business.

Since many of those buyers, purchasing agents, foremen, minor department heads, and so on who fall prey to kickbacks and payoffs are generally not well paid in comparison to senior management, it would be simple to blame their superiors and say, "If you paid them better, they wouldn't be crooked." But as some of the initial examples of those who misused company funds would indicate, the temptation isn't necessarily greater for those who are only paid moderately. If anything, corruption seems to intensify in proportion to salaries drawn, no doubt a reflection of the bribe taker's own mounting standards of greed and need.

Management, unfortunately, often closes its eyes to the rip-offs that either occur around it or on down the line. On a superficial level, many companies will publicly condemn it, even taking ads to advise suppliers at Christmastime that employees aren't allowed to accept gifts. Some companies seek out cases in which employees have stepped over the line. But in most cases, action is only taken, usually in the form of an investigating unit, when someone has blown the whistle on a perpetrator within the company. Based on stories I have researched and written over the years, I've learned that such employees are tagged by so-called friends of theirs who really aren't friends, by disenchanted wives or resentful girl friends happy to get "lover boy" in trouble, by other employees who aren't sharing in the largess, and by other salesmen who aren't paying the bribes and are incensed that they have lost out on their quota because competitors are providing "gifts" to business customers whom the unhappy salesmen wanted to sell.

In fact, most such cases surface not only because management has taken action on its own but because letters and telephone calls came in which apprised the company of misbehavior. And these outside notifications—as in cases where the press becomes aware of them and suddenly reports on internal corruption—infuriate management and cause it to take sterner action than if it had all remained an internal family affair, most frequently discharging the employees involved.

Unfortunately, while the American business drive and success mentality have long been the envy of the world, although it has eroded in recent years, the bribe instinct and the corrupt behavior seem to be very much part of it. I have over the years run across such instances as: district managers earmarking part of merchandise shipments for their own use; one manager maintaining an interest in a brothel, stocking it with goods that he sold, so he could get buyers in a happy frame of mind to buy his merchandise; and retail-store buyers accepting gifts over the years from more than one supplier and building a sizable estate from it.

Who Will Be the Watchdog?

If most chief executives are honest and tend to be upset when outsiders have to inform them of internal wrongdoings, but not infrequently contribute to an atmosphere of "anything goes" within their own companies, what's the solution?

It's obvious that top management, already under fire for a variety of things including its unabated love of perks and privileges, should curb baser instincts and set a stern example of behavior and morality. That will involve not merely stellar personal propriety but also the creation of a company ambience that management at all levels are stewards of an institution that belongs to its stockholders and has strong social and moral obligations to society and its customers.

No company should be without an internal audit or inspection unit. In cases where such a watchdog system operates, the advantages have been very great, not only saving the company losses that would otherwise go undetected but also avoiding the embarrassment, even harassment, that outside informers seem to create. Of course, for a while the installation of such a unit will be criticized and condemned. But if it operates efficiently, without "fear or favor," it will soon be accepted and the sound moral climate will become clear.

In addition, disclosure of internal abuse should be prompt

and forthright. Nothing creates more suspicion than a hesitant, delayed, or hedging admission that there have been improprieties. There may be good reasons for an initial, vaguely couched communiqué, primarily because it takes time to determine the extent and the manner of white-collar crime and misbehavior. But in such cases, the intent to investigate further and an indication in general terms of what is involved will allay at least some suspicion.

But no rules or precautions will accomplish what is needed unless those who ultimately exert the power—such as directors or stockholders—act as a matter of principle.

That didn't happen in May 1976 at the first annual meeting in three years of the Northrop Corporation in Hawthorne, California. The meeting had been held up because of varied scandals in which the big aircraft manufacturer was involved. Thomas V. Jones, Northrop's chairman, had already pleaded guilty to felony charges of making illegal contributions to former President Richard Nixon. The company had illegally given $150,000 to Nixon's campaign, of which at least $50,000 had been used to ensure silence from the Watergate burglars.

In addition, the company had kept an illegal political slush fund of more than $1 million used to contribute to other politicians. In 1972 and 1973 Northrop had admitted paying $450,000 in bribes to Adnan M. Khashoggi, a Saudi Arabian with a checkered career of investments and influence. Two Saudi generals were to be the recipients of the payments but may not ever have received them.

Despite all these admitted illegalities, Northrop's stockholders gave Jones an enthusiastic round of applause because of the company's excellent financial report. Profits had climbed 83 percent for the quarter over the previous year, and annual sales were expected to exceed $1 billion for the first time. After the applause dwindled, stockholders rejected the efforts of a handful of dissenters who urged that the company be required to adopt stricter rules of behavior.

So Jones stayed. He was luckier than a bunch of executives at other companies, such as Gulf Oil, American Shipbuilding, Lockheed, and Minnesota Mining and Manufacturing. They lost their jobs or their outside directorships because of their failure to prevent political activities or the giving of bribes by companies in which they were prominent.

Those who might deplore the Northrop stockholders' zeal for profit at the expense of morality might easily feel the same about the behavior of management at Columbia Pictures early in 1978 in defending one of their errant own. After announcing on October 3, 1977, that David Begelman had "resigned" as senior executive vice-president, a director and head of its motion-picture and television divisions, Columbia reinstated him two and a half months later. The disclosure by Columbia that Begelman had "obtained through improper means corporate funds in the amount of $61,000 for his personal benefit" was not sufficient to keep him unemployed, the company said. "The emotional problems which prompted these acts, coupled with ongoing therapy, will not impair his continuing effectiveness as an executive," said Columbia from its Burbank, California, headquarters.

The additional disclosure that Begelman allegedly forged the name of Cliff Robertson, the movie actor, to a check for $10,000 and cashed it also did not appear to prejudice the company against Begelman. What may well have created Columbia's bias in his favor, however, was the success that the former talent agent turned movie mogul had had in producing Columbia's science-fiction hit movie *Close Encounters of the Third Kind* and the large revenue Columbia derived from it. Soon after, however, Begelman resigned and became an independent producer—with Columbia as a key client.

So both Northrop's stockholders and Columbia Pictures' management came to the same conclusion: profits were better than ethics.

Who or what is best equipped to curb corrupt business acts? Two years before President Carter asked him to come to Washington as Secretary of the Treasury, W. Michael Blumenthal, then president and chief executive of the Bendix Corporation, suggested an answer in a speech at the University of Detroit.

"The business community needs a more intimate and meaningful dialogue with its critics as well as its constituents," he said. "What we have today hardly deserves the name of dialogue. On one hand, we have the scandals, the charges, the countercharges and the suspicions so characteristic of the post-Watergate atmosphere. On the other, we find business spokesmen defending business as if it were a monolith, all of a piece, as if every suggestion of corporate wrongdoing, every proposal

169

for change, were an attack on the free-enterprise system as a whole. The result is nothing but confusion."

What is needed is a new approach, Blumenthal said, "a frankly moral approach that would begin with business taking a long, hard look at itself." Businessmen, together with representatives of other segments of society, should organize an institute or an association that would promote the idea of responsibility and ethics in business practices, Blumenthal said. The monitor organization would focus on devising new ethical behavior codes to which all business would be expected to subscribe. The founding members could be business leaders, he explained, but the new group could also draw on lawyers, the clergy, statesmen, philosophers, and others whose views would represent the moral concerns of American society. "This, indeed, would be the very point of the new departure," Blumenthal said, "that it would be and would be seen to be operating on behalf of society as a whole."

So far as is known, Blumenthal's concept was never taken up, although the idea has a precedent in several other fields, particularly advertising, the legal community, medicine, and architecture. Perhaps the principal reason the Blumenthal recommendation never led to action was that creating such a body would tacitly acknowledge that American business needs a self-employed watchdog. But another reason may have been the growing realization that corporate corruption and abuse have come under such a vivid spotlight that the practices may have become prohibitive.

"The moral climate in American business is improving because the risks have increased enormously," said Herbert Robinson, the New York lawyer who is much involved in investigating and preparing litigation against white-collar crime. "The climate is changing," he went on. "People realize that the perks that used to be winked at aren't proper. And the government is so attuned to the problem that at least one or more agencies are certain to take action. Conditions are dictating what conscience hasn't been able to—a more honest behavior by the nation's businessmen."

11

Getting There, Poor or Rich

"There I was," said J. Peter Grace, Jr., "the poor little rich boy. Twenty-three years old, just out of Yale, where I had my own twelve-cylinder Packard and my own horses, and I was thrown into the family business. My father, who had had a stroke and thought he was going to die any day, just shoved me down the directors' throats. Suddenly, I was to be the head of a big business that looked like it was going broke. What was I supposed to do?"

That day in 1936 when he joined the company was just as vivid more than four decades later to the president and chief executive of W. R. Grace & Co., the $5-billion-a-year chemicals, natural resources, and consumer-goods conglomerate.

"So I was a rich kid, but can a poor kid make it to the top nowadays?" he mused on a gray afternoon in 1978. "A lot easier than he could before, I think. . . .

"But what could I do? I had always been handed everything, but when I became president a few years later there was nothing left in the company that had any future. I had to become a maverick and I did.

"What prepared me for it? I came from a home with sixty-eight servants, a yacht with a crew of twenty-eight, my own Chris-Craft, and twenty-eight polo ponies with five grooms. I had to become a nut, sufficiently independent to do what was necessary. Everything seemed to be going wrong, especially all of our businesses in Latin America. We had bad, bad management there. I flew one day to Lima, the next day to Germany, then back to the United States. But I began to straighten things out, unloading this company, unloading that one. I made it, even though many of my first cousins were fired. . . .

"What a young man needs today, rich or poor, is the willingness to work hard, to take criticism, and to learn. So many today won't do any of those things. I go today on the assumption that most people have equal intelligence. The difference is their desire to work, their initiative, and whether they are willing to refuse to accept defeat."

There aren't too many geniuses—only people whose personal traits and attitudes determine whether they will succeed or fail in their careers, Grace said.

But in today's increasingly complex, beleaguered business world, can a red-blooded, work-oriented, ambition-driven young man or woman still make it in a dazzling sweep upward in a decade or two? And when the summit or near-summit is reached, can he or she reasonably hope for a long, happy stay there without being dislodged by company upheavals, politics, mergers, and the like?

On a simplistic basis, CEOs say yes on both scores. The opportunities are great and growing even better. New markets are beckoning. Old, tired concepts are blowing away. The demands for qualified and eager executives are booming even in professional fields that only yesterday were crowded—engineering, education, communications, science, electronics, construction. And across the country major demographic changes are bringing new life to city cores, a new maturity to suburban areas, and an agri-industrial-commercial complexion to the corn and wheat fields of rural America.

But one senses a hesitation, an uncertainty, as the typical chief executive finishes. Later, he speaks of some counter trends. The shifting to egalitarianism, everyone wanting to be at least as equal as the next one without necessarily waiting to qualify. The increasing love of the coffee break, the days off, the longer vacation. The impatience of the young, especially those with a master's degree in business administration. The declining motivation of many employees, age notwithstanding. The social-welfare system, with its umbrella from womb to tomb. The overcompensation of the affirmative-action and equal-opportunity laws. And the drive to legalize the working age to seventy and even preclude mandatory retirement.

In all that flux, the simplistic answers cannot hold. Career entry and career success are both easier and harder and will become more so. "It's easier today in business than it used to be," asserts Peter Grace.

But Peter Redfield, president and chief executive of Itel Corporation, says, "I notice that in large companies there is a lid on the growth of young people. Performance counts more. In my own company, we aren't inclined any more to tolerate mediocrity. Executives get a year to two years to show what they can do. Salesmen get one year. And there's no small problem with people who have topped off in their ability. If we can't find them something else that is productive, we let them go. Why prolong their agony and ours?"

On the other hand, it's likely that new opportunities will take seed working down from the chief executive's office.

"The company chief executive has to rely on more and more people," observes Carl Menk, president of Boyden Associates. "That's why the personnel manager has been upgraded to vice-president for human resources or the company brings in a more qualified man to do this job. This means a need for people close to the top to help him. In addition, companies are going more to the outside for their chief executives, probably because there are whole new industries since the last few wars and the rapid growth didn't allow lots of companies to develop their CEOs. And don't forget all those fatalities in the last three wars, men who might well have qualified for top jobs.

"So what it all means, I think, is that there are opportunities at the top and on down because of changes at the top," Menk said. "But at the same time, there are fewer guys who want to be CEOs. Maybe it's because they just don't want the responsibilities that go with the jobs and they can live pretty well without being hassled in lower jobs."

The chief executive's role will undoubtedly only become more complex, notes James Davant, the CEO of Paine Webber, "and he will need more delegation. I don't know how you will ever minimize the risk of relying on people and that must mean many opportunities for everyone if they are willing to meet the challenges. The personal equation will always be endemic, but performance will mean more than ever."

Making It—Or Else

In a great sense, then, reaching the summit in American business is more difficult because the demands are more stringent. In another sense, increased passing on of responsibility makes it easier.

These two factors, which appear so divergent, cross when the corporate needs and the individual's qualifications meet in a supply-and-demand situation.

In essence, the difficulties with which American businessmen have been grappling—a declined productivity rate, inability to cope with inflation, a lowered profit trend, and a competitive decline on the world scene—require more effective, more productive chief and senior executives, and that in great part is why the advancement to the heights is tougher than it has been. While this complicates the advancement process, the importance of finding the best is probably more vital now than at any time since the end of World War II.

As mentioned earlier, however, the problems of shortened sights, the desire for security, peace of mind, and leisure time, and the reluctance to accept the pressures of top-level responsibility work against the challenges of upward mobility. Evidence is the trend of increased job movement of executives. And evidence of the tougher requirements in contemporary American business is the unprecedented turnover in the CEO's office in the last decade.

The conclusion to be drawn from all this is that while the opportunity is greater, so are the job requirements. But whether individuals will respond to the call and the opportunities remains an open question and, not so incidentally, an essential one.

"Whatever one can say in criticism of our American system," asserts Reuben Gutoff, the president of Standard Brands, "it is inherently strong. There is no class structure and it rewards excellence. On the other hand, I buy the thesis that the Establishment is in trouble not so much for the external pressures on it as for its own failures. The worst is the creeping conservatism, the decline in imagination, and the conformity to the norm. The biggest challenge is to create an orderly nonconformity that will give the corporation structure but enough freedom and vitality to do what is needed. And that, of course, comes down to people."

Doesn't that imply that the leadership quality is missing? The Standard Brands president agreed and wasn't alone in citing it.

"The attitudes of people inside the corporation make it increasingly difficult to get the job done," said Marvin Schiller of A. T. Kearney. "There's a shortage of effective people at the top who know how to win in the business environment or how to make money. As the merger mill keeps churning, there are so many big companies—a three-billion-dollar United Technologies buys a two-billion-dollar Otis Elevator—and they gestate ranks of automatons—young men who know how to follow but not how to lead. Like bureaucracies, big corporations breed followers, implementers, not builders."

Can a skilled, ambitious executive or young man make it and remain happy in a conservative company that has only a moderate growth rate and is satisfied with it? Or, conversely, would such a company want to promote such a nonconforming aspirant? Not likely, in either case.

If the situation isn't one of oil-and-water, however, the prognosis is naturally quite different. Much has been written and debated about the chemistry in business as an important success factor. It has two elements and only one is the personality fit of the boss and the aspiring underling. The other is the chemistry between the hopeful executive and the nature of the company. The mixture must be harmonious or it has no cohesive substance, consisting instead of separate brooding layers.

As a result, the cautious, well-balanced, nonabrasive young man or woman and the middle-aged executive with that type of personality will do well in a company suited to them. The hustling, restless type will not only feel out of sorts there but will certainly be made to feel he will do better elsewhere.

Unfortunately, such fit-or-go situations aren't readily apparent. One reason is the traditionally lax communications between managements and mid-levels and another is the uncertainty that seems to dog company policies in many businesses. A long, wondering process descends from the top to the middle, each side remaining uncertain about the other until time and circumstance either bring them together or break them apart. A third reason lies in the aspirant's own uncertainty, which can only be removed when he makes his moves, testing the water to find how it feels before he plunges in.

Early in his career the confrontation doesn't really matter unless the young executive's personality is so abrasive or different in tone, or if his personal habits are so questionable, that he is promptly hustled out. The real confrontation takes place later, for better or worse. And there are likely to be periodic confrontations and even departures if career goals don't mesh with the company's needs.

As far as young men are concerned, the question of corporate/personal chemistry is even more vital because a wrong judgment can easily delay or sidetrack an otherwise promising career. The danger, of course, is a too rapid judgment on the need to move. And in a period when youth and education are in high demand, it's likely that many ambitious young executives are jumping too quickly from job to job in search of the right corporate home.

How can one tell early in the game if his chances of reaching the top are good in the company that employs him? There's no easy way to tell this, and a personnel counselor who could chart the ways would probably find hordes of executives beating a path to his door. But common sense and experience suggest a few possibilities:

First, make your performance effective and preferably superior.

Second, discuss personal ambitions with superiors.

Third, seek a frank discussion with superiors as to how you can satisfy the company's goals and relate that to specific higher jobs you can attain.

Fourth, make your work speak louder than you do. Obvious loyalty and motivation are prerequisites to being considered for promotion. And keep improving your value by additional in-house training and education.

Fifth, don't be a loner. Maintain a proper rapport with everyone—your peers as well as your superiors—and strive always to be helpful, even if it hurts.

Sixth, develop a resilience to disappointment. Employers respect and do not easily forget those who can bounce back from failure to get a raise or promotion and do even better than before. Is that asking too much? Not really.

In time—set your own deadline—all that should pay off. If it doesn't—

Seventh, go elsewhere, and this time don't hesitate.

The Big, Bad Game of Company Politics

But, many will say, aren't all those rules just a lot of hogwash when most promotions are actually won by playing the game of company politics? That, unfortunately, is a very valid question.

One of the most nonproductive of company practices, internal politics—the jockeying for position, calumny, falsification, and toadying to pit oneself against another—is often a function of the management. If the chief executive, the senior managers, and others engage in it, it's likely that everyone else will. Sad to say, there's scarcely an American company in which politics doesn't exist, its scope varying on the temperament of those who run things, but the practice regardless has the same effect. It wastes time and effort and keeps too many people away from the important factor, job performance.

Here is what some CEOs say about it, and it's not very reassuring:

"Internal politics are one of the toughest problems any chief executive faces," said Philip I. Berman, chairman of Hess's, the Allentown, Pennsylvania, department-store chain. "Sometimes, it's probably best to take your biggest company politicians and lock them up in a room and let them beat each other into a pulp. They'll come out better men and better employees," Berman says. "When I first took over Hess's, I asked the six top executives to put down their own job descriptions. When I read them, I saw that we had titles but not a team. I told them I wanted them to get together, to divide up the company's responsibilities so that we would have total coverage. They started at nine A.M. and concluded at three P.M. the same day. There were some harsh words, but they wound up pooling their talents and common sense. That happened six years ago, and we have had no reason to change any of their mutual decisions."

"I cope with company politics by not facing it—I ignore it," reported Laurence Tisch of Loews Corporation.

His brother, Robert, Loews president, added, "We try to put the right people in the right jobs. If they have failings, we try not to show favoritism and tell them what those failings are. That's what I get paid for, to see that everyone does their job properly. I gave up a long time ago trying to get everybody in the company to love each other. And you try to do the best you can to remove the problem that could create the jealousies and the jostlings."

Isn't one of the prime causes of company politics the frustration that employees feel when their efforts aren't recognized?

"That's one of the big problems," replied Laurence Tisch. "In many cases, it's true. You try to keep the company small enough. Sometimes it's not easy. You pat the wrong guy on the back and a hundred people get mad because of it.... We travel and talk to people. You do the best you can. We believe in maintaining our internal relations. But it could be better."

"Certainly there is competition among executives," declared Robert T. Quittmeyer, president of the Amstar Corporation. "But those who are wise compete without climbing on the back of the next man. That's how they really stand out. The biggest challenge to the CEO is to use people in their own best interests. When it comes to physical properties, you make a decision on the basis of facts. People are very complicated but they make the country and the corporation work. The real objective should be to assign them responsibilities in the best manner for all concerned. But I don't think it is possible to do it well all the time."

James Davant, chairman of Paine, Webber, Jackson, and Curtis, said, "Politics emerges to the extent that you permit it to. It's foolish to allow it to flourish, particularly when the biggest problem many companies have is to find enough people to serve the business. So we must concentrate on motivating them, keeping them directed and set on the right track."

William Olsten, founder and chairman of the Olsten Corporation, Westbury, New York, which provides temporary-help services, said, "In general, it is true that businessmen handle people badly. The chief execs are more committed to the whole, their companies, than to the parts, the people. People are the guts in the corporation, but unfortunately people come and go —they're replaceable—but a corporation remains. People do make a difference, but the corporation needs a leader. A business almost manages itself. It can go along on momentum, but never more than a few years."

Most other CEOs express themselves in the same vein but prefer not to discuss the subject in any detail. Still, we can make a few general observations, based on long observation of and participation in corporate life, on why there is so much company politicking.

Many top executives simply ignore company politics, either because they believe they can do nothing about it, since human nature is intractable, or because they tacitly condone it. Many others invite internal politics in the belief that it keeps everyone on his toes—alive and kicking, in other words. They see in the bickering, pushing, and sycophantic process a sort of checks-and-balances system at work. Others secretly encourage it on the basis that it will cut down any threats to them, a self-defeating theory that really helps no one.

In a large number of situations, the seeds of niggling politicking are sown when the boss in direct or subtle ways displays favoritism. The tricks used to do this are varied and creative. One department head will give a gift to one employee and ignore all the others sitting nearby. Or he will take the same people to lunch day after day. Or the boss will invite the same people to his home. Or he will make praiseworthy mention only of the same favored group. The others don't exist. What does all this do? Nothing much more than needlessly upset most people and spread discontent.

Will involving oneself in company politics boost a career? Probably, if the senior executive is inclined toward it and responds favorably to an employee's blandishments. Those bosses who don't like it will more likely insist on performance as a promotion requirement. "If two men are constantly in agreement," observed David Mahoney, the chairman of Norton Simon, "then one of them is unnecessary." That principle should be a good offset to the problem of company politics, but of course it won't be.

Communications, or Public and Private Relations

"Your job is to take ---- and turn it into applesauce," the company's executive vice-president told one of the string of public-relations men who regularly paraded in and out of the giant conglomerate. No one today will admit to making that statement, but the public-relations man who was so instructed swears that that is what he was told.

"What did he mean?" the PR man said. "He meant that both he and I knew that the so-called hot company we worked for really was nothing but a giant mess, but my job and that of my staff was to convince the world at large that it was in fact a well-run, effective company and that the chief executive was in fact a statesman of business.

"But that wasn't an easy thing to do," he added, "and we had trouble convincing a lot of people of our case. That's why I was soon asked to leave and joined a platoon of others who had to look for a new job. The company was actually a big network of companies, loosely run with only a thread of fear and uncertainty keeping them together. The CEO? He spent only one third of his time on business but made it look like it was nineteen hours a day. Most of the time, he would be busy in his office, playing the stock and commodities markets for his own benefit. But we—we were supposed to turn it all into applesauce."

This situation, as described by an obviously bitter ex-executive, is probably an exception but, unfortunately, only in degree. The principle of making everything look like applesauce appears to be the rule in corporate public relations. And this, as many reporters have learned, turns into a double standard. The corporate PR man will break down the doors to foist a favorable story on the media. But when there is an unfavorable development involving the same company, try to find the PR man or, if he can be located, try to get a forthright answer. He is suddenly too busy—the boss is away or at an important meeting. And if the reporter manages to get through to a senior executive, he will indignantly be told, "You know, I can't possibly comment on that."

Now all that, like company politics, is nothing more than human nature. And, like company politics, anyone who wants to get ahead in the corporation should know something about external and internal communications because he will inevitably be involved in it, even if indirectly.

The irony of the PR double standard arises from the self-righteous complaint by businessmen that the media have an anti-business bias. The simple fact is that it would be difficult not to have it purely on the strength of that super-defensive and hypocritical corporate practice. As a newspaperman for more than thirty years, I personally do not blame the public-relations men. Most of them are, after all, only able to keep their jobs based on their ability to manufacture applesauce. I blame their superiors, who have their finger on the applesauce button.

Yet recently a strange thing has happened. Two of the most conservative corporate PR men I know, both of whom carried vice-presidential titles in their large companies, retired. In both cases, they expressed an entirely different view of the press's obligations. Before, as their employers' principal press representatives, they would cooperate on routine stories but would object to any prodding on what were essentially unfavorable aspects, such as why the earnings fell or why top executives were shuffled. Now, when I sought out their attitudes about the media, one replied, "You have to keep digging, digging, like Con Edison. That's what you're there for." And when I countered, "You didn't always feel that way, did you?" he smiled vaguely, scarcely the Buddha he thought he was.

Replying to the same question, the other PR man said, "Boy, give us the inside story. That's the fascinating stuff. That's what I want to read and so does everyone else." When I reminded him that that was quite a change in attitude, he shrugged. "Do you think I'm crazy?" he asked. "How could I be otherwise? What do you think a public-relations man is all about?"

Despite all the disclaimers that chief executives and their PR people will make, it is a fact that an intensifying adversary relationship has erupted like a festering sore between business and the media. Much of it is unnecessary if businessmen will realize that the media have a strange desire not to be taken in. And though business chiefs complain that it simply isn't true they lie to the press, I, as one newspaperman, can testify to those company heads who have lied to me and later admitted it. And when I reminded them of it later, at least two of them blithely replied, "I had to lie to protect the company and the individuals involved. You understand that, don't you?"

"Maybe. But naturally you won't expect me to believe anything you tell me from now on," I said, turning sarcastic. "You understand that, don't you?"

If corporate public relations leave much to be desired (and I have only scratched the surface of that problem here), private or internal relations aren't much better. References to it were included in chapter 8 on the 80/20 syndrome. But a few more points won't be out of context here.

"Egalitarianism" worries many management people, but they might well consider the possibility of offsetting it by generating a more open society within their own companies. In most, the delay between policy formulation and its dissemination is long, painful, and ineffective. I have never understood why the intelligence factor is considered to diminish as the hierarchy descends layer by layer. One may be hung for saying it, but responsibility and intelligence are not mutually exclusive. But many companies operate as though they are mutually exclusive when they make decisions that affect a great number of people but allow only a tiny group to formulate them, and then mark time before the news is passed along. The inevitable results are employee dissatisfaction, frustration, and eventual loss of interest.

There is perhaps nothing that more clearly shows the unhappy state of internal relations than company meetings. They are often stilted, restricted, tortuous, and invigorated only by the competition to make points with the boss. Everyone present seems to have two challenges: (1) to contribute something meaningful and (2) to do so without riling his superiors, whether present or not. When such meetings actually produce worthwhile results it is unusual and refreshing.

This is even true among the CEO's peers. At board meetings, for example, open, frank discussions are largely inhibited for fear of acrid debate. But at least one chief executive recently took action to change things. William M. Agee, who in 1976 at age thirty-eight succeeded Michael Blumenthal as chairman of the Bendix Corporation, early in 1978 removed the giant wooden table used in the company's boardroom in Southfield, Michigan. The table was a "security blanket" for the directors, he decided, placing a wedge among them and hampering free discussion. The directors, not warned in advance, were nonplussed when they assembled at a tableless meeting, while the furniture industry wasn't happy about the resulting publicity, either.

More from Peter Grace: MBAs, CEOs, and Youth

Quixotic, hyperactive, and unconventional, the sixty-five-year-old Peter Grace has a montagelike aspect in American business. Some consider him a genius. Others call him flaky. Others say he was just born with a silver spoon in his mouth and a string of polo ponies waiting for him. Some say he acts first, talks next, and thinks last. But few will deny the dramatic success he has had in turning a struggling company into a profitable giant and a major employer. He is also one of those not-infrequent cases of a strain of restless entrepreneurism beginning with a founder, skipping a generation, and renewing itself in the grandson. Grace's grandfather, William R. Grace, fled the Irish potato famine in 1854 to start a business empire in Peru, and when his health began to fail in the hot climate he moved to the United States where he was twice a reform mayor of New York City and built a new company.

An interview with Peter Grace is a run-on affair, questions and answers tumbling over each other. But unusual perspectives and insights come out of it, the only real problem being to control it:

Q: How can people make it in business today? What do you look for in an executive?

A: I think it's easier today than it ever was. Each decade is different. Today the competition is much easier. The people don't work as hard, they don't have the same ambition, they don't sacrifice the way people used to sacrifice. What are we looking for? People who work hard, show initiative, and refuse to accept defeat. There's less and less of that around today. It's much easier, therefore, to get to the top than it used to be.

Q: People used to have better work ethic and motivation?

A: Absolutely. Today if a young man in our company comes in with a study that's lousy—he didn't think about it or give his all—and you give him hell, he gets mad, walks out, and he'll have another job within a week. The MBA or anyone else could get a job almost at will if he has any ability at all. There's no reason to stay here if you feel that people don't like you so much or you've had it with the boss. And so the real essentiality of employment in any given place is no longer there because everyone has too many alternatives.

Q: What's your feeling about MBAs generally?

A: I believe that the best people by far are self-educated. If you had to learn by force of circumstance, what you learned is so much more retained and so much part of you compared to somebody who's trying to be a synthetic expert and goes to college or business school just because that's the thing to do. I don't know what they teach in business schools, but the graduates seem to think that the world is just waiting for them to come out and they don't realize that they have one hell of a lot to learn when they get out and furthermore that they are impractical, and they get quite annoyed when they're told that. . . . By and large, I find them quite unsatisfactory. I'd rather take any day a kid who is a high-school graduate, a good athlete, with reasonable leadership qualities and good grades. I'd take him in here tomorrow and wouldn't give a damn if he never went to business school.

Q: Do you think that some foreign businessmen are showing more skill, more vision, more drive?

A: In Japan, yes, but not in Europe.

Q: Not in West Germany?

A: Not particularly. I find there's quite a bit of bureaucracy in West Germany, too.

Q: But you respect the Japanese . . .

A: Very definitely. And I can't believe the way they work. I've gone there many times. You go into Mitsubishi on a Saturday morning and here's a room ten times as long as this and a director of Mitsubishi is sitting at the head table and clerks are working alongside of him

there, all of them working as hard on a Saturday as they do any other day of the week. . . .
Q: And we . . .
A: We have lots of things that we could do in our company, that we don't have anybody to implement. I mean that there's three things that make the world go round in business. One is ideas, the other is people, and the third is money. Now the easiest of all to get is money. If you've got a good idea and a couple of good guys to carry it out, you could always get the financing. No way of not. The hardest thing in the world to get is a good idea and the next hardest thing, not very much less difficult, is to get good people. And it's getting harder and harder and harder.

12

The Pivotal Crisis

The telephone's shrillness rips into the night's tranquillity. At the first ring he is awake and rising, dread brushing his temples with icy fingers. Who the hell can be calling at three in the morning? he wonders. He speaks into the phone and the brutal voice assaults him and then is gone.

His wife's hand is at his shoulder. "Who was it?"

He answers slowly, "I don't know."

"What did he want?"

"Nothing much."

"Well, what did he say?"

He hesitates and says with perverse humor, "Just that he wants . . . to kill me." . . .

Troubled, confused, weighed down by his business problems, the stolid, well-dressed man listens to the sermon but doesn't really hear the words. He is smothering in a cocoon of worry. Then he senses a change around him. A silence from the pulpit has also fallen over the congregation. Staring around, he is surprised by the repose and softness on every face. It brings him outside himself. Is he wearing the same expression? And isn't even aware of it? A small smile rounds his square face. He sighs. . . .

Carefully closing the boss's door behind him, the taciturn executive silently makes his way along the plush hallway to his own office and passes his secretary without a word. He stands at the window and stares bleakly out wondering, Why him? Assigned to cast the key vote on the continuance or disposition of a heavily losing company division, he must decide on a move that will affect the lives of hundreds of employees and their families. The irony is hardly lost on him. He was one of those who only a few years ago advocated that the giant company start that very division. Is there, he wonders, a message, a warning, or an omen in being singled out to make the deciding vote when a more senior executive should have been given the responsibility? Of course there is, but what is it? . . .

The prolonged drive by the national labor union to thrust its way into the giant corporation has been bitter and burdensome. Weeks of turmoil preceding the union bargaining election have only made the situation less clear. Late on the night before the voting will be held, the chief executive receives one more call. It is the fifth threatening message. *Keep your hands off.* Opposing factions, splintered amongst themselves, have clearly declared themselves. Does he value his wife, children, home, safety? Would he have protected them all by having taken a trip or leave of absence or even early retirement? Of course, but how could he? . . .

The chief executive, his heart pounding, listens with disbelief to his senior controller. The message just delivered couldn't have been more shocking to him. An audit has found that the company's engineering vice-president has been accepting kickbacks amounting to several hundred thousand dollars from suppliers over the last three years. Can there be any doubt? Definitely not, assures the controller. But just who is the culprit? Only one of the CEO's best friends. Their wives are good friends, the children . . . "There's no way around it," the controller insists. "We've got to take action. Otherwise, we'll be accused of a cover-up." The CEO nods slowly, with pain. . . .

The Perception of a Non-Crisis

In the pressurized world of the chief executive in the last quarter of the twentieth century, frequent, small crises are normal, even expected. Many filter up to him through the organization and many others are absorbed below. But the major crisis always comes at him with a rending jolt, reawakening him to the reality that he sometimes forgets. He is the man in the "ultimate job" with the ultimate responsibility that can't be passed on or ignored.

The most difficult of those major crises is the pivotal one, on which a career, even a life, hangs, and it can be as traumatic as the most personal crisis faced in a lifetime. Many businessmen have had them, but those with the maximum authority in a company are likely to have more of them.

Yet some chief executives do not see such crises as more than challenges, their degree and variety representing no more than the constant stream of confrontation of decisions and issues with which a CEO normally contends. Some challenges are bigger than others, they admit, but most if not all must be handled as though they are hardly crises.

Edward F. Gibbons, an advocate of that thesis, has had a lot to grapple with since 1976, when he became chairman and chief executive of the F. W. Woolworth Company. He was the first outside executive to be brought in by the big retail company, and his appointment as financial vice-president no doubt caused some noses to go out of joint in that conservative company. But the word quickly went out that he was slated for even higher things. Two years after his arrival, he was elected Woolworth's president. But suddenly he became seriously ill, and the prognosis for a time was uncertain. When he improved he returned as a part-time consultant and soon after reassumed the president's post.

Three years later, he finally moved into the CEO's chair. But Woolworth's profits promptly fell apart because of the effect of the weak dollar on the company's far-flung international operations. Thus Gibbons's succession to the highly sought-after CEO role at Woolworth was rocky and hardly auspicious.

The short, scrappy, restless Gibbons insisted, however, "We often perceive crises where none exist. We forget that we have a God-given adaptability to unusual things. After all, my occupancy of a certain chair presupposes that I have an adaptability to handle unusual situations.

"In any such situation," he said, "the best approach is by contemplation and research, and those are best accomplished by soliciting input from others. No amount of hysteria will make any contributions.

"I have to have a certain equanimity, a certain calmness to

maintain in carrying out this job, and part of that is to avoid a crisis or an apparent crisis by using a proper perspective," Gibbons added.

Achieving such a perspective requires an ability to relax and to devote at least part of one's life to helping others, he said. As a deacon in the Catholic church, he maintains a ministry at hospitals, where he provides counsel and performs a variety of functions, including the giving of Communion.

"Providing spiritual and humane help also helps me. It's a form of purging anxiety. It gives me a sense of peace and better relative values," Gibbons said. "There's nothing that clarifies one's confusion and clears the head more than to find that the problems of other people are greater than yours."

Smiling, he added, "There are other ways to relax and get some of that perspective. I like to do creative things with my hands. I make clocks, tables, even dressers, and give them to my kids or to other relatives. Using my hands and tools, combined with a lot of reading in philosophy, theology, and history, also gives me the equanimity I must hold on to."

After his twenty-two jobs in his thirty-six years at AT&T, John deButts still doesn't regard some "tough situations" he had as full-blown crises.

"I never had one that I looked at quite that way," he told me. "I had one such situation when the Teamsters Union tried to invade us in 1962 and they picked my particular division, Illinois Bell, to do it. It happened two months after I took the job in Illinois. We didn't want the Teamsters. We didn't think that they had a place. We were already unionized. Most of the employees were represented by the Communications Workers, a lot of them by the International Brotherhood of Electrical Workers and quite a few independent unions."

"And your crisis was how to cope with the Teamsters?"

"How to cope with it and how to get what I felt was more-responsive union representation," deButts said. "There were bodily-harm threats."

"Threats to you?"

"Yes. And to my wife and family. But we won."

"How?"

"We won by using people. We went to the first-line supervisors and I personally met them with outside lawyers to tell them what they could and could not say under the law but to let them know that there were a lot of things they could say. And they were the contact with the crafts. They were all clerical people in the accounting department. . . . I couldn't quite see the Teamsters moving into that group. So I went to the supervisors and they in turn talked to the employees and we beat them three to one. . . ."

"What was your toughest challenge? Was it the morale problem when you became chief executive?"

"That wasn't the toughest, because I think I knew what had to be done there," said deButts. "It was just a question of getting it done. I think one of the toughest periods I had was when I went to Illinois Bell. I had never worked there. I knew very few people out there. I knew two or three of the officers. I and my family didn't know anybody in the community. And I was one of the few non–Illinois Bell people who had ever moved into that company and the first non–Illinois Bell person to become president of that AT&T company."

"That was against their policy?"

"We hope we've cracked that, but that provincialism just doesn't work. But anyhow, it was a real challenge for me to operate in such a way as to be accepted by the people in the company and in the community and at the same time accomplish our objectives on earnings and service. I spent an awful lot of time in the field. I went to every central office in Illinois Bell. I never will forget. I went to an office in Peoria and I spent about an hour in there talking to the switchman, the foreman, and so forth, and I got up to leave and the foreman said, 'Mr. deButts, you know I've been in this business for thirty-five years and you're the first company president I've ever seen in my life.' That was not a crisis. Obviously, if I had failed, I wouldn't be where I am today. It was a tremendous challenge and it was a tough one. But it worked out all right," deButts said.

"I don't visualize my career in terms of crisis," said Irving S. Shapiro, chief executive of Du Pont. "But my early days as a lawyer were full of uncertainty because I didn't know what my capability was. When I came to Washington, I was an unwashed young lawyer who didn't know what he could do. I had to develop self-confidence. I had left a sheltered existence in Minneapolis and I was a shy, retiring youngster.

"So I had to demonstrate my ability. I wanted to become

the best lawyer I could be. And I was lucky. I got a fair amount of responsibility in the Justice Department, but I remained uncertain about myself for quite a while. Writing, in particular, was for me a traumatic experience."

But after twenty-five years at Du Pont, where he moved up to the post of vice-chairman after starting as a fledgling lawyer in the legal department, Shapiro found himself facing what was an undeniable crisis. For the first time in its long history Du Pont was offering its top post to a Jew—only the second time it had elected to go outside the family. And the offer had gone to him.

Should he take the post? Still vividly recalling the situation, Shapiro said, "It wasn't that I was concerned about taking the job because of the ethnic consideration. It was whether I should take the job when it was obvious in 1974 that we were heading into a recession. If it would be hard to prove myself as it was, it would be much harder if the economic climate were adverse."

But he took the job anyway.

After Small Ones, the Pivotal Crisis

In the never-ending confrontation between organizations and men, challenges build up to crises and small crises mount up to big ones.

Such was the case with Reginald Jones, who at General Electric was always given jobs he didn't want, objected to edicts handed down that he felt weren't necessary, or found himself forced to make a big decision he didn't want to make.

For years, Jones worked under such chief executives as Ralph Cordiner and Fred Borch, who must have seemed awesome and bigger than life-size to the determined younger man. But they apparently saw in the lanky, zealous Jones someone who would figure in GE's future. After a thorough, fifteen-year stretch in finance and operations, he was shifted into general management and appointed a group executive.

"At that point," Jones recalled, "I came to the attention of headhunters. Each approach from them represented, in a sense, a crisis. There were one or two instances that seemed so appealing that I looked into them. But I decided that the grass wasn't really greener on the other side."

Perhaps his decision to stay had been reinforced by the

results of an earlier, full-fledged crisis. It had occurred when GE's top brass had issued a set of edicts on reducing expenses and inventory in an effort to improve profits. In his own bailiwick, Jones had already undertaken to accomplish the same objective, and after studying the new set of controls he decided that they were unreasonable.

"I phoned the boss and told him I was tendering my resignation," Jones said. "I also told him that I was not accepting any absolute edicts, especially since I had already taken the necessary steps on my own initiative. I guess I was more incensed about that than about anything that I had ever encountered at GE."

Top management's answer was terse: Resignation not acceptable. The edicts are absolute only where similar action has not been taken.

Jones faced his next crisis when he was asked to become the company's financial vice-president. Why put him into general management, letting him taste the wine of the big view only to shunt him back into finance? Explaining that he liked his current job more, he refused. But the pressure was applied and he was forced to take the post. Then he found he liked it so much that he refused the next job he was offered, and this time he got away with it.

The ultimate crisis descended upon him in 1970 when General Electric decided it had to act to stem the severe losses of its computer division. Jones, then financial vice-president, had been one of those who had recommended some years earlier that GE get into computers. But in the effort to reduce the drain, the company set up a task force and asked Jones to be one of its members. Studying the reasons for the loss of several hundred million dollars over the years, the severe competition, and the immense impact of IBM over the entire field of computers, Jones reluctantly came to the decision that there was only one way to cut the losses and that was for GE to get out of the computer business.

"It was a terrible decision for me," Jones said. "I had been instrumental in GE's getting into the field and now I was convinced that we should get rid of the entire venture. It dawned on me, too, that I was the key man on the task force because of my financial responsibility. Was that why I was put on the task force? I didn't know. But I knew that GE traditionally never gives up on anything."

But his conscience wouldn't let him be dissuaded. His recommendation was approved by the full task force and presented to the board of directors. When the directors approved it they added a touch of irony. Jones was to be in charge of implementing the divestiture of a division he had helped to originate.

GE's divestiture wasn't quite that. It was more of a merger, true perhaps to the tradition that the company never liked to give up on anything. Most of GE's data-processing operations and the business of Honeywell, Inc., a more successful computer producer, were combined in a new company in which Honeywell would have an 81-percent ownership. For GE it was a humiliating experience, but at least the price of the transaction, about $240 million in notes and Honeywell common stock, repaid General Electric for most of its losses since the ill-fated division had begun in 1956. Together, the two companies had accounted in the premerger year of 1969 for only 8.7 percent of the industry's total shipments against IBM's 70-percent domination. And the Justice Department, which was already preparing an antitrust suit against IBM, didn't object to the birth of a new competitor, even though its market share would still be a puny one in contrast to IBM.

The merger news had a dramatic effect on the computer industry and that ever-increasing segment of Wall Street which was enamored with the potential of electronic data processing. Some analysts saw it all as a positive move for GE, which, they said, had now gotten "the albatross" off its neck. But others were very hard-nosed about it. They perceived it this way: GE, which enjoyed a reputation for showing considerable courage and vision in venturing into aerospace, nuclear energy, and advanced pollution-control systems, was now in the awkward position of virtually going out of the world's fastest-growing business, one that would probably be the world's biggest industry in the not-very-distant future. Was that any way, the critics wondered, for a dynamic company with multi-billion-dollar resources to behave?

The media coverage, basing it on the companies' releases, only quoted the two chief executives. But it was Jones who was in the middle of it all, although he was very much behind the scenes.

"It was," Jones said, "the toughest thing I ever had to do." When it was all over and he continued to advance in GE's hierarchy, he learned that it was his behavior during that critical time which had spurred the directors to tap him for the CEO post. Within a single year, 1972, he was successively advanced from vice-chairman to president to chairman of the board.

In 1973 and 1974, Americans were outraged by the stunning jump in sugar prices. At the supermarket level, a pound of sugar had traditionally sold for about twenty cents. But in that two-year period, shortages and speculation drove the price up more than 400 percent, bringing considerable resentment against cane- and beet-sugar refiners, Congressional investigations, and housewives' boycotts. Astronomically high refiner profits didn't soothe feelings much either.

The crisis came to roost in the offices of the principal American sugar refiners. For more than six months in 1974, Amstar Corporation, the largest (formerly known as the American Sugar Refining Company), was in the eye of the storm. Its president and chief executive, Robert T. Quittmeyer, found himself under the most intense pressure he had ever experienced.

The usually unflappable Quittmeyer had already been through an earlier crisis, one similar to that of John Bunting, chairman of the First Pennsylvania Trust Company. In a traumatic career shift, he had been thrown into the breach when Amstar's chief executive became seriously ill.

One of those people who seem always to be singled out, Quittmeyer grew up in Peekskill, New York, was a salutatorian in Peekskill High School, and held honors scholarships all through his undergraduate years at Columbia University. He graduated with a bachelor of arts degree and took honors in economics. At Columbia Law School he was editor of the *Law Review* before taking his law degree in 1946.

After some years with a New York law firm, he was hired in 1956 by Amstar's legal department. He rose to administrative vice-president and in 1971, as Quittmeyer himself put it, was "plucked from that post in answer to an emergency situation" when William F. Oliver, president, took ill. Oliver had already tapped him as a comer five years earlier when he had made Quittmeyer a vice-president and his own assistant in order to understudy the company's top management. Then Quittmeyer, at fifty-one, who had never suspected that he would someday head the company, found himself not only running it but without the support of his sponsor. Oliver died at age fifty-seven before the year had ended.

The new president quickly began applying one of the principles Oliver had taught him by example: remain committed to a policy of maintaining the company on its chosen track despite any unexpected occurrences that might jolt management. It was, of course, a principle that was to come into good use in the sugar crisis. He had seen Oliver demonstrate it a decade earlier.

In 1960, Fidel Castro expropriated $83 million of Amstar assets in Cuba, consisting of two large modern refineries and five cane fields. Undismayed by the adverse effects of this act on the balance sheet, however, Oliver geared Amstar for its future growth by building the country's most modern sugar refinery in Boston.

When the sugar crisis boiled up, however, Quittmeyer had difficulty understanding why Amstar and the other refiners were being so harshly condemned for their high earnings. For decades the industry's return on investment had been low compared to American manufacturing in general. Only in the early 1970s did that return on capital begin to creep up. But it was not a telling argument against the raw emotion Quittmeyer met.

"We came under very heavy criticism," he told me. "Everyone had to find a devil and we were it, as the biggest company in the industry. It didn't matter that it was all a simple supply-demand equation that had caught up with reality. World consumption in the previous four years had exceeded production and world stocks were short. We felt a severe frustration. How could we make them see? Would it be possible to get through all that emotion?"

Especially disconcerting was the fact that no one seemed to accept on faith the frequent explanation by Amstar and other refiners that in a volatile world market it was becoming increasingly difficult to obtain a desired price. The market was setting its own price and in a great sense the refiner was in the same boat as the consumer. Bitter editorials appeared, and at least four separate government investigations were launched with fanfare.

He lost sleep, grew nervous, and received anonymous calls threatening his life. "I was beleaguered, it seemed to me, on every front," said Quittmeyer. "But against the advice of friends I took no tranquilizers. If you hold a job that sometimes has fire under it, you should be able to handle it without artificial aids. It was—rough. There were the toilet-paper brigades in front of the supermarkets. My neighbors demanded explanations. . . ."

But, he recalled, he found some escape and support, even calmness, in prayer while attending church. "I'm not pious," he said, "but I think there is a great deal in prayer—in church services and in a fine sermon. It sustains you and helps you get away from strains and stresses. I knew, too, that I had done all I could."

Years later he could add, "It was the most difficult crisis in my career but it matured me. Maybe American consumers had never been without sugar or much else in the previous few decades and it was hard for them to accept it. But in retrospect I think I made the right decisions, especially to maintain our normal policies through the turmoil, to sustain supply, remain confident about the future, and not run away."

The Crisis-Packed Days and Nights of David Wallace

One of the more pertinent examples of crisis-prone lives caused by a reluctance to forget ethical beliefs is that of David W. Wallace, the chief executive of Bangor Punta Corporation. The Greenwich, Connecticut, concern is a rapidly growing conglomerate with interests in recreational boats, handguns, industrial and agricultural products, and aircraft.

Wallace's family had lived in Brooklyn since 1840. His grandfather had a bakery there for years but switched to building contracting. That may have been the reason for young David's decision to enter the Yale University School of Engineering in 1942. Halfway through his second year, he enlisted in the United States Army, became an infantry corporal, and was wounded twice. He was awarded a commission as an infantry officer, and after World War II ended he was assigned to guard prisoners at the Nuremberg war-crimes trials.

After returning to Yale in 1946 to get his engineering degree, he decided to change to law and five years later graduated from Harvard Law School. For three years he worked for the New York law firm of White & Case, where he was assigned to corporate law.

During the next two decades, Wallace was to know and work closely with four chief executives, each one among the nation's best known at the time, whose influence on the young lawyer helped to permanently mold him. He was also to be involved in the crises in each of their lives and in turn to face his own crises because of most of them.

The four were Robert Young, a Texas financier who amazingly emerged from the 1929 stock market crash with $1 million by selling short; Allan P. Kirby, a backer of Young in the Texan's successful move to acquire the New York Central Railroad and one of America's richest men in the mid-1960s, with a personal fortune of $300 million; Eli Black, the former rabbi who became chairman of the United Brands Corporation; and Nicolas Salgo, the founder and chairman of Bangor Punta. Both Young and Black were to commit suicide, self-destruction that Wallace recalled years later as acts of conscience by men unable to accept the unpredictable whims of reality.

Articulate, frank, anxious to balance his appraisals, Wallace explained in careful detail the crises in his professional life in terms of the four men:

"I first met Robert Young in 1954 as a young lawyer for White and Case. Mr. Young was going to try to get control of the New York Central with the backing of Mr. Kirby's holding company, the Allegheny Corporation. Mr. Young asked our law firm to handle some sales of Allegheny's which would help him to get the money to go after New York Central, and I was assigned to work with him.

"At that point, I was three years out of law school, earning all of seventy-five hundred a year. When Mr. Young got my bill for handling the sale of some key subsidiaries that had brought in millions of dollars, he said to me, 'I just paid the bill to White and Case. What are you earning?' When I told him he said, 'How would you like to come up here as general counsel? If you stay here, you'll have a good career, but I can't make you any promises because you're too young yet to be partner material.'

"I was fairly old, thirty, for where I was because I had spent four years in the army and had gone to college twice. My wife said, 'Stay with White and Case, you like it so much.' But I figured, what the hell, go for broke. So he lured me up there by doubling my salary. I became general counsel of a five-billion-dollar empire, earning fifteen thousand a year, but I thought Mr. Young was a great man.

"Shortly afterward, we got involved in some very difficult litigation stemming from the New York Central proxy fight, which we eventually won although the legal fight was sticky. During its course, I was down in Washington and on a Saturday called Mr. Young. He said, 'I was in our Washington lawyer's office the other day and we discussed different aspects of the case. I got advice from him that what you're saying is not right.' He didn't mean, of course, that I wasn't telling the truth but that my legal judgment was not right. I said, 'I would like to know who told you that because I don't think it's right and I would like to debate it.' He said, 'Well, never mind.' But I said, 'I can't be your lawyer if you are going to confront me with legal advice and I don't know the basis on which that advice was given.'

"We got into some pretty hot discussions on the telephone. Finally, he said, 'David, I think you had better come to my apartment at the Waldorf Towers as soon as you can get here.' 'Well,' I said, 'I have my car here in Washington. I can be in your apartment at nine o'clock Sunday morning.' I had taken my wife down with me—we didn't have any children at that time—and I said to her, 'Jean, it looks like I'm gonna get canned.' So we drove back. When I got there, Mr. Young said, 'I know what you said to me. You are trying to do the best job for me. And that you are loyal and honest. And I respect that. But the reason I wanted you here is to tell you that I don't like yes-men and I never want you to change. I want you to say exactly what you think. And I'm going to back that up by telling you that at the next board meeting you are going to be elected a vice-president. And I'm doubling your salary.' And that afternoon, I can tell you, I had more than one cocktail.

"On January 25, 1958, Mr. Young took his life with a shotgun. He was the chairman of the New York Central and he did well but his problems mounted. On January twentieth, the board decided against declaring the regular dividend. And I can tell you that he committed suicide really over remorse that he couldn't fulfill the promises he made to the New York Central shareholders when he won the proxy fight. He told them that he would put the stock on a two-dollar dividend basis and keep it on it and when that became impossible it just broke him. When he died, he had two million dollars in his checking account. He wasn't going busted. . . . But the situation kind of left me in charge of protecting the Young family. I was his personal lawyer as well as the general counsel for the Allegheny Corporation, New York Central's holding company, and I remain a close friend of Mrs. Young. I run all of Mrs. Young's affairs.

"And that, I guess, led to the next crisis. On Mr. Young's death, the New York Central-Allegheny empire was in a terribly chaotic state. Allan Kirby, Mr. Young's silent backer, was off on an around-the-world trip and I was really the senior person there. I had a group of directors who were trying to carve up the empire for themselves. I had to preserve Mr. Kirby's position. I felt he was the best man to take over the position of Mr. Young and I had to quiet down the operating people and I myself was pretty young at the time. Shortly after, Mr. Kirby made me executive vice-president and I was really the number-two man to him in Allegheny.

"Mr. Kirby seemed grateful for my efforts. But in the fall of 1959, he came to me and made a proposition. He was preparing for some changes at Allegheny, possibly for A. M. Sonnabend, the financier, coming into Allegheny too and because of my relationship with Mrs. Robert Young, Mr. Kirby wanted me in effect to promise him that Mrs. Young would support him in whatever happened in the company. I told Mr. Kirby that I had no brief against Mr. Sonnabend. I liked him, in fact, because he had been a friend of Mr. Young's. But I was not going to be a party to saying to Mrs. Young that she was going to vote in any particular way or that she had to pledge her stock.

"Mr. Kirby, though, was being pressed by some of his own people to get a commitment, come hell or high water, that was the way it was going to be. And then Mr. Kirby finally said to me, 'If Mrs. Young and I don't get along, whose side are you on?' I said, 'Well, I'm executive vice-president of this company and I would hope that I will be on nobody's side but the company's.

But if you ask me to take sides, I can't desert Mrs. Young. It wouldn't be fair. Mr. Young made me what I am. And as long as she wants my help, she is going to get it. And if that conflicted with your personal desires, then the conflict would have to be.' He said, 'I don't think that you can serve as an officer any more.' And that was it.

"Later, he relented and we kissed and made up, and he gave me a consulting arrangement. If I had wanted to betray the trust I felt I had with Mr. Young, I could have and none of that would have been. I think it was the best thing that ever happened to me. I realized after that that no one really gets hurt in the long run by sticking to what they believe because everything that happened after that has really helped me."

Wallace had known Eli Black for some years previous as head of a small company, the American Sealcap Corporation, with sales of about $30 million in milk-bottle and glass-bottle caps. After the ambitious, hustling Black acquired control of United Brands, the big produce and banana growers and marketers, he decided to invite Wallace to join the company. In 1960, Wallace became executive vice-president of United Brands and a member of the board.

"We were very good friends, but I felt that my experience was such that I was in a position to run a company myself," Wallace recalled. "I became United Brands' chairman of the executive committee. But Eli said that he would never make me president and chief operating officer or president and chief executive. He wanted those posts for himself. He said, 'I'll pay you any kind of money you want but I want those jobs for myself.' So there was an impasse, but when I left, though, I stayed on his board and his sudden suicide hit me very hard. I was especially distressed when some of the media went overboard and referred to him as 'Black Eli.'"

Wallace met Nicolas Salgo while both were on the board of Webb & Knapp. An energetic entrepreneur who had put together Bangor Punta in 1960, Salgo invited Wallace seven years later to become Bangor's president and chief operating officer. But, said Wallace, "I told him that I would come but you understand that if I had my druthers, I would prefer to be the CEO. And if I come, that's what I'm working for!" Salgo smiled and agreed and Wallace joined him. But by the end of six years,

Salgo no longer had any choice. His daring acquisitions and other zealous moves made his directors edgy. In 1973, they asked for his resignation and elected Wallace chief executive. And so the gangling, methodical baker's grandson found himself at the helm of a company made up of an odd combination —the remainder of the Punte Alegre Sugar Company that wasn't expropriated by Fidel Castro with the historic Bangor & Aroostook Railway of Maine.

But in spite of his triumph, what Wallace didn't know was that he was hardly done with crises. His greatest lay ahead to blot out much of his days and nights.

In 1969, Chris-Craft Industries acquired more than 200,000 shares of Piper Aircraft Company for some $11 million. The Piper family, which owned about one third of the 1.64 million outstanding shares of the aircraft manufacturer, wasn't anxious to sell to Chris-Craft. With the assistance of First Boston Corporation, the New England investment bankers, the family approached the Salgo-Wallace team as a rival contender to block Chris-Craft.

Bangor Punta and Piper signed an agreement, one that became highly controversial, particularly since part of it included offering for sale unregistered securities. When the SEC protested the violation of its regulations, both companies agreed not to engage in further violations and proceeded with their merger plan. But Chris-Craft wasn't sitting idly by after having built up its Piper investment to about one third of the aircraft company's stock. Litigation ensued, and in spite of Wallace's own legal background, Chris-Craft in 1976 won a stunning $36-million damage suit against Bangor Punta.

For Wallace, it was the most bitter disappointment of his career. When the judgment was issued, bank lines to Bangor Punta were immediately canceled. "Banks, you know," said Wallace, "give you an umbrella when the sun is shining and take it away when it's raining. But, as you can understand, we were deeply disturbed by the court decision. We were jointly and separately liable with First Boston, as well as the Piper family, for all of it. But if Bangor had to pay the whole thirty-six million, which was quite possible, when our net worth was only in excess of one hundred million— Nobody, you know, can come up with thirty or thirty-five percent of their net worth in cash to pay for damages. That would have put us out of business. The issue that decided the judge was that intent and good faith were not matters of concern. It's only a matter of whether you've technically violated the law. You are liable for damages, but whether it was justice is something else.

"I don't know how we could have avoided it, especially when our lawyers and our investment banker told us that what you have done is right," Wallace added. "But it is something that troubles me a great deal, that we are seeing a departure from the old traditions of common law where the idea was that you should be able to look at what the law has said in the past and have a pretty good idea of what the law is going to do in the future.

"Why is it happening?" Wallace asked. "I think it is all part of the attitude toward business where you get this great feeling on the part of a lot of courts of populism, courts which are the courts of the public, in other words, and not the courts of precedent. . . . All during the Chris-Craft litigation I had a number of people who kept telling me, 'Settle, settle, settle.' But I said we were right, we had done right, and eventually the law would vindicate us. For a while, I didn't look too bright. But I think if you're going to get some place and what's more important after you get there if you're going to respect yourself, then dammit, you've got to have the courage of your convictions."

On February 23, 1977, the U.S. Supreme Court overturned the $36-million damage award against Bangor Punta and also voided another lower-court ruling which barred Bangor from voting Piper shares that it had allegedly obtained by illegal means. Chris-Craft vowed to continue the fight in the state courts.

For David Wallace, the big crisis was over. It left him shaken but relieved and understandably bled.

13

The Private Company—Dynasties Without Stockholders

It may come as a surprise to those who believe that the Dow Jones industrial index of stocks and its tracking of Wall Street's gyrations of the bluest of blue-chip companies represents all American industry.

But the fact is that privately held or family-owned businesses, some with annual sales of as much as $2.5 billion, constitute an understructure in the national economy that accounts for one quarter of all jobs, one third of all sales, and one quarter of all profits.

So much time and attention have been paid to the publicly owned companies by the government, the financial community, and some 30 million investors that the private firms have remained largely invisible, except in their communities and in the promotion of their products and services. Yet in a number of ways, the family-controlled businesses have rendered even more important services to the American economy than merely their largely unsuspected contribution to the country's gross national product.

In the last three decades, large public companies have had unprecedented growth largely from feeding on the small- and medium-sized companies, acquiring thousands of them and absorbing their sales, profits, and staffs to swell their own operations. And because of the innovativeness and flexibility of these smaller companies, the metabolism of the ever-increasing public ones has been enriched, yielding a wealth of new products as well as entry into new markets. In addition, many private firms that have spurned the merger lures have grown at least as well as big public companies, often providing leadership in creativeness and marketing that has benefited entire industries.

How do chief executives of private companies function in terms of management, style, and effectiveness compared to the CEOs of public companies? Very differently indeed.

The main differences arise from the varied nature and structures of the two types of companies. Both strive for continuity. In the case of the public firm, it is continuity in profits and growth. If one professional management doesn't deliver it, another is promptly ushered in to try. In the case of the private firm, it is continuity of the family or the same management. Accelerating profits and growth are desirable but not essential to the management's survival. Nonetheless, an upward profit trend in an inflationary era is important for the private firm too. In any case, privacy isn't surrendered.

"Our way of safeguarding our principles and beliefs is to remain a privately held company," says Samuel C. Johnson, II, chairman and chief executive of S. C. Johnson & Son, Inc., of Racine, Wisconsin. "Our way of reinforcing them is to make profits through growth and development, profits which will allow us to do more for all the people on whom we depend," he adds.

Johnson, in his mid-fifties, is the fourth-generation member of the Johnson family to head the one-hundred-year-old company, maker of Johnson Wax and other well-known household and personal-care products. Its $1-billion-plus sales put it among the ten largest private American companies.

What differentiates the private-company experience from the public one is "the intimate sense of being part of a unified family," reports CCMP Management Consultants, New York. "By contrast, what shapes a public corporation most powerfully is not unity but competition. The very word takes on a holy ring when mentioned within earshot of the investing public—that vast, remote, impersonal, constantly changing and often ignorant 'Great Beast' that owns and theoretically controls the public company."

In its study of private versus public companies, CCMP said, "from the corporate viewpoint, the Beast's interest is strictly material: It is continuity of financially measurable growth in profits and earnings-per-share that is key. Consequently, the chief concern of corporate management, the focus of planning and information systems, and main criterion for executive advancement is the ability to demonstrate such steady continuity, regardless of the business's natural ebb and flow. The contest thus created is often fiercer internally than externally, deadlier to fellow executives, than to rival companies.

"Some say such internal warfare is what powers commercial creativity," the consulting firm said.

Given those differences of competition and continuity, the natures and drives of the two CEOs make for these divergent characteristics and internal corporate environments:

With a survival rate of roughly six and a half years, the head of a public company has only a short run on the stage and gears his decision-making to achieve quick success. He knows that if his performance is to be extended or to lead to bigger and better roles elsewhere, he must show a dramatic skill in building the company's assets. As he pushes himself to deliver an unqualified success, his executives are consciously whipped to help him achieve it in a constant process that they too know only allows them a short-run opportunity. The challenge they have to meet often involves them in a frenzy, the more so the higher they climb the corporate ladder.

But the CEO of a private company must only satisfy himself and his family members, who also hold substantial interest in the company. If he is a professional manager employed to run a business, his only major need is to continue to have the approval of the owners. In any case, he doesn't have to suffer the nit-picking of small investors or the barbs of their advocates. He doesn't have to concern himself with scrutiny of the Securities and Exchange Commission, an agency whose increasing investigations give public CEOs nightmares. Above all, the private CEO, especially if he is a member of the owning family, is frequently the absolute ruler of his kingdom, able to create and carry out his own laws. If he wants to, he is able to act as judge, prosecutor, and jury over his own employees, but mostly he takes a softer stance, performing a paternalistic role, alternately humane and stern.

His executives—unlike their counterparts in a public company, where though always uncertain they may always hope to become CEO themselves—know that the top spot in a private company will probably never come within their grasp. So the internal competition among them is lessened, the ambience is friendlier, and there is often a warm camaraderie. But much of this also depends upon the private CEO. Even if he is given to playing one man against another, a trait that marked many of the earlier entrepreneurs but seems to have diminished in their sons, his executives can only jostle one another and occasionally rap one another on the butt, locker-room style.

Invading Three Famous but Private Enclaves

But if the style and traits of the private chief executive set the pattern for those of his executives, the bigger question is what those traits do for the company itself. In most large private companies, policies and dictums laid down by the founder often persist into later generations but are necessarily refined in the light of new economic and social conditions. This earmark of largely unchanging business and personal credos is much truer of the private company than it is of the public company, where succeeding managements tend to dilute and radically alter the founding policies.

Imbued with such patriarchal instincts, how do private companies behave in terms of marketing, product innovation, research, diversification, employee relations, and customer communications? And how do these methods differ from public companies?

Hallmark: Controversial Moves from Mid-America

"My father, Joyce C. Hall, at eighty-six is still rather active. He comes into the office three times a week," said Donald J. Hall, president of Hallmark Cards.

"My people and I spend time with him when he is in, often half of each day that he shows up. And besides my father, who founded our company, I'm answerable to a board of directors that has both inside and outside members. So I'm not quite an absolute ruler. I believe in total input from our people—and it has helped our business immensely," Hall said.

Hallmark's sales in excess of $500 million a year derive

mostly from the greeting-card business, in which the company commands about 35 percent of the national market. The concern, based in Kansas City, Missouri, has one of the largest creative staffs in the world, considerably larger than any advertising agency. Three hundred design artists work with about 150 others in various other creative and technical functions.

"With creative marketing, production, and selling staffs of large size," Hall said, "we have more than the usual amount of meetings with groups. In Kansas City, for example, we attach representatives from our personnel department to the various divisions and plants (two or three to each), who spend their entire time with the employees. We don't want to circumvent our managers, but we find that the input grows from allowing our personnel field men to sit in with groups of about thirty to forty employees.

"We figure that about sixty percent of the suggestions that come upward are prevented from being cut off by the presence of the personnel reps," Hall said. "This is no reflection on the departmental and divisional managers but merely shows that the presence of a staff representative on the line frees communications. Maybe it makes the workers eager to show that they can think too. But in any event it's a policy that has worked well."

In 1966, Hall, only thirty-seven then, succeeded his father as Hallmark's chief executive, having put in a twenty-year apprenticeship. It was the first time in more than half a century that the indisputable leader of the greeting-card industry (Hallmark in its desire for dignity calls it the "social expression" industry) hadn't been run by Joyce Hall.

(True to the American canon of success, that is, an idea and a man devoted to it must succeed if both are good enough,) Hallmark emerged from a tiny business in 1907 in which the three Hall brothers, Joyce, Rollie, and Bill, sold imported picture postcards in the town of Norfolk, Nebraska. Joyce, the youngest, was also the most ambitious and restless. At the age of nine he had started working, selling perfume from door to door. By the time he was eighteen he had decided he was ready for the big city, and he departed from Norfolk with a battered suitcase and two shoe boxes full of picture cards and checked into the Young Men's Christian Association in Kansas City. His youth and frail inventory failed to cut much of a swath. Every day

207

was a survival test for his tiny store. But persistence helped and a year later, in 1911, he was joined by his two brothers. In 1916, they were wiped out by a fire. However, a local banker was impressed by the brothers' diligence and lent them $25,000 to buy an engraving firm that had done some work for them.

During the Christmas season of 1915, Hallmark showed its first original designs—simple, unfolded cards only 2½ inches by 4 inches in size. Friendship and inspiration were the themes. "When you get to the end of your rope," one read, "tie a knot in it and hang on." In 1923, Hall Brothers, as the company was known until the name was changed again in 1954, took a new six-story building as its headquarters. In 1922, paper gift wrappings were added and shortly afterward self-adhering colored ribbon.

Hallmark's success was steady, but even three decades later it was still the same three-product company. New facilities had been added. In 1945 a small plant was opened in Topeka; two years later another began operations in Leavenworth, Kansas; and in 1958 a third was devoted to making the shiny, sticky ribbons in Lawrence, Kansas. But, looking back on fifty years of gratifying but unspectacular success, Joyce Hall now girded the company for dramatic moves.

Propelled into new product lines in the 1960s—party goods in 1960, stationery in 1964, puzzles and Hallmark books in 1967, candles in 1968—the quiet, private company seemed to be exploding with creative new efforts. Computerized distribution centers and giant new plants spewed forth a tide of goods to dealers who capitalized on the public's growing faith in the products labeled Hallmark. Company sales tripled in the decade.

Yet Hallmark, the epitome of solid, basic midwestern values and virtues, took two if not three dramatic steps that seemed out of character. They caused company watchers impressed with Joyce Hall's firm judgments to wonder if his balance hadn't slipped with age. Why would a businessman who often declared, "Good taste is good business," carry it out in a series of moves that seemed daring, foolhardy, and impractical?

The first move was the company's television series, the "Hallmark Hall of Fame," started in 1951, which cost the company more than $50 million within the next dozen years. The TV dramatic specials drew mostly mediocre audience ratings, despite enthusiastic reviews by critics. Yet despite the lackadaisical attention most TV viewers gave the series, Hallmark confidently backed it. In 1972, Donald Hall, now ensconced in the CEO's chair, announced that Hallmark would spend another $60 million to maintain for another decade the show which critics had labeled "an oasis in television's wasteland" but from which viewers largely flipped the dial in favor of crime, soap operas, and talk shows.

The second move, taken in 1963, involved the opening of the Hallmark Gallery, an elegant showplace for the firm's products on Fifth Avenue in Manhattan, one of the country's highest-rent business districts. The general reaction was: good taste, yes, profits, no. At best, the store designed by Edward Durrell Stone, one of the outstanding American architects, never did more than break even. And so it stands, a tasteful testimonial to faith amid the confluence of some of the world's best-known, posh stores—Tiffany, Cartier, Bergdorf Goodman, Henri Bendel, Saks Fifth Avenue, Harry Winston, and Bonwit Teller.

But it was the third and latest move which really threw observers and no doubt convinced advocates of public companies that they were indeed blessed to have curbs on management. No monarchies, benevolent or otherwise, for them. The subject of the new controversy and the object of some derision was Hallmark's $400-million Crown Center, a twenty-three-square block of real estate that the eighty-year-old Joyce Hall had erected to surround Hallmark's Kansas City headquarters. Now almost complete, the vast redevelopment complex will eventually include a 730-room hotel, a shopping center with sixty-five stores, apartment houses, a motel, office buildings, and a bank. Fully conceived and financed by Hallmark, the project has already won praise for its architectural beauty and its replacement of urban blight. But for a variety of reasons, including its location and the meticulous care Joyce Hall insisted be lavished on it in spite of the expense, Crown Center will probably take twice as long to earn a profit as most other large real-estate projects.

The three moves might never have been taken if Hallmark had been a public company, subject to the scrutiny of big and little stockholders or a board of directors. "We have a board much like a public company's and it is objective," says Donald Hall confidently. And it is true that most large private companies have taken pains to ensure that their boards maintain a sense of independence. But in the case of Hallmark it's safe to assume that unbridled success, a policy emphasizing quality, efficiency, and dramatic entrepreneurism, would be especially hard for a board, however independent, to contain. At a time when the director's role has become more important than it ever was, that may spell one of the biggest differences between private and public companies.

There is another side to this. Burdened with the censoring effect of militant directors and unhappy stockholders, Hallmark as a public company might also have had trouble pushing through with its emphasis on quality which, as Donald Hall puts it, "intrigues us so much. If we can't do something that is top quality, we just don't do it." Bottom-line consideration, whether profit margin on sales or the return on investment, often dominates directors' thinking. And yet much of Hallmark's success, despite the doubters who scoff at such apparent idealism, comes from its internal standards. And that—the results themselves—most likely is the answer to the question of whether private companies or public companies are better structured to yield results.

Johnson's Wax: A Product to Lead Every Market

"As a private company, we have the competitive advantage of not having our guts laid out every fiscal quarter or our strategies exposed to the world at large," declared Samuel C. Johnson, II, of S. C. Johnson & Son. "Our competition are all public companies, so while we're a mystery to them, they are not to us and have to tell us how they are doing."

One of the few chief executives interviewed for this book who did not insist that his press-relations man be present during the talk, Johnson was asked whether his competitive advantage of corporate privacy wasn't being defeated by his executives' exchanging information with those of the competition and by the so-called trade grapevine.

"Our guys have been told not to talk to competitive executives," he replied. "They have been repeatedly told that—and that I only believe in beating the competition, not tipping our hand to them. As far as the grapevine is concerned, we're headquartered in Racine, not New York, Chicago, or Los Angeles, and that makes the grapevine rather long."

Johnson stressed that the main difference between CEOs of private companies and those running public companies comes from "the requirements for public-company disclosure of operating results. These push the chief executive into making decisions that will always thrust their results upward. But in private companies we make decisions primarily for the long term, the long pull. I know that some CEOs of public companies would argue the point, but I believe nonetheless that this is the case. It's especially true considering the relatively short tenure the public CEO has compared to his private-company counterpart."

Considered by market analysts a singular blend of the traditional and the unusual, S. C. Johnson may treasure its privacy like other family-owned businesses, but it is quite aggressive in communicating with its two publics—its trade customers and the millions of consumers who have made its products the number-one sellers in four product areas: floor care, furniture care, insecticides, and air fresheners. The company is also number two in auto wax and shoe polish.

"Retailers and consumers are the most important audiences to us," says Johnson. "We communicate through our five-hundred-man sales force to our retail dealers, especially the major chains, and we spend something like fifteen percent of our sales on advertising to tell the public about our household products and their qualities."

A great-grandson and namesake of the company's founder, Johnson said he is willing to take risks, and he claims that unlike public-company CEOs he isn't afraid to make mistakes. Several years ago he introduced four new products—all toiletries to compete in the frenetic personal-care market—and promptly failed on three of them. Recalling, he said, "I take more risks because my mistakes aren't as visible as in the public company. Well, I've been wrong a lot as well as right a lot. But let's face it, you can get too conservative if you always want to be right."

That risk principle apparently began some ninety years ago when Samuel Curtis Johnson changed the original intent of the enterprise and started a business dynasty, the members of which still own 90 percent of the company's holdings.

In 1886 in an old shed in Racine, S. C. Johnson and two young helpers began making parquet flooring, selling with each installation a container of wax that Johnson had also manufactured. Homeowners also received instructions how to use the wax to clean and protect the new flooring. As the tiny company grew, Johnson attracted more orders for his paste wax than for his flooring. He began concentrating on Johnson's Wax and it became the mainstay of an eventual 150 products and a vast company with twenty major field installations in major American markets and forty overseas subsidiaries. Yet even today that original product still dominates the home floor-care market.

In several ways, founder Sam Johnson resembled Joyce Hall. He displayed a similar zeal to issue new products, to seek individual "franchises" in specific product categories, to ferret out consumer needs and meet them with better items that could quickly capture leadership, and to develop them through a large research arm, which in Johnson's case eventually numbered more than six hundred employees. Although he liked to refer to his business as "a backwoods chemicals mixer-upper," his ambition and innovativeness were far greater than the homey term indicated.

Products streamed out of Racine across the country and abroad. In 1914, the company opened its first foreign subsidiary in Great Britain, and the more than three dozen that followed remained all virtually wholly owned by S. C. Johnson. Foreign sales mushroomed to account for more than 50 percent of total sales. But Sam Johnson and his three descendants who later filled the chief executive's chair didn't always click with new efforts. A move into household paint, a product subject to sharp price rivalry, produced only puny profits. Invading the automotive-care market, the Johnson firm stubbed its toe on a line of antifreeze, radiator cleaners, and lubricants. In 1958, the company suffered a costly failure with a venture into specialty industrial chemicals and also later with an unsuccessful lawn-care product.

But it succeeded brilliantly with others. Many of its products, either number one or two in national sales, are household names: Pledge furniture polish, Future acrylic floor finish, Rain Barrel fabric softener, Edge shaving gel, Glo-Coat floor polish, and Agree creme rinse and hair conditioner. The company boasts that Agree, introduced in January 1976, forged to the top position in its field within six months, beating competitive products by Revlon, Clairol, Breck, and Alberto-Culver—all more experienced cosmetics producers. Industry data backs up the claim. A high initial $7-million advertising budget helped boost Agree to its speedy success, along with some solid market research.

All in all, it's probably not difficult to understand why the Johnson firm was recently referred to as the sort of company investors would love to invest in if they could. And whether one views the starkly modern Frank Lloyd Wright–designed Racine headquarters, the company's long subsidizing of American art competitions, its heavy radio sponsorship starting with the early Fibber McGee and Molly series and later television shows, its employee profit-sharing plan of 25 percent of pretax profits, and its long efforts to help improve urban conditions, it's also hard to see what S. C. Johnson is losing, if anything, by remaining a private company.

But Sam Johnson sees it the other way—what it has gained from staying family owned.

"In the closely held company where there is a continuity of management, there is also a continuity of philosophy that bridges the generations," he observed. "This encompasses employee benefits—our profit-sharing plan has been in effect since 1918; new product policy, never just a me-too effort but carefully studied by our unusually large research team; and community relations, which is helped by the fact that family-run businesses tend to be closely integrated into the community. We give five percent of our pretax profits to charity—only one percent is the national corporate average."

How does a private company borrow money, make acquisitions, and in general finance its way without common and preferred stock that have easily traded market values?

"We don't have access to the equity market," Johnson said, "but we do to the debt market or the private-placement debt market. You have to manage yourself to have enough reserve borrowing power by not leveraging the company too much. Our policy is to borrow no more than up to twenty-five percent of our net worth plus debt, although, frankly, we could get up to seventy-five percent as some public companies do. But we have extensive banking relationships in which we freely furnish our figures, and it has worked well. In the last five years, we have bought sixteen companies, and all for cash through increasing our debt."

What's the big disadvantage in remaining private? Estate taxes, he said. "The tax laws are set up to prevent companies from being passed on to succeeding generations of ownership and that is a major problem for us. Estate taxes are essentially punitive, and so we have had to make plans to continue our ownership. But tax problems could well affect that."

Aside from his conviction that private companies can do everything public ones do—and maybe better—he believes that as CEO (and owner-entrepreneur) he has fewer reins on him than his public-company counterpart. But, he added, "What drives my engine is probably the same as his—competitive spirit and a drive to make the company grow. But then," Johnson went on with a broad smile, "I've had an advantage. I was born into the business and it would have been difficult to fire me. Maybe that helps me take risks that public CEOs might easily hesitate over."

Beech-Nut: Natural to Be Different

Beginning a new career at fifty-three, buying a losing division from a giant food conglomerate, and thoroughly revamping it and casting forth into uncharted territory would be unusual enough for someone well equipped with funds and suitable experience.

But Frank C. Nicholas, a lawyer with no sizable funds of his own and only a year's professional experience in the baby-food business, did all those things, helped by the entrepreneurial freedom allowed in the private company and the happy streak of the gambler. In 1973, a year after he and two partners had bought a tiny baby-cereal company, Nicholas borrowed $16.5 million to buy the baby-food division of the Squibb Corporation. And then he started the $400-million industry by marketing two radically different products, both controversial enough to arouse the resentment of traditional companies and to bring him prime-time national publicity.

Nicholas, however, is one of those super-confident salesmen who seem to know they have half the battle won. He generates such evident sincerity that what might be unpleasant abrasiveness in others is accepted as the behavior of an arm-waving enthusiast interested only in elbowing reluctant mountains.

Growing up in Minneapolis, Nicholas started his entrepreneurship early as a somewhat overage undergraduate at

Northwestern University in Evanston. His later serious intent may have come from his abrupt medical discharge from the U.S. Army Air Force when the plane he was navigating flew 350 miles off course over China. When the aircraft ran out of gas, he bailed out with the rest of the crew, got badly smashed up, and was given a discharge and pension. Living "more or less on candy bars" at the university, Nicholas noticed that the vending machines were constantly running out of candy and convinced the campus administration to give him the candy concession. By refilling the machines four times daily in between classes, outrunning and outmaneuvering a faculty competitor, Nicholas in due course was selling 90,000 candy bars monthly. His success allowed him to take over such other concessions as laundry and flowers. Shortly after enrolling in the university's law school, he was earning $1,000 a month in profits.

Receiving his law degree in 1952 at the relatively advanced age of thirty-two, he was in a hurry to take on the world. But the $250-a-month starting salary for young lawyers didn't suit him. He had to make some money and he did, but it took a while. In the next twenty years, holding such jobs as sales manager for the Brunswick Corporation, the leisure-time products producer, as executive vice-president of Alcoa Corporation, the aluminum giant, and in several other sales and marketing jobs, he wound up a millionaire. During the latter years of those two decades, however, he quit working for others and became a lawyer in Bucks County, Pennsylvania, where he acquired a 250-acre farm on which he now lives with his second wife and six children.

The lawyer's life wasn't active enough for him. In 1972, using some of his own money, he and two others bought Baker Laboratories, a maker of baby formulas, from Pfizer Inc. But it was only a tiny contender in a huge marketplace. Soon, Nicholas was ready to expand his toehold, but this wasn't the case with the bankers whom he approached to help him.

The problem was that Nicholas had sighted in on a loser—Squibb's Beech-Nut baby-foods division, on which the otherwise profitable company had lost $8 million that same year. "I went to just about every major bank in the United States," Nicholas said. "Squibb Beech-Nut had a net worth of twenty-seven and a half million dollars. I tested an offer of sixteen and a half million on them, eleven and a half million in cash and a note for five million—and they didn't say no or yes. But every banker I got to came up with the same question. 'If Squibb with all their resources and talents lost eight million on it, what makes you think you can do better?' And then they asked another question. 'What's your background again?' I just couldn't answer those questions to their satisfaction."

But a Milwaukee bank that had turned him down referred him to the Walter E. Heller Company, a commercial finance firm. Heller took a good, hard look at the ebullient salesman-lawyer-businessman with the heavy white sideburns, at what he had already done, and decided to take a chance. "I was absolutely delighted," Nicholas said. "Squibb accepted. It was a bargain-basement price but I think Squibb was glad to get off the hook."

Once over that hump, though, he found he now had to climb a few more. The newly acquired company, it turned out, had a selling cost of 15.4 percent of sales. It should have been about 6 percent to turn a profit. Promotional costs ran to almost 20 percent of sales, more than twice what they should have been. In other words, 35 percent of the company's volume was being swallowed up by salesmen's and sales manager's salaries, their automobiles, fringe benefits, advertising, and promotion.

In addition, the internal climate was restricted, unproductive, and not inclined to expense budgeting, Nicholas found. "Regional executives and others never talked to anyone one or more rungs below or above them," he said. "And there was a bunch of MBA-type executives who had developed Machiavellian instincts for spending the company's money. Why not? It wasn't their own."

Nicholas's scythe promptly swept hard and wide. Some top executives were let go. The 750-man sales staff was cut to 200. Nicholas switched major distribution from total reliance on a sales staff to substantial use of food brokers, who are manufacturer's agents and unlike salesmen are only paid when they sell his goods.

Within a few years, the 15.4-percent selling cost had been cut to a viable 6.5 percent.

But the big controversies on products were still ahead. Early in 1977, Nicholas purged all Beech-Nut's baby foods of added salt and sugar. He did this in the belief that the two ingredients were conducive in later life to hypertension, obesity, dental problems, and allergies. "For forty years," he said, "the baby-foods industry made its products to suit the mother, who has a totally different taste sense than a baby. Babies have almost none at all until they are five or six months old. Why give them something that can't mean much to them but can hurt them later?"

The move was anathema to the traditional competitors. Most immediately blasted Nicholas, but some quickly followed suit. As far as the public was concerned, however, Nicholas realized that he had a major educational job ahead of him. For nine months he traveled around the country, appearing on television and radio talk shows, giving interviews, and speaking before women's groups. He appeared on the "Today" show and other major TV talk shows. But sales slowly moved up, first from curiosity and then more quickly from the growing acceptance of the health aspect of the Beech-Nut effort. Within six months the revitalized Beech-Nut was pushing Heinz for the number-two spot and was beginning to concern Gerber, the market leader.

The next controversial move was to take the baby fruit juice out of a can and put it into a bottle with the top threaded to fit the store-bought rubber nipple. It was a small change but daring in a market in which change was glacial. Competitors scoffed at the step. Two medical groups—the American Academy of Pediatrics and the American Academy of Pedodontics—issued statements warning that the fruit-juice bottle could lead to increased tooth decay if babies get to like the bottle too much and drink more fruit juice than they should. In less than a year, however, sales of the bottled juice jumped 400 percent. Nicholas, flushed with that success and happy letters from mothers, quickly reformulated all the company's cereals.

"Why didn't Heinz, Gerber, or even Squibb do it all?" asked Nicholas in an interview during which his excitement kept him on the edge of his chair, gesticulating and almost shouting. "I'll tell you why they didn't. It would have been a risk, that's why. I think that the majority of public companies make their decisions based on the effect on the stock market. They're afraid to rock the boat. Well, we're not."

Given his degree of push, salesmanship, and ambition, he was asked, how can anyone be certain that Nicholas and Beech-Nut won't suddenly go public?

Shrugging his heavy shoulders, he replied with a grin, "Look, we need the financing and the assets to move up and get bigger. We're not that far from one hundred million dollars in sales now, and that's a big jump but it's just the start. We certainly aren't going to stay where we are, right? So we may go public someday. But I'll tell you this—if I do sell to the public or sell the business to a bigger company, I'll make my freedom a condition of either step. That's a must!"

Private Dreams, Public Realities

Behavior comes from motivation and life-style. If the varying behavior between chief executives of private companies and those of public companies depends upon one single factor, however, it is obvious that it is the effect of both individual motivation and corporate life-style. The private-company CEO retains direct entrepreneurial responsibilities while the public CEO, who is mostly a professional manager, is a caretaker of limited entrepreneurial initiative. That primary initiative may well be vested in a team.

But the private-company chief executive not only makes and implements his own decisions but also decides who will serve as the filter or sieve for those decisions.

Every characteristic of either type of company is molded by that basic difference, allowing these conclusions:

Since the head of the private company is a despot or can be one, each such institution represents a monarchy, benevolent or absolute. Executives and employees are taken care of, depending upon the whim of the chief executive. But generally, in order to retain people, the private company's policy toward employees is paternalistic. No private-company "family retainer," as CCMP puts it in its study, "goes unrewarded for loyal service."

Yet the private firm cannot live in a vacuum. In many cases, it strives to attract proven executives from public companies. The S. C. Johnson firm has many. In fact, its president, William K. Eastham, came to it from the American Home Products Company, rising in twelve years to the private-company's second-highest post. Hallmark also has a number of key executives from public companies.

But despite the privacy that it savors, the family-owned business must compete with the public ones in its markets. The enlightened private firm, knowing that entrepreneurship is its secret weapon, gives constant challenges to its executives to ensure constant motivation. "Give me some guys who seem to have a thread of dynamism in them and I'll throw responsibility at them far beyond what they ever had," Frank Nicholas says. "I have nine guys like that and they're doing a fabulous job."

Compared with the public company, there is some basis to say that the large private company treats its employees better and takes a clearer overall interest in them. Is it despotic benevolence or a protectiveness to assure its needs in the human marketplace or simply a more sensitive instinct on what each individual contributes in a quasi-family atmosphere?

Asked the question, Donald Hall of Hallmark replied that it could be all these but added, "Late in 1974 my parents signed an agreement to sell—upon their deaths—a substantial portion of their Hallmark holdings to the employee stock-ownership trust. This agreement assured the employees that their fund would have the opportunity to become a substantial shareholder in the corporation. When my mother passed away in March 1976, her estate sold more than $28-million worth of Hallmark stock to the employee ownership fund."

More than fifty major American companies with annual sales of more than $100 million remain privately owned. They include companies as large as Cargill, Inc., the big grain and commodities concern with sales of $2.5 billion; Hearst Corporation, with sales of more than $600 million; Milliken Corporation, the textile giant with $1 billion in sales; Reader's Digest Association, with sales of $350 million; and the E. J. Gallo winery, with sales of about $150 million. And among smaller companies there are thousands that remain private, a greater number than those that sold their stock to the public.

Some that pursued the public route have been attempting in recent years to buy back their stock and "go private." This trend, as well as the more pervading one to remain private, will undoubtedly continue as long as the equities market remains erratic, trapped in its four-year slide from the 1,000 Dow-Jones level. But even then there will remain a substantial share of American business that will prefer its own privacy, its ability to move without all the strings on the public company, and, in short, to go its own way.

14

How They Live

Now You See Him, Now You—

In their private lives, America's corporate elite inhabit fishbowls with walled-in sides.

Although many are among the best-known Americans, most have unlisted telephone numbers, do not give out their home addresses, live in apartments or homes with tight security, and do not like to mix their home and business lives. Those who live in suburban enclaves have a standing arrangement with local police, sheriffs, state troopers, and county attorneys to keep their presence inviolate and make it difficult for outsiders to intrude on their privacy. A prying tourist or stranger may soon find that he is stopped by a suspicious trooper or local policeman and asked for his identification.

Conversely, the same chief executive out on the town with his wife, girl friend, or male friends will be hurt if eyes do not curiously follow him, if there isn't a hushed stir at the restaurant, nightclub, concert hall, or opera as he makes his way through it. He does not openly invite the maître d' to announce him, but he probably won't chastise him if the word is spread that "the big man" has arrived.

A paradox on the surface, this behavior isn't hard to understand for those who watch and know the American CEO. Part of his psychic reward is personal recognition, even a modicum of notoriety. But harassed and put upon by a host of complicated pressures and obligations, some of them either inappropriate or unfair in his view, he finds that he must protect his privacy and even preserve a portion of his business day for himself. In that sense, he has the celebrity syndrome of here I am, there I'm not. By seeking the limelight while also hiding from prying eyes, the contradictory traits of his private personality give him a mystique that confuses people and probably reduces their sense of empathy with him.

Yet, as though tempted by the challenge of understanding him, Americans are fascinated by the personal lives of the rich and the powerful. They read with avid interest newspaper stories about the industrialist's marital adventures or problems, usually when a divorce suit hits the courts and the press. Features about corporate jet-setters on deep-sea adventures or safaris are read with wide eyes and sighs. The splurge of "People" columns in newspapers and magazines across the country and similar capsule news segments on television is an attempt to satisfy the appetite for the hungry glimpse into the private lives of celebrities of all kinds. And nothing, it seems, piques as much curiosity as the family affairs of the tycoon, whether it involves an errant son, daughter, or grandchild, or charges of adultery by husband against wife, or vice versa.

Do we shed as many tears over the personal problems of the most successful as we would over the faceless, average man? Not likely. Our interest in the celebrity's fallibility is no doubt a combination of curiosity and envy rather than sympathy. There may also be an inverse relationship between that envy and the satisfaction of seeing the mighty plagued by the same problems and irritants as you and I.

And many businessmen seem to sense it. They know that envy, probably one of the most undiluted of human traits, turns the attitude toward them more critical and less sympathetic than if they were viewed simply as ordinary citizens. But they too are human and have the same instincts. The very gossip columnists whom they avoid draw their eager attention as if they were just another wide-eyed, panting reader or TV viewer. And when the CEO reads some feisty gossip about one of his own kind, he may regret it but he reads on avidly.

The walled-in fishbowl lives of many chief executives are reflected in a variety of forms, the extremes of which make the head spin.

Early in 1978, the New York City police department mounted an elaborate kidnapping exercise, more detailed than three earlier ones, involving the close participation of a major company. The identity wasn't disclosed but its anonymity was explained by the claim that the company had become very sensitive over past kidnapping threats.

That sensitivity had grown because of a wave of kidnappings of industrialists in Western Europe and Latin America, leading to fears that American chief executives might be next. Some in this country had already begun to take preventive measures such as the use of armored limousines with drivers who doubled as bodyguards. One head of a large company already knew about violence. A year earlier he and his wife had returned late one night to their suburban home, surprising two burglars who were looting the house. The couple was gagged and chained to their refrigerator while the thieves completed their work. Terrorism, in fact, is a growing fear among American CEOs. Though he is a happy bird-watcher, Clifford Garvin, chief executive of Exxon Corporation, the world's largest refiner of oil, decided in spring 1978 against any further interviews, including a requested one from *Audubon* magazine, which left the publication's editors sorely disappointed. Such is the fear over terrorism.

The Manhattan police exercise was, in its mobility and unexpected twists, not unlike something out of "The Late Show." The police dashed after "Kidnapper One" when the ransom drop was made to "Kidnapper Two," but somehow "Kidnapper One" changed clothes and disappeared into the crowds at the World Trade Center. And then "Kidnapper Two," a member of a special police unit, evaded the clutches of the pursuers. The theory behind it all was to study mistakes made in the pursuit in order to ensure that they weren't repeated when and if the real thing happened.

But the same chief executives who might have participated in or invited such police war games aimed at protecting them are just as prone to project themselves—or be projected—into the limelight. Besides the publicity and hoopla involved in civic and philanthropic events, corporate sponsorship of the arts often places the CEO in the role of host and thus in the spotlight.

A typical such event occurred only four months after the police exercise. SCM Corporation, the business-machines, paint, and food conglomerate, sponsored a retrospective showing of the works of painter Saul Steinberg at the Whitney Museum of Modern Art. Paul Elicker, SCM's president, drifted through the colorful ranks of about 180 personalities, artists, critics, academics, and writers. Besides Elicker and his wife, Jane, the heady gathering, which tried not to fawn over Jacqueline Onassis, Woody Allen, and of course Saul Steinberg, included Thomas Carroll, president of Lever Brothers, Oscar Kolin, the chairman of Helena Rubinstein, and other not-as-well-known businessmen. Jane Elicker, surveying the variety of people and the gaiety, mused out loud, "I think that artists have learned that business people aren't so bad."

But even on that exposed stage, life can take a hazardous turn. At a similar gathering only months before, John W. Christian, Jr., the president of B. Altman & Company, the New York department store, slipped at the head of a museum stairway and plummeted down, striking his head severely on the steps. He was incapacitated for more than ten weeks.

The CEO's exposure at such events represents part of his company's community relations, recognition that goodwill must be earned not just from good intentions but from participation as well. Retailers go further than most companies, with such as Bloomingdale's in New York, Neiman-Marcus in Dallas, and I. Magnin in San Francisco tying in store openings with charitable or cultural happenings. Industrial companies, too, are following this route, underwriting various community events while allowing their products and services to be exposed along with it.

But the presence of the company chiefs at such affairs, and their appearances on talk shows and public-broadcasting seminars, is neither wholehearted nor the rule. The pressure to emerge from the insulated offices grows at an irritating rate, forcing a sense of urgency on the man inside that makes him crave every iota of privacy he can squeeze out of his life.

"Being a CEO is a lonely business," observes Kenneth Randall, president of the Conference Board. "On his side of the desk there is no one else there with him. But on the other side it is excessively populated. There are too many demands on him, too many people and too many organizations that want his time. So he has to parcel it out and be very selfish about his private life."

Where He Lives and How He Relaxes

Most chief executives have several homes—an apartment in the city or suburbs, a house in the suburbs, an apartment in the Sun Belt states, mostly Florida, and a condominium or villa in the Caribbean, on the Riviera, or on another European sun island. Not every one has all these, but most have at least two and some have as many as nine.

Why two and why nine? The difference is between the new money and the old money. CEOs from modest circumstances never really try to catapult out of the more modest way of life. A good example is perhaps the segment that follows on William M. Batten, chairman of the New York Stock Exchange. They like to live comfortably but not lavishly. Others, such as J. Peter Grace, who is reputed to have nine homes, could hardly live in less than the baronial life they were accustomed to now that they have strengthened the family's business and brought it within survival distance of the twenty-first century.

The demise of the big Long Island, Maryland, and California estates, although some fine examples still exist, is due to factors other than family background. The huge mansionlike or colonial homeplace has given way to the need for executive travel, to working late in the city, to pursuing a frequent round of nights out. Gone are the days of retiring for the weekend and burrowing away amid one's family, horses, quiet cocktail evenings, and personal memorabilia.

But some chief executives, in a recent trend that has worried many urban authorities, have picked up their corporate headquarters and moved it twenty to fifty miles away from the city to a quiet suburban site. And because at least some of those moves have brought the company close to the CEO's home location, the suspicion has grown that it was all for his convenience. This has been roundly denied. But the question lingers, especially when executives who have been compelled to come along will insist while remaining anonymous that a certain measure of excitement has departed with the shift out of town.

The CEOs involved attribute the move to prohibitive working conditions in the city—high corporate taxes, crime, poor transit facilities, a waning labor pool—whereas the suburban locations in Connecticut, Shaker Heights, or Beverly Hills apparently have none of these.

Whether the suburban conditions will become more like those in the city is probably not as important as whether the transfer to more bucolic areas isn't as conducive to the push for more business, better marketing, and a closer touch with the marketplace. What might be suitable for the planner, the researcher, the financial man, and the computer technician might not be for the marketer, the sales manager, and the creative staffs. A growing number of companies, recognizing this, are setting up in-town sales and marketing offices, while the parent company resides in green splendor out where the interstate highways meander.

How do CEOs relax? What sporting or spectator activities do they prefer? What do they read? The questions were posed to a number of them and here is a sampling:

James Davant of Paine Webber has three homes: a handsome house in Mill Neck, Long Island; an apartment in New York; and a beach house in Delray Beach, Florida. "In the winter, I mostly stay in New York," he said. "In the summer, I spend a lot of my spare time in my pool on Long Island, or fish and shoot, mostly pheasant and duck releases. In Delray we swim and play golf and tennis.

"I like music, classics mainly. My idea of a perfect afternoon of relaxation is to listen to Mozart and read history. Books I've liked include Admiral Nimitz's biography and John Toland's *Adolf Hitler*. I'm currently reading the two-volume set on Captain Cook. I'm happy to read a mystery while traveling by airplane. Frankly, reading a lot on a weekend is a withdrawal. I'd like to travel. One day I'd like to wake up and have an open day to look forward to."

Robert Quittmeyer of Amstar Corporation jogs "at least" one mile every day, starting at about 7 A.M. "At night, I swim about thirty laps in my backyard pool, thirty-two feet long," he reported. "I used to sail and play tennis, but not as much any more. I spend my evenings reading the work I bring home. When my children are there we talk or I watch a few idiot programs on TV. I like the public-broadcasting channel, though. As for books, I liked *The Imperial Presidency*. Those perks and grandiose trappings only build mistrust. I don't need them. I don't have a car to travel with while at work. I use the subway."

Peter Redfield of Itel Corporation walks a good deal.

"When I'm at home in Atherton, California," he said, "I will walk every night about two and a half miles, but I also like to walk in New York City, starting out from our apartment at Sixty-first and Madison. I'm not frightened about walking alone at night. At home, I play tennis, golf. . . . I love to read fiction, mostly the best-sellers."

The Tisches of Loews both play tennis. Larry prefers bridge. Robert likes to travel. Both spend a lot of time reading, mostly newspapers, particularly the *New York Times* and the *Wall Street Journal.* Larry particularly enjoys the writings of Irving Kristol, the conservative writer on economics, as opposed to the "liberals, who believe in pie in the sky."

Irving Shapiro of E. I. du Pont works most weekends at home, mostly looking at material he hasn't had a chance to read before and analyzing policy judgments, reports, and recommendations from the company's executive committee. "My general reading time as a result is more limited," he said. "I read three or four newspapers a day and six to seven magazines a week, but where I miss out are books. I'd like to read more books but I can't. I go to sleep at eleven P.M. sharp because by that time I've pretty well had it."

How do American businessmen behave on a night out compared to the Europeans? Robert Coppenrath, the Belgian who heads Agfa-Gavaert's photographic operations in the United States, has entertained both types of chief executives in his New Jersey home over the last decade and makes these observations:

"The Americans seem to lack background in civilization, such as literature, music, philosophy, even food. I must have had a thousand executives in my house in the last ten years and it is clear to see the differences. The Europeans love your rugs, knowing the difference in Orientals, for example. But not many Americans comment on my paintings or my rugs.

"The Americans are beginning to know something about wine," he went on, "but really aren't making the great effort about it. That sort of thing perhaps makes him a better businessman because it removes the periphery from him. Europeans in my home talk about Hegel, Kant, Schopenhauer, and John Locke, kicking it around, so to speak, but Americans are more prone to talk about golf, football, baseball, politics, and barbecuing. So the conversation with each is quite different, but this is subtly changing. The Americans are trying to talk more about wines and art. But there is still a vast gulf."

How Much Is He Worth?

A goad both to unions pressured to keep wage demands down and to Washington administrations seeking to control salaries from pushing inflation higher, compensation of American chief executives has been rising 12 percent and more in the most recent years. Bonuses greater than the CEO's salary itself have become a favorite way for company directors to give the chief executive the kind of raises that keep him happy and forging ahead.

In 1976, for example, Chrysler Corporation, rebounding to the black after a $260-million loss in 1975, lavishly rewarded John J. Riccardo, chairman, and E. A. Cafiero, president. Riccardo, who had earned $216,000 the year before, received not only a $30,000 boost in salary but a whopping bonus of $445,900. And Cafiero got a $401,000 bonus on top of his $219,000 salary.

Astronomical money increases aren't unusual in the automobile industry. Henry Ford, II, chairman of the Ford Motor Company, was the beneficiary in 1976 of one of the industry's highest salaries ever: $970,000, almost three times his 1975 salary of $333,750. And General Motors' chairman, Thomas A. Murphy, struggled along that year on compensation of $950,000 against only $320,000 in 1975. As in Chrysler's case, Ford and GM rewarded their CEOs for a much better profit than the year before.

Other industries weren't far behind. Irving Shapiro of Du Pont received an 84.6-percent salary rise in 1976 to $457,752; Reginald Jones of GE was given a 24-percent increase to $620,000; and Revlon's Michel C. Bergerac obtained one of the highest percentage boosts, 98 percent, to $693,567.

That was in 1976, a fine vintage earnings year, and the salary boom continued in 1977 and was expected to similarly perk along in 1978 and 1979.

Is a corporate chief worth all that money? CEOs think they are—and more. Stockholders generally don't think so. And most activists believe that corporate executives are paid too well, especially the CEOs.

The average company president and/or chief executive earns $111,000 in annual base salary, plus about $40,000 in incentive pay, according to a survey of 127 American corporations by the Gallagher Presidents' Report. Sources of their income in 1977 involve 66.5 percent salary, 14.1 percent incentives, 10.5 percent dividends, 6.8 percent outside investments, 1.2 percent capital gains, and 0.9 percent other remuneration such as serving on outside boards.

Other Gallagher findings: Most CEOs plan to step down before they reach age sixty-five, anticipating an annual retirement income of $96,284. Currently the chief executives carry life insurance of $340,807, own stocks with a present market value of $652,644, and own real estate worth about $319,411 in market value. They also have tax-exempt securities worth $254,186 and maintain an average $36,418 in savings. In 1977, the corporate chief's average tax bill was $79,753.

In other words, the average company chief executive is worth well over $1.5 million and many, perhaps most, are even better set up financially. Yet sources who deal closely with them, such as Pierre Rinfret, the economist, say that CEOs feel robbed by inflation and claim they are underpaid.

How the Big Board's "Mil" Batten Built His Dream House

Despite their curbs and pressures, America's chief executives still continue to enjoy many of the perks, privileges, and power they have always savored. Some, listening to the encomiums of their colleagues and even more to their own demands, aren't reluctant to let certain elements of their professional lives make their private lives more convenient and enjoyable.

What follows has never been told before, perhaps because it pertains to the twilight zone between those professional and private worlds. But there are more than a few people at the J. C. Penney Company who for a time were just bursting to have it told. To them, it was an example of how American top executives arrogate the best perks to themselves, taking advantage of their high roles. Although it is a vast company with sales in excess of $9 billion, with 184,000 employees and 79,000 stockholders, Penney itself has not seen fit to bring it to the public's attention, perhaps because the company doesn't think it worthwhile or important enough to do so.

William M. Batten is a much-respected, fatherly type who has had the unusual distinction of rising to the top of two famous institutions. In the 1970s he was the chairman of the J. C. Penney Company. And in 1976, two years after he retired from Penney at age sixty-five, he was elected chairman of the New York Stock Exchange, also known as the Big Board, filling a role that combines the best elements of a baseball commissioner and a guru.

Batten's life at Penney has more or less become part of recent history, but early in 1978 certain elements of it came to life again. Two former Penney internal auditors filed a $10-million suit against the company and eleven former and present top executives, including Batten, claiming that they were fired for uncovering improper expenditures, fraud, and bribery. The suit filed in the New York federal court by Preston Perdue and Patrick Grimes charged that the defendants conspired to fire them to conceal their own fraud and wrongdoing in connection with renovations done in Penney's New York headquarters. The complaint also charged that some of the defendants, including Batten, had construction work performed in their homes which was charged to Penney's.

For the unflappable Batten, the charges must have resembled an unpleasant dream that returned to haunt him. . . .

In 1964, after thirty-eight years with Penney's, Batten was elected chairman and CEO of the nation's second-largest retail company. Retirement was still a decade away, but it was not so remote that he didn't begin to think about it and where he would eventually live.

His promotion was considered fitting recognition. The onetime shoe salesman had performed loyal, sometimes brilliant service, moving up through Penney's field and staff ranks with solid contributions, all the while observing the founder's famous "golden rule" credo. And so, when he became Penney's chief, it all seemed natural and proper. He proved he was the right man for the job by quadrupling Penney's sales and trebling its profits in the decade that followed.

In 1969, perhaps in belated recognition of his important role and of Penney's ongoing efforts to become a more sophisticated company, "Mil" Batten, as he is more familiarly known, decided to build his "dream house." It proved a difficult decision.

Although he was then, as he more recently described himself, a "frustrated architect," he was sometimes admonished by friends for living so modestly and so long in a thirty-year-old colonial house in Manhasset, Long Island. He simply had no grand pretensions for the new home. He knew that he wanted a larger place for his wife, Katherine, where his two children and his grandchildren could come. But his negative reaction to suggestions that it might have some dramatic, modern lines was strong.

Edward Gorman, Penney's marketing vice-president at the time and a friend of Batten, prodded him for preferring simply another, if larger, colonial house. Then he showed Batten a tiny scale model of an unusual contemporary house that Julian Neski, the well-known avant-garde architect, had designed for him. Batten seemed to recoil from it. Soon after, however, the Penney CEO asked to meet Neski. Preliminary plans were drawn up for a large white structure on four distinct platforms on a plot owned by Batten in Mill Neck, Long Island. A protracted period of construction followed over the next three years and seven months, drawn out partly because of the constant involvement first of Batten and increasingly of his wife.

From early 1970 through early 1972, Batten extensively used the services of Ronald S. Barnum, Penney's home furnishings design director, and of Terry Martin, his assistant, to help him design and furnish the exterior of the house.

It cost just under $500,000 to build. To furnish it, Batten in that same two-year period ordered through Barnum and through Penney's buyers about $100,000 of household furnishings at a standard Penney's discount that ranged, depending upon the merchandise, from 15 percent to 50 percent of the normal tagged retail price.

Penney's executives frequently bought clothing, home goods, and other items through the company at similar discounts. Batten's purchases were so extensive, however, that Robert B. Gill, then Penney's vice-president and general merchandise manager for home goods, took the unusual step of suggesting that a special account be set up for the purchases in Penney's accounting department. Gill proposed that Barnum send and endorse invoices to the accounting department from various suppliers from whom merchandise was obtained. Batten agreed, and the system was put into effect.

Over a period of eighteen months, Barnum spent between 15 and 20 percent of his company time on the Batten home, in addition to occasional evenings and portions of weekends. Sometimes, as he said later, he spent entire days away from Penney's on the project. Miss Martin was also similarly involved but did not spend as much time in Mill Neck as Barnum.

The use of the two Penney employees and the large-scale purchases through Penney suppliers were related by Batten and Gill to two factors. "We were trying hard at Penney to stress our new at-home-decorating service," said Batten in an interview, "and Mr. Barnum was hired to help in that connection. So we decided to have Ron Barnum tie in that effort with my needs. Also, we thought it made sense to have as much Penney merchandise as possible used by Penney people."

"When Mr. Batten first talked about his new house," Gill said in a separate interview, "he asked to have in it items of Penney merchandise. It was to be a change in his life-style, but he wanted appropriate Penney goods in it, although obviously there would be items in his home that wouldn't be available in our stores."

But the use of the two staff people for what could have been viewed as a personal need and the amount of purchases through Penney suppliers produced some consternation throughout Penney ranks, according to some present and former employees who asked not to be identified. That concern remained latent after Batten's 1974 retirement but it erupted two years later, six months after the former Penney chief began his second career on Wall Street.

The subject arose in November 1976, when the Justice Department impaneled a federal grand jury to investigate alleged contractor kickbacks to Penney employees during renovations at the company's New York headquarters.

According to Richard H. Kuh, Batten's attorney and previously acting district attorney for the borough of Manhattan,

Batten voluntarily appeared for an interview with the U.S. Attorney for the Eastern District of New York to discuss those renovations. As far as Batten's interview was concerned, Kuh said, "they appeared completely satisfied."

Two former Penney employees were indicted in February 1977 for evading federal income tax on alleged kickbacks amounting to $1.4 million during 1971 through 1974. H. L. Lazar, Inc., a prominent building contractor, was indicted for allegedly giving bribes. And Penney's filed a suit against Lazar and one of the Penney employees to recover the amount of the kickbacks and any overcharges.

During the investigation, Kenneth S. Axelson, a Penney senior vice-president for finance and administration, withdrew his name from consideration as deputy secretary of the Treasury Department after learning of a pending article in the *New York Times* citing possible misconduct on his part. Federal officials had raised questions about Axelson's payment of $6,000 to a contractor, which turned out to be Lazar, to remodel his Central Park West apartment, actual costs of which were later estimated to have run as high as $10,000. But no action was taken by the grand jury on Axelson. He was also exonerated of any misconduct by Penney and was returned to his post there.

During the investigation, however, the U.S. Attorney's office received calls from Penney employees and from anonymous individuals calling attention to Batten's use of the Penney staffer and his purchases of Penney's goods. The SEC also called on Batten and Gill to discuss the matter, both executives said.

In reply to a query by this writer, a spokesman for the U.S. Attorney's office said, "We heard the allegations about Mr. Batten. But since they did not come within our jurisdiction, we did not investigate them. We consider it an internal Penney matter."

The house in question, nestling in a series of small hills scattered through a highly wooded enclave, is in a lovely area about twenty-five miles from the New York City line on Long Island's North Shore, overlooking Oyster Bay and Long Island Sound. Considered one of the most affluent sections of Nassau County, Mill Neck has a number of imposing residences, as well as some small, shabby ones, few stores, and hardly any industrial area. Its hub is a combination post office, village hall, and police department. But its tiny administration sternly protects the residents.

The plot had been acquired by Batten three years earlier. It was a portion of the former estate of the late Arthur Vining Davis, who had been the chairman of the Aluminum Company of America. After Davis's death, local residents bought component plots through a real-estate syndicate set up to dispose of the land. "I bought the plot with no real purpose in mind," Batten recalled, "except that the land there was a pretty scarce commodity."

Although Batten's initial plans for the house were traditional, his enthusiasm for something very different soon surprised the architect he selected. "Mr. Batten told me that he wanted a house as a final move for him," said Julian Neski, the architect. "He said that he was interested in a different kind of structure. For me, it came as a surprise that a man who was head of a conservative company like Penney would want a different kind of house. We got into a long period of discussion. He seems to give absolutely deep thought to everything."

The result of their consultations was an eleven-room painted-white-brick contemporary residence with four connected structures surrounding a central courtyard and driveway. The wings of the house included a garage, kitchen-and-dining room, living room, study, and four master bedrooms.

"Mr. Batten had always talked about a swimming pool, but that would have required extensive clearing and grading," said Neski. "It would also have disturbed the natural quality of the immediate surroundings. So toward the end he suggested putting in a pool underneath the terrace, an indoor pool, and that's what we did. That was an example of his input into the project."

Batten still commutes back and forth every day from Mill Neck to his Wall Street office. But he preserves his privacy. His telephone is unlisted. The only indication that the two-level, three-balcony house is his is his name on the mailbox at the driveway's entrance. A scale map in the village hall identifies the Batten plot and others in the village's Heather Lane enclave.

Other homes there range from modestly lavish to sumptuous, but they cover a wide spectrum of design. A neighbor perhaps a quarter mile away is James Davant of Paine Webber. Both Batten and Davant are longtime acquaintances.

Ron Barnum, prior to working with Batten on the house, had met the Penney chief when Batten had asked him to help select new china and tablecloths for Penney's renovations of its

New York offices. But the then thirty-year-old decorator had been attracted to Batten when he had read in a *Fortune* magazine interview that Batten was interested in improving the fashion content of Penney's home furnishings.

Contacted in Chicago, where he is now an independent interior designer specializing in corporate work since he left Penney's in 1974, Barnum said that he had become involved with Batten's house after having performed similar work for the late Whitney Young, the executive director of the Urban League. "Mr. Young was building a new house in New Rochelle, leaving a much more modest home," Barnum said, "and Mr. Batten knew Mr. Young through their work together in civil rights. When Mr. Young asked if someone at Penney could help him with the interior of his new house, Mr. Batten recommended me." That type of cooperation "happens a lot within large corporations," he said, "and they do it largely as a PR matter."

The efforts of the Barnum-Martin team on the Whitney Young house lasted about six months in 1970, and when they finished, Young expressed satisfaction with their work to Batten. "Mr. Batten then told me that he would like Terry and me to design the interior of his house," Barnum recalled. "Everyone thought he was crazy to build such a house, but he seemed so concerned about the quality of the architecture and the need to shift from 'the ruts' to something fresh that I could understand.

"From a design point of view, it was certainly the highlight of my career. Maybe only once in a lifetime do you get that kind of opportunity. I felt flattered by it. . . . When it was all over, there were several parties and Terry and I were invited. They were mostly for the Penney people who were most involved in the building and furnishing of the house, and there was also a summer open house for the Penney people," Barnum said.

Terry Martin has since been shifted to Penney's public-relations department, where she is an interior designer for special projects. This represents a promotion, she said in a discussion in which she was joined by an attorney from Penney's legal staff. "My career at Penney was aided by the work I did on Mr. Batten's house and other projects at about the same time. I spent some time in 1970 and 1971 helping on Mr. Batten's house," she went on. Although she put in time outside Penney hours on the Mill Neck house, she was never paid for it, "but the promotion I got more than compensated for it," she said.

Batten said that obtaining household objects through Penney's was in line with company policy. "I could have been within company policy to go to fifteen showrooms and order goods and have them shipped to my home," he said. "But Mr. Gill decided it would be more efficient to have Ron Barnum coordinate it and also to add five percent to my cost to cover Mr. Barnum's time away from his duties."

He said that goods ordered for him received the standard Penney discounts. Merchandise ordered including anything in the Penney suppliers' lines, not merely what was being sold in the Penney stores. "But to my best knowledge the suppliers did not know that the goods were being ordered for the chairman of the board," Batten said.

Replying to a question on whether he was aware of the amount of time both decorators put in on his house, he said, "I had no way of knowing how many hours Ron Barnum spent on the house, and Terry as well. I only knew what I could see. The girl put in less time. . . . I was not aware that my use of those two people produced any complaints at Penney."

As to the service provided to Whitney Young's house, he said that it was no different from an advertiser's use of O. J. Simpson, the professional football celebrity, or Jack Nicklaus, the golfer. "In Mr. Young's case," said Batten, "he was a very important person with high visibility in the Urban League, which then had more than eighty local chapters, and he did a lot of entertaining with them." Young, he said, paid for the Penney services he obtained.

As far as the Batten purchases were concerned, Gill said, "Our feeling was that important people would come to his home and it would help Penney business."

Asked about the amount of time Barnum spent working on the Batten house, Gill said he would be surprised if "he spent more than twenty percent of his time during the most intensive period of about six or seven months." However, Gill conceded that "there was some time that Ron spent that could be characterized for Mr. Batten. But the extra charge of five percent would account for the period of time expended by Ron Barnum."

Although it was later decided that photographs of Batten's home should not be used for promotional purposes, Penney believes that the effort was worthwhile in terms of the benefits received. Barnum described the Batten home in a talk shortly after it was completed at the Chicago home-furnishings trade market. And as far as Gill is concerned, "people might misinterpret it, but if another situation like this develops, if another house is being built from the ground up, we would do it again."

Asked if he had any regrets about the use of the two decorators or the extensive purchases through his former company, Batten replied that he had none.

In its own investigation of the alleged contractor kickbacks to Penney executives, the company's audit committee also looked into the matter of Batten's use of the employees and his purchases. Walter Wriston, chairman of Citicorp, New York, and chairman of Penney's audit committee, said in a telephone response, "The audit committee reviewed everything that was turned up based on a lot of rumors on Mr. Batten. But the audit committee doesn't believe that he engaged in any impropriety." A request to peruse the committee's findings or the invoices of Batten's purchases wasn't granted, however.

The at-home decorating service involving furniture, for which Batten's home was to be a sort of showcase, was dropped in 1975 after more than three years, mainly, according to Gill, "because it was ahead of its time."

15

The Passing of the Imperial Chief Executive

The Demand Imperative

In the first half of the twentieth century, the United States was propelled from a loose collection of regional economies into a powerful national economy with high international ranking.

In the century's second half, an interdependent world economy emerged. A stiff, even bitter, competition for international markets embroiled American, European, and Japanese world companies.

And in the final quarter of the twentieth century, this economic scramble, fueled by the oil-swollen coffers of much of the Middle East, will intensify to a boil, creating a new international pecking order with mighty winners and some bedraggled losers.

While this economic war will create significant changes in many nations, whether they are industrial leaders, developed, or less-developed countries, it will not of itself constitute the most sweeping new characteristic of the century's final decades. Ideological and political tides will take that role. Whether they will favor the differing communistic styles of the Chinese or the Russians or the proliferating European version, or the nationalistic strivings in Africa and Asia or the democratic political models of the United States, the United Kingdom, Israel, or Scandinavia, those tides will wash across the face of the world, bringing peaceful or militant change and altering governments, economies, and life-styles everywhere.

But even more important than that will be a more fragmented but encompassing class struggle. Both within nations and penetrating outside them, people—majorities and minorities; differing races and ethnic strains, economic strata, sexes; varying age groups; management and labor, office and factory workers; and others with less categorical differences—will jostle one another in a complex rivalry for a better place under the sun.

Forced to respond, governments will adjust, shift position, try to transform themselves, and inevitably reflect a tortured effort to cater to the many pressures. Most of those government feints and moves will be errant, in effect a testing of the sentiment, leading to further convulsive feints and moves before more sound decisions are reached.

In the natural process of all this flux will be inevitable effects on millions of people, Americans no less than those throughout the world. And in the demand imperative that emerges clearly in all this, it is obvious that American businessmen will be challenged more than ever before. Inveigh against or resign to the difficulties of operating within a pluralistic society, the nation's chief executives are in the uncomfortable but strategic position of constructively reacting to their state of siege or of pulling back from it or of using their positions and strengths in a narrow or broad sense to counter the challenge.

Beleaguered yet still much honored, CEOs have in recent years tended to forget in the midst of their mixed reviews that they are still largely regarded as leaders, if for nothing else than their roles as heads of large corporate institutions. But there is another reason for their still-high place in the American scale of achievement. In a country in which individual attainment has remained an ideal, the man who rises to the top of the American corporation is still viewed as a sort of folk hero, even though he may have been battered and scorned through the years. He is still a hero, notwithstanding the fact that in recent years his capricious and sometimes downright bad judgments have created harm which extends far beyond the confines of his own company.

As leaders, American businessmen will be buffeted in the decades ahead by some of the most conflicting and complex forces they have yet encountered. But the imprimatur of leadership isn't a mantle for the weak or indecisive. How they will react to those forces as individuals and as a group of leaders will depend not merely on whether the siege against them will be lifted by its own erosion but on how millions of Americans, and indirectly billions abroad, will fare in the years to come. Like it or not, the doors of the American corporate chief executive have been permanently flung open by forces in the world outside.

"Some of today's managers seem to be uncomfortable with their new social responsibilities, but it's like fish swimming in new waters—either we'll adapt or we won't survive," observed Reginald Jones of General Electric. "The successful managers of tomorrow will be those that swim as comfortably in the societal waters as their predecessors swam in the waters of technology and finance.

"These are some of the changing demands on business management," Jones said. "But some things don't change. In the end, it comes down to character.

"Successful leaders in business, government, academia, or any other field will continue to be those who somehow carry within them the impulse to serve the larger destinies of mankind. Competence is necessary, but it is not enough. People will forgive many failings if they sense that one is trying his or her very best to serve their nobler needs and aspirations."

What are some of the needs and options under the demand imperative to meet the many-headed challenges of the century's final quarter, to compete in the global village, and to "serve the larger destinies of mankind"?

Strategists, Not Technicians

If American business is to remain responsible for two thirds of the gross national product and if the shape of the GNP remains a function of production, inflation, and employment, it's axiomatic that businessmen see their role as the pacemakers of the nation's pulse beat. Given a few serious mistakes, some substantive misjudgments, a handful of massive, unpleasant surprises by major corporations, the United States can reel under an economic turndown that takes years to rectify.

Such was the case in late 1974 and early 1975, when business inventory accumulations and high productivity far exceeded consumer expenditures. Automobile makers fell into a three-year trough. Retailers dumped goods and took frantic markdowns on the rest. Many producers cut back their operations if they could or went out of business if they couldn't. And the stock market began a precipitous slide that hasn't yet been fully reversed. It was the worst recession since the big depression of the 1930s.

Could it have been predicted? It's difficult to say for certain, even if one puts store in the economic trend cycles in which—partly in fact, partly in theory—soft-lines sales mount after a prolonged durables uptrend. Some of this thinking is based on consumer shopping preferences—the credit-buying habit sating itself on autos and furniture so that cash buying, that is, the buying of clothing and other nondurables, is a natural next step. And when this occurs, the other declines.

Whether business learned much from the 1974 recession isn't easily verified because no similar situation has occurred since then to show it. But what has emerged from the experience is the clear need for a business strategist or a policy of corporate strategic planning that would avoid unpleasant surprises whether economic, social, or political.

Describing W. Michael Blumenthal's CEO performance at Bendix, William Agee, his successor, told me, "Whether it's a small problem or a major question of acquiring some company to expand, most people come at the problem on the basis of their own bias—financial, engineering, or whatever. But Mike Blumenthal will think about more of the variables quicker and more thoroughly than most people, and he'll come at a problem less biased."

Blumenthal is not only "a pragmatist and bottom-line guy but doesn't have to work at learning what the social consequences are of a business action," Agee said. "He acquired a tremendous overview and seems naturally to think of strategic and international considerations."

What can other CEOs learn from the former Bendix chief? "He brought orderliness and a sense of consistency to the company," said Agee. "He gave it additional balance, built in more countercyclicality in our various market areas, and took dimensions of the business that didn't fit either the financial or the operating mold and cut them back."

Perhaps understandably enthusiastic about the man who tapped him as his successor, but also expressing obvious sincerity, Agee in his paean to the Treasury official added, "He also built more of a sense of people-awareness by humanizing the organization and by upgrading personnel policies toward both the salaries and hourly workers."

Is all that—the foreseeing of variables, the absence of bias, the improved awareness of people, and the implementation of countercyclicality—tantamount to corporate strategies? How do most companies behave in that regard?

Marvin Schiller, of A. T. Kearney, a respected consultant, observed, "In too many cases, managements concern themselves with the symptoms rather than the actual problem. They fight fires rather than solve problems. They look for an aspirin to alleviate a headache when they need more sophisticated therapy to stay alive. More specifically, I am reminded of a firm that hired and fired seven presidents in eight years. The problem was in convincing the chairman of the board that the real culprit was the firm's marketing strategy which he formulated many years ago but which was basically misdirected and outmoded, and not its personnel. It was like telling someone that his child is ugly; that may be true, but it's hard to accept. Businessmen these days have to be managers of change."

"Management is still more of an art than a science," said GE's Jones, "but the managers who fly by the seat of the pants will find themselves outclassed. Much that passes for long-range planning in business today is little more than a projection of past experience, with perhaps a *soupçon* of wish-fulfillment.

"Real strategic planning involves a careful, analytical examination of all the major factors that enter into the business process—and the external factors are probably of greater importance than the traditional internal factors. Social obstacles, political constraints, and competitive counterpressures must be anticipated. Issues must be surfaced. Alternative futures must be imaginatively constructed. Alternative plans must be prepared to match the contingencies. And hard choices must be made, because investments today will determine the character of the enterprise for years to come," Jones said.

For that type of planning, added the GE chief, "the imperial chief executive closeted in his private chamber will not suffice. It requires not only a capable and imaginative staff but also the participation of management at every level of the organization."

The Loss of the Dominant Personality

An increasing number of American corporations are already set up for strategic planning, owing to the necessary delegation of management and the formation of the multi-headed chief executive's or president's "office."

Although some companies such as General Electric and Montgomery Ward have placed the strategic planning responsibility with one man, it may be at least as suited to a committee whose members could pursue the function from the standpoint of their specialties or specific roles.

The probability that this will happen in many cases is supported by two parallel developments: the growing belief in strategic planning and the increasing delegation of senior management. The two are also synergistic, since as the tip of the corporate pyramid reshapes itself to a three- or four-man executive "office," it is natural that planning for change in order to avoid unforeseen contingencies will receive a prominent place in the group's agenda. And conversely, as the corporation's management is divided among more people, the ability to engage in strategic planning is rendered easier and more efficient.

The democratizing of the top responsibility is taking various forms, including not only the CEO's office but military-style restructuring along parallel lines proceeding downward deep into the company's extremities. In any version, the passing on of responsibility recognizes in spirit, if not in mechanics, the difficulty of dominating the total thought and implementation processes covering the wide range of disciplines required in the contemporary corporation.

Yet in one of those ironies that often befall progress, the blurring of individual responsibility has raised fears among many people that the loss of the single strong personality who for years dominated the American corporate scene will remove much of its leadership stamp. Driving, often irascible, demanding, and not at all known for his organizational ability, the tough, mentally sinewy, and forceful CEO, often a founder and sometimes an antecedent, pushed his company into broad directions that gave it pith and permanence. His leaving, by death or long-overdue retirement, bequeathed the business a momentum that in a good many cases is still continuing. But increasingly, the succession of the committee management is slowly turning that momentum into a more cautious, considered movement and, in the process, often robbing the company of its difference from many others.

"In the past, the strong individual personality exerted a marked personal influence on business which will now be diverted," observed Bernard L. Schwartz, president and chairman of Loral Corporation, the New York producer of electronic systems. "Totally, there will probably be a dilution of our effectiveness as a corporate society as the chief executive's personality is spread from the hard-driving individual to the consensus management. But this can be improved by the quality of the committee arrangement. If managements are conscious of the void left by the dynamic individual leadership, they will act to foster it among their top members so that the loss will not prove harmful," Schwartz said.

Another means of offsetting that loss, in the view of Schwartz and others, is through a more aggressive, more responsible board of directors. Already imbued with a more independent spirit and more outside representation, directors are increasingly showing that they recognize their moral and fiduciary responsibility to watchdog the management better. But, it is only a step further than taking a more forthright hand in the policy-making function.

"In the years to come, directors will begin to run the policies of the company in conjunction with management," asserts economist Pierre Rinfret. "For twenty-five years or more, directors would mostly only agree with management's recommendations. Now they will really begin to share in the running of the company. Managements will still recommend, but the board will decide, in effect saying, 'Prove it, even if it entails a delay in the procedures.' "

American management, too, will accept the more militant director more readily than it will the SEC's controversial proposal to convert corporate boards to outsiders only and thus exclude management directors. By doing so, contends the SEC, managements will be put on their own mettle and the nonemployee directors will without any strings be better able to act independently as evaluators of management's proposals and performance.

But whether chief executives take actions to inject vitality into their delegating processes, or whether they are separated from boards that themselves will exert more personality, it's safe to say that little can be done to replace the strong, central focus that has mostly departed from the American corporate scene. How much that void may have caused some of the complex problems that plague American business or whether the strong man in the boss's office would have further aggravated them if he were still around are open questions. Hypotheses, needless to say, are always frustrating.

One conclusion is certain, however. Regret it or not, the dominant chief-executive figure is quickly fading in corporate America. And because of the pressures and complexities that have so directly fallen on him, the passing of the imperial chief executive isn't far behind.

How Much a Self-Correcting Society?

In all my interviews, in variations of conviction or resignation, chief executives expressed the belief that most of the problems facing them, especially those of an external nature, would worsen in the years ahead.

Government would become more encroaching. Foreign companies would be able to compete better than Americans because of restrictive U.S. practices on foreign payments and because of the nationalistic tendencies abroad. The entire range of vocal constituencies, from stockholders to activist church groups, will become more diverse, more loud, and more onerous. And down the road lay not only increasing strictures on the corporation but an inevitable drift in our form of government to socialism.

But here and there a different sentiment is voiced.

"Four or five years ago, I would have come close to agreeing with the contention that the American corporation was an endangered species," declared John deButts. "But now I think that the business community has come alive and is no longer as reluctant to face the nation and tell it the facts in a credible manner. We are talking more and we are beginning to see a change in public attitude. I believe that as the public becomes more knowledgeable it will be more reasoned in the demands it makes on business. There has to be a trade-off—if not, the public will be forced to pay for all the costs and restrictions foisted on the public companies. After all, who owns AT&T? Isn't it our one million stockholders? And who uses it but our one hundred million customers?"

Observed Loral's Bernard Schwartz: "What will happen, I believe, is that our society will act in a self-correcting manner, swinging back on government oversight and rectifying the over-regulation, at least partially.

"There are already detectable signs in Washington," Schwartz said. "Businessmen are being placed in important cabinet and regulatory roles—G. William Miller at the head of the Federal Reserve System, Blumenthal at Treasury. And the defeat in 1978 of the consumer bill—I think it means that the public is beginning to recognize the cost of all the corrective devices. Regulatory agencies are also starting to self-correct—like the delay in some environmental controls and the softening of some of the toughest OSHA regulations. But the biggest self-correcting development may be the public's growing perception that inflation is a bigger problem than unemployment, which used to be the prime national economic priority."

A "born" optimist, Russell Banks of Grow Chemical nonetheless thinks that the United States will have its own homegrown version of socialism but that business will adjust to it. "It's already with us to a certain extent," he said. "As corporations grow bigger, it will be easier under that form of government to control them, so our system will become semi-free enterprise. But I see small business still being an important arm of the business community, a creative, innovative arm that will splinter off and then eventually become part of a big company."

But, said others thinking aloud, will business—which occasionally seems to find its voice in Washington but fears this is only an aberration—want to continue to find the time, energy, and stimulus to compete in the hardening adversary relationship? The question, at first blush, seems farfetched. American business has the vast preponderance of economic power in that relationship, but so much effort, money, and ill feeling go into its programs to lobby and fight against the adversaries that some businessmen admit to losing heart.

Said one, who requested anonymity, "I see the end result of this already happening—a failure by some company heads to offer their viewpoint and others who have cut back on new ventures where the economic and social risks have already hurt.

"That's the rub that all the pressure-makers create," he said. "We should be doing everything possible to encourage new economic ventures to provide a better way of life and upward mobility. Look at it this way: If there hadn't been economic opportunity when I decided to get into this company, where the hell would I be now and what would my thousands of employees be doing?"

Dynamic Choruses

Into this querulous debate and breast-beating filters another strain too. A voice. A chorus. Many choruses.

In a nation that prides itself often in the midst of strife on its sense of equality, sometimes the polyphony reaches a Babel-tower pitch. Yet one of the saving graces of the American system has been the freedom of that often harsh counterpoint, allowing steam to siphon off and emotions to cool without resort to violence. Without getting maudlin about it, the wonder of the world may well be how the American form of government survived without upheaval during at least four terrible times in the last four decades—the Great Depression, the assassination of President John F. Kennedy, the Vietnam invasion, and the Watergate scandal and subsequent resignation of President Richard M. Nixon.

The reason, of course, is that the pressures were allowed to overheat at least in terms of vocal, even political, energy. If any had been deliberately and completely capped, although some misguided attempts were made to control some beyond reasonable means, any of those four potentially chaotic situations could have exploded into violence and even revolution. And what would have happened then is beyond prediction.

In attempting to relate that principle to the matter of functioning within a pluralistic society and whether that society is capable of correcting its own abuses, it is possible perhaps without emotion to see a clear parallel. Indulging one's point of view, whether it is business's or the needs of the old, the young, the sick, the weak, or just the willing is proper as long as the indulgence doesn't go beyond reasonable bounds. It may even overheat, as long as the proponents do not force any one-sided commands on the other segments of society. If business has its problems, and it does, most of the other segments of American society do as well. If each makes its voice heard and presents its case with logic and credibility, chances are that that voice will be listened to. Businessmen's inability to achieve their objectives either with Washington or with any of their other constituencies comes from a basic failure to establish its case, either because that case was faulty or because the lack of openness created suspicion. In a great sense, however, the resources American business has place it in the paramount position to obtain its goals, much more than is the case with some of the other adversaries in the push-pull arena of public opinion. What business has lacked has been an ability or willingness to talk to, rather than down at, its adversaries. Pragmatic candor will go a long way, as will the desire to listen openly to others.

There is nothing wrong with rational debate, even if at times it became irrationally vocal. During those four terrible times, if it hadn't it's probable that recent American history would have been tragically different.

Needless to say, business and human considerations are not antithetical. In the most simplistic terms, people are business and business provides them the livelihood to exist. Business may no longer be the business of America in the full sense of the tired phrase, but it keeps the country going.

"How many checks and balances do we need?" asks one disgusted businessman. The answer, which one may offer at the risk of being charged with facetiousness, is as many as the businessman can handle to remain honest, productive, and sane. And that is no more than any other member of the American community should have to face or accept. If it is all too much, he can—and should—object, and his voice will, if the past is any prologue, be raised in chorus with others. The resulting polyphony may be hardly musical, but it will be effective again if one may trust the past.

Americans have the right to expect the same from their corporate elite, whose state of siege, when all is said and done, may be the best thing that has yet happened to them. Character, after all, emerges best under pressure and then either cracks or reaches to unprecedented heights.

The next few decades will doubtless reflect the full passing of the imperial chief executive, a victim of rapid change, as was the demise of the strong personality who imparted his own feisty flavor.

And while the mantle is slowly passing to a group, a consensus management, it is probably still true, as Ralph Waldo Emerson, said, that "every great institution is the lengthened shadow of a single man." What this may mean, one can only hope, is that every member of that managing committee will if he cares to reach his fulfillment behave as though he individually will be the lengthened shadow of the institution he works for. Courage, unless it can be proven otherwise, isn't really old-fashioned, in spite of all the changes that have altered the business scene.

"I happen to think that the United States," a foreign businessman told me, "is ready for a major new drive to capitalize on its tremendous assets. It will certainly be accomplished by the year 2000. But by then the political evolution will have taken place in a slow but definite form. An evolution, mind you, not a revolution. Now that, if I am right, is an amazing thing because it will be the reverse of the norm. Usually, political evolution follows economic change. In the case of the United States, it seems that economic evolution can actually absorb political change, and that is a strength in my opinion that is truly worth thinking about."

Index

Agee, William M., 11, 119, 182, 240
Agfa-Gevaert, Inc., 99
Air France, 44–45
Alcoa Corporation, 215
Allegheny Corporation, 197–99
Allen, Woody, 223
Allied Chemical Corporation, 103
Altman, B., and Company, 223
American Academy of Pediatrics, 217
American Academy of Pedodontics, 217
American Bankers Association, 124
American Bar Association, 84
American Home Products Corporation, 218
American Jewish Congress, 79
American Petroleum Institute, 88
American Sealcap Corporation, 200
American Shipbuilding Corporation, 168
American Telephone and Telegraph Company, 12, 13, 40, 46, 51, 60–61, 80, 90, 111
American Women's Economic Development Corporation, 152
AMF, Inc., 103
Amstar Corporation, 46, 194–95
Amtrak, 21
Anti-Defamation League of B'nai B'rith, 107
Applied Synergetics, Inc., 115

Arab boycott, 79, 107
Arnold, John D., 115–16
Asamera Oil Corporation, 160
Ashland Oil, Inc., 103
Audubon Magazine, 222
Avis, Inc, 27, 53, 54, 55, 127
Axelson, Kenneth S., 27, 232
Ayer, N.W., & Son, Inc., 51

Baker Laboratories, 215
Bangor Punta Corporation, 11, 196, 200–2
Bankers Trust Company, 49
Banks, Russell, 11, 137, 245
Bank Secrecy Act, 103
Barnum, Ronald S., 230–31, 233–36
Barwick, Eugene, 26
Barwick Corporation, 26
Bates, C. Wallace, 15
Batten, William M., 224, 228–36
Baxter, William A., 160
Beech-Nut Foods Corporation, 16, 215–18
Begelman, David, 169
Bell Laboratories, 13
Bell System, 13
Bendix Corporation, 11, 182
Berezin, Evelyn, 151–52
Bergerac, Michel C., 105, 141–42, 227
Berman, Philip I., 177

249

Black, Eli M., 57–58, 102, 197, 200
Bloomingdale's, 223
Bluhdorn, Charles G., 49
Blumenthal, W. Michael, 11, 12, 63, 95–96, 100–101, 169–70, 182, 240, 245
B'nai B'rith, 12
Board Room, The, 18
Boards of directors, 19–20, 142, 243–44
Boise Cascade Corporation, 11
Bonwit Teller, 27
Borch, Fred, 191
Borman, Frank, 40
Boyden Associates, 118
British Airways, 44–45
Bronfman, Edgar, 52
Brook, Thomas L., 160
Brown, Courtney, 78
Brunswick Corporation, 107, 215
Brzezinski, Zbigniew, 52
Bunting, John R., Jr., 121–26, 195
Burger, Warren, 89
Burns, Arthur, 13, 64
Burroughs Corporation, 152
Business Council, 10, 62
Business profits, 81–82, 96, 110
Business Roundtable, 10, 15, 52, 107
Business Week, 15

Cafiero, E. A., 226
Carbine, Pat, 14
Cardozo, Benjamin, 161
Cargill, Inc., 219
Carnegie, Andrew, 34
Carroll, Thomas, 223
Carter, Jimmy, 12, 13, 52, 62–64, 65–69, 95, 169
Carvel, Tom, 40
Castle & Cooke, 101
Castro, Fidel, 95, 195
Castroism, 10
CCMP Management Consultants, 204–5, 218
Celler-Kefauver Amendment, 66

Census Bureau, U.S., 148
Center for the Study of American Business, 68
Chamber of Commerce, U.S., 164
Chris-Craft Industries, 201–2
Christian, John W., 223
Chrysler Corporation, 227
Citicorp, 62, 236
Civil Aeronautics Board, 66
Clarke, Richard, 146, 153–54, 156
Clayton Act, 66
Close Encounters of the Third Kind, 169
Coca-Cola Company, 84
Collier, Calvin J., 84
Columbia Graduate School of Business, 78
Columbia Pictures, 169
Committee for Economic Development, 77
Communications, 39–40, 87–90, 99, 118, 134, 180
Communications workers, 188
Company politics, 177–79
Concorde, the, 44
Conference Board, 30, 37, 43, 53, 110, 137, 223
Conrad, Anthony, 26
Conrail, 21
Consolidated Edison Company, 49
Consumer Product Safety Commission, 50, 67
Coppenrath, Robert, 99–100, 226
Cordiner, Ralph, 191
Cornfeld, Bernard, 43
Cost-benefit analysis, 69
Crown Center, 208
Cybernetics, 35, 99

Dance, Walter D., 130
Davant, James, 81, 87, 173, 178, 225, 233
Davis, Arthur Vining, 233
Davis, Evelyn Y., 80
deButts, John D., 12, 13, 40, 46–47, 51, 60–61, 131, 189–90, 244

250

Depression, Great, 246
Diebold, John, 112, 113, 115
Diebold Group, 112
Del Monte Corporation, 101
Department of Energy, U.S., 67
Dorsey, Bob R., 102
Dow Chemical U.S.A. Corp., 68
Dow Jones industrial index, 203, 219
Dresser Industries, 104
Dun's Review, 164
du Pont de Nemours, E.I., & Co., 12, 13, 14, 51, 52, 190–91
Duquesne Club, 18

Eastern Airlines, 40
Eastham, William K., 218
Economic Club, 10
Economic productivity, 110, 113
Economists, young, 37–38
Eisenhower, Dwight D., 64
Elicker, Jane, 223
Elicker, Paul, 223
Emerson, Ralph Waldo, 248
Energy use, 92, 94, 97, 98
Environmental Protection Agency, U.S., 67, 71
Equal Employment Opportunity Commission, U.S., 67
Equity Funding Corporation, 20, 21, 22, 24
Executive compensation, 30–31, 55, 114, 149, 153, 227–28
Exxon Corporation, 88, 222

Federal chartering of companies, 78–79
Federal Communications Commission, 66
Federal Power Commission, 66
Federal Reserve Bank of Philadelphia, 123
Federal Reserve Board, 13, 245
Federal Trade Commission, 83–85
Federal Trade Commission Act, 66
Federated Department Stores, 50

Fiedler, Edgar R., 110–11
First Boston Corporation, 201
First Pennsylvania Corporation, 121
Fitzpatrick, Beatrice, 152
Food and Drug Administration, U.S., 66, 71
Ford, Henry, II, 227
Ford Motor Company, 227
Foreign payments, 101–7, 244
Fortune 500, 162
Fortune magazine, 234
Friedman, Milton, 38

Galbraith, John K., 38
Gallagher Presidents' Report, 228
Gallo, E.J., Winery, 219
Garvin, Clifford, 222
Geneen, Harold S., 126–29, 130, 131, 132, 140–41
General Electric Company, 13, 34, 40, 80, 111, 128–31, 191–94, 242
General Motors Corporation, 34, 68, 111, 227
Genesco Inc., 27, 107
Gibbons, Edward F., 188–89
Gilbert, Lewis D., 77–78
Gill, Robert B., 230, 231, 232, 235
Goldblum, Stanley, 22
Gorman, Edward, 230
Government intervention, 65–75, 83–87, 247
Grace, J. Peter, Jr., 140–41, 171, 183–85, 224
Grace, William R., 183
Grace, W. R., & Company, 140, 171
Graham, Katherine, 151
Grant, W.T., Company, 20, 22, 23, 24, 134
Greenbrier Hotel, 10
Greenspan, Alan J., 16
Grow Chemical Corporation, 11
Gulf & Western Industries, 49
Gulf Oil Corporation, 102–3, 168
Gutoff, Reuben, 16, 137–39, 174–75

251

Hall, Donald J., 206–10, 219
Hall, Frank B., Inc., 160
Hall, Joyce C., 206–9, 212
Hallmark Cards, 206–10, 218
Hallmark Gallery, 209
"Hallmark Hall of Fame," 208–9
Hamill, Pete, 44–45
Handy Associates, 149
Hanigan, John L., 107
Hartford Fire Insurance Company, 127–28
Harvard Graduate School of Business, 11, 122
Harvard University, 18, 81–82
Hearst Corporation, 219
Hefner, Hugh M., 43
Heidrick & Struggles, 116, 119–21
Helena Rubinstein, Inc., 223
Heller, Walter, 38
Heller, Walter E., Company, 216
Hess's, Inc., 177
Hewlett-Packard Company, 62
Hoadley, Walter, 16
Honeywell, Inc., 193
Horatio Algerism, 14
Hubert M. Humphrey School of Public Service, 52
Hugh Wilsonism, 10

IBM Corporation, 89–90, 92, 105, 122, 152, 193
Industrial kidnappings, 222
Inflation, 76, 245
Interfaith Center on Corporate Responsibility, 79
Internal Revenue Service, 24, 25, 87, 159, 162
    "Eleven Questions," 162
International Brotherhood of Teamsters, 188
International Monetary Fund, 93–94
International Telephone and Telegraph Corporation, 126–29, 132
Interstate Commerce Commission, 66–67

Investors Overseas Services, 43
Itel Corporation, 12, 118

Jefferson, Thomas, 66
Jennings, Eugene, 116–17
Johnson, Lyndon B., 64
Johnson, Samuel C., II, 204, 210–14
Johnson, S.C., & Son, Inc., 204, 210–14, 218
Jones, Reginald H., 13, 34, 40, 74–75, 96–98, 121, 126, 127, 128, 129, 130–32, 191–94, 227, 239, 241
Jones, Thomas V., 168
Justice Department, U.S., 12, 13, 66, 87, 89–90, 159, 164

Kaiser, Edgar F., 50
Kaiser Industries, 50
Kearney, A. T., Inc., 17
Kelly, William, 124–25
Kennedy, John F., 64, 246
Keynes, John Maynard, 38
Khashoggi, Adnan M., 168
Kirby, Allan P., 197, 199–200
Kirkpatrick, Miles W., 84
Kirstein, Hilda, 14
Kissinger, Henry, 52
K Mart Stores, 23
Kohler, Jonas, 56
Kolin, Oscar, 223
Korn, Lester B., 90
Korn/Ferry International, 90
Kreps, Juanita M., 63, 77, 147–48
Kresge, S.S., Company, 23
Kristol, Irving, 226
Kroll, Jack, 164
Kuh, Richard H., 231–32

Land, Edwin, 34
Lang, George, 41–42
Lansing, Jack, 161
Lauder, Estee, 14
Lawrence, Mary Wells, 14
Lazar, H.L., Inc., 232
Lazarus, Ralph, 50

Lever Brothers, 223
Levitt and Sons, 127
Links Club, 18
Lobbying, 87–90
Lockheed Corporation, 102, 168
Loews Corporation, 70
Lopez Arellano, Oswaldo, 102
Loral Corporation, 11, 243
Luce, Charles F., 49

Madison Avenue, 11
Magnin, I., 223
Mahoney, David J., 10, 53–55, 178
Malthus, Thomas Robert, 38
Mark Hopkins Hotel, 10
Martin, Terry, 230, 234–35
Maryland Cup Corporation, 115
Mayer, Richard W., 22, 23
MBAs, 14, 184
McCracken, Paul, 38
McNamara, Robert, 37
Menk, Carl W., 118, 173
Meyer, Pearl, 149–51
Michelson, Alphonso, 52
Miller, G. William, 245
Milliken Corporation, 219
Minnesota Mining and Manufacturing Company (3M), 168
Minority advancement, 145–48, 152–57
Mobil Corporation, 89
Montgomery Ward & Company, 242
Morgan, J. P., & Company, 29
Morgan Guaranty Trust Company of New York, 29
Multinationals, 91–92, 100
Murphy, Thomas, 34, 227

Nader, Ralph, 39, 68, 78–79
Naftalis, Gary F., 163
Nathan, Robert R., 77
National Association of Manufacturers, 77
Neiman-Marcus, 223
Neski, Julian, 230, 233

New York Central Railroad, 21, 197–98
New York Daily News, 44, 51
New York Stock Exchange, 127, 151, 224, 229
New York Times, 27, 49, 50, 51, 96, 147, 232
New York University (NYU), 18
Newsweek magazine, 151
Nicholas, Frank C., 16, 214–19
Nixon, Richard M., 64, 84, 113, 168, 240
Northrop Corporation, 168–69
Norton Simon, Inc., 53, 55

Occupational Safety and Health Administration (OSHA), U.S., 67, 68, 71–72
Office of Price Administration, U.S. 12
Ogilvy & Mather International, Inc., 103
Oliver, William F., 194
Olsten, William, 178
Olsten Corporation, 178
Onassis, Jacqueline, 223
Oreffice, Paul F., 68
Organization of Petroleum Exporting Countries, 94
Otis Elevator Company, 175

Pacific Power and Light Company, 161
Packard, David, 62
Paine, Webber, Jackson and Curtis, 81
Parker, Jack S., 130
Paterson, Ellmore C., 29
Penn Central Transportation Company, 20, 21, 23, 24, 134
Penney, J.C., Company, 27, 228–36
Perdue, Frank, 40
Perlman, Alfred E., 21
Perquisites, 24, 29, 159–61
Pertschuk, Michael, 83–84

Petroleum Club, 18
Pinnacle Club, 18
Piper Aircraft Company, 201–2
Plant investment, 15–16, 73, 97, 111
Playboy Enterprises, 43
Polaroid Corporation, 34
Potter, John T., 160
Potter Instrument Company, 160
Princeton University, 18
Pritchard, Charles, 160
Pritchard, William, 160
Pritchard & Baird, 160

Quittmeyer, Robert T., 46, 178, 194–96, 225

Ramos, José Abraham Bennaton, 102
Randall, Kenneth A., 37, 43, 223
Raytheon Corporation, 127, 132
RCA Corporation, 26
Reader's Digest Association, 219
REA Express, 134
Real-estate investment trusts, 37–38
Redactron Corporation, 152
Red Baron of Lufthansa, 9
Redfield, Peter S., 12, 118–19, 173, 225–26
Reuss, Henry, 101
Revlon, Inc., 105, 141–42, 212
Revson, Charles, 141
Riccardo, John J., 227
Rinfret, Pierre, 32, 113–14, 228, 243
Ritz Carlton Hotel, 10
Robert Hall Clothes, 49
Robertson, Cliff, 169
Robinson, Herbert, 159, 163, 170
Rockefeller, David, 34
Rockefeller, John D., 34
Roesch, William R., 50–51
Roosevelt, Franklin D., 64

Salgo, Nicolas, 197
Sarnoff, David, 34
Saunders, Stuart T., 21

Schiller, Marvin, 17, 135–36, 140, 175, 241
Schlesinger, James, 62
Schultz, J. Robert, 26
Schumacher, John, 27
Schwab, Martin, 49
Schwartz, Bernard L., 11, 243, 245
SCM Corporation, 222
Seagram's Distillers, 52
Sears, Roebuck & Company, 92, 105
Securities and Exchange Commission, U.S., 23, 24, 25, 66, 78, 79, 83, 85–87, 101–2, 127, 159, 160, 162, 205, 243
Shahmoon, Solomon E., 161
Shahmoon Industries Inc., 161
Shapiro, Charlotte, 51, 52, 53
Shapiro, Henry, 115
Shapiro, Irving S., 12, 13, 51, 52, 63, 131, 190–91, 227
Sheraton Corporation, 127
Sherman Antitrust Act, 66
Siebert, Muriel, 14, 151
Simmons, Grant G., Jr., 50
Simmons Company, 50
Simon, Norton, 11
Simon, William, 94
Smith, Adam, 38
Sonnabend, A. M., 199
Soss, Wilma, 80
Squibb Corporation, 215–17
Standard Brands Corporation, 16, 138
Standard Oil of California, 89
Stanford Research Institute, 53
Steinberg, Saul, 223
Stieglitz, Harold, 30–31
Stillman, Charles A., 162
Strategic planning, 137–38, 239–42
Sugar crisis, 194–96
Swope, Gerard, 34

Temple University, 123
Texas Instruments Company, 92
Thatcher, Margaret, 52

Tisch, Laurence A., 69–70, 73, 104–5, 136, 177–78, 226
Tisch, P. Robert, 136–37, 178, 226
Transamerica Corporation, 12
Trans World Airlines, Inc., 103
Treasury Department, U.S., 27, 103
Trudeau, Pierre, 52
Truman, Harry S., 61, 64
21 Club, 18
Tyler, Robert, Jr., 50

United Brands, Inc., 20, 57–58, 101–2, 200
United Merchants & Manufacturers, Inc., 49
United States government:
 Census Bureau, 148
 Chamber of Commerce, 164
 Department of Energy, 67
 EPA, 67, 71
 FDA, 66, 71
 Justice Department, 12, 13, 66, 87, 89–90, 159, 164
 OPA, 12
 OSHA, 67, 68, 71–72
 Supreme Court, 202
 Treasury Department, 27, 103
 see also entries under Federal
United States Steel Corporation, 51
United Technologies Company, 175
University of Idaho, 11
Urban League, 234

Vietnam War, 37, 246
Volkswagen of America, Inc., 71

Waldorf-Astoria Hotel, 10, 45
Wall Street Journal, 22, 26, 51, 104
Wallace, David W., 11, 57–58, 196–202
Wallace, Jean, 198
Washington Post, 151
Watergate break-in, 169, 246
Weidenbaum, Murray L., 68
Westinghouse Corporation, 131
Wharton School of the University of Pennsylvania, 128
White & Case, 197–98
White-collar crime, 164–67, 170
Whitehead, Arch, 154–56
Wilson, Joseph, 152–53
Women's advancement, 14–15, 145–52
Wood, Arthur M., 105–6
Woolworth, F. W., Company, 188
World Bank, 94
Wright, Frank Lloyd, 213
Wriston, Walter, 62, 121, 236

Xerox Corporation, 92, 122, 152–53

Yale University, 18
Young, Mrs. Robert, 199–200
Young, Robert, 197–99
Young, Whitney, 234–35

255